The Evolution
of Pitching in
Major League Baseball

The Evolution
of Pitching in
Major League Baseball

WILLIAM F. MCNEIL

McFarland & Company, Inc., Publishers
Jefferson, North Carolina, and London

Library of Congress Cataloguing-in-Publication Data

McNeil, William.
The evolution of pitching in major league baseball / William F. McNeil.
p.   cm.
Includes bibliographical references and index.

ISBN 0-7864-2468-0 (softcover : 50# alkaline paper)

1. Pitching (Baseball)   2. Baseball — United States — History.   I. Title.
GV871.M43 2006   796.357'22 — dc22   2006006091

British Library cataloguing data are available

Cover illustration by Mark Durr, based on the original by Rudy Zallinger

Manufactured in the United States of America

McFarland & Company, Inc., Publishers
Box 611, Jefferson, North Carolina 28640
www.mcfarlandpub.com

This book is gratefully dedicated to my family
for their support and encouragement:

My wife, Janet;
my children, Michael, Danny, Jeanne, and Eileen;
my grandchildren, Jessica, Jamie, Jeffrey, Jenna,
Morgan, Shannon, Shane, Katie, Connor, Rachel,
Joe, and Ari; and my great-grandson, Anthony.

Acknowledgments

My daughter, Jeanne Kruger, was an immense help with this project. She solved many computer problems that were frustrating me, and she continually tried to educate me in the correct operation of my software.

Debbie Matson, director of publications for the Boston Red Sox, went above and beyond the call of duty by working around several obstacles to provide me with photographs of Schilling, Martinez, Clemens, Lyle, Eckersley, and Lee Smith.

Thanks also to Jim Madden, Jr., Jay Sanford, John Outland, the New York Mets, the Montreal Expos, the New York Yankees, and Mary Brace for photographs and for permission to publish them.

Dave Smith generously permitted me to use his statistics on the number of runs scored in a game, inning by inning, since 1901, from a paper he presented at the Cincinnati SABR meeting in July 2004. His article "From Exile to Specialist: The Evolution of the Relief Pitcher," was also utilized extensively.

Dick Kramer's statistics in "The Effect of Relief Pitching," which appeared in the 1975 edition of the *Baseball Research Journal*, were extremely valuable in evaluating the changes in pitching over the years.

Table of Contents

Introduction

There has been a lively debate making the rounds in the baseball community for several years, concerning the quality of pitching in the major leagues today. Are today's big league pitchers as good as the pitchers who toed the rubber 40, 50, or 60 years ago? Are they less talented? Or are they the most talented pitchers the game has ever seen? Those questions and more have been discussed, and argued about, for most of the past decade. The supporters of today's pitchers being the best ever point to Roger Clemens' and Kerry Wood's 20 strikeouts in a single game, Nolan Ryan's 5,714 career strikeouts and his seven no-hitters. The detractors point out the drastic drop in complete games thrown by today's pitchers, which hit a low of 4.3 percent in 2003 compared to 26.9 percent in 1960 and 44.3 percent in 1940. They also talk about the overall dilution of major league talent caused by the expansion that has resulted in an increase of 88 percent in the number of big league teams. Before 1960, there were 16 major league teams, eight in each league. Today, 30 teams make up the major league roster, 16 teams in the National League and 14 teams in the American League.

There have been many changes in the game from the inaugural National League season in 1876 through the 30-team pennant races of 2004, and the state of pitching has had more than its share of ups and downs. The first major modification to the pitching position occurred in 1884 when the rules committee legalized overhand pitching. Before that change, pitchers were restricted to having their hand no higher than the shoulder when they released the ball. And, in fact, before 1881, they had to pitch underhand. There were also several changes in the ball and strike counts over the years before they were finally established at three strikes for an out and four balls for a walk. In the 1880s, while most pitchers threw off the flat ground, a few enterprising hurlers began pitching off a built-up mound. Originally, mounds may have evolved as a matter of groundskeeper maintenance for better drainage. Photographs taken during the 1890s show that pitching mounds varied considerably from city to city. Philadelphia's Shibe Park was said to have had a 20" mound at one time. To rectify the nonconformity in mound height, the rules committee permitted a mound to be built as long as it did not exceed 15". In 1969, to offset an apparent pitching advantage that resulted in Bob Gibson's 1.12 season ERA, the pitching mound was lowered to 10", where it remains. Earned run averages, which were in the 3.40 range in the National League during the 1960s, are now running about 4.40, but much of that increase seems to have been caused by expansion rather than the lower mound. American League ERAs are about one-half run higher than their National League counterpart due to the establishment of the designated hitter in 1973, a move that, according to Palmer and Gillette's *Baseball Encyclopedia*, resulted in a 23 percent increase in scoring, the largest increase since 1911. Probably one of the most important areas of contention regarding pitchers is the location of the strike zone. This is constantly in a state of flux and shows no sign of being resolved soon. The baseball commissioner's office has ordered umpires to call the strikes as defined in the rule books, but the umpires, kings of their domains, refuse to adhere to the rules. Each umpire has his own strike zone and continues to call the pitches the same way he has for years.

Some of the more recent pitching changes have nothing to do with rules. For instance, there has been a fundamental change in the hitting mentality of batters that began in the 1950s and reached a peak in the 1970s. Until players like Mickey Mantle and Harmon Killebrew arrived on the scene, batters considered it humiliating to be struck out, but Mantle and Killebrew changed that mentality. And a new generation of hitters, led by Bobby Bonds, Dave Kingman, and Reggie Jackson, were determined to hit home runs at any cost, and they didn't care how many times they struck out. As Sammy Sosa said, "I get paid to hit home runs." Other changes revolve around new philosophies embraced by baseball managers and general managers to protect the valuable pitching arms of their pitchers, many of who are under long-term contracts. The most questionable area now is that of the pitch count and the pitch count limit. Most managers, following a decade of discussion about the value of pitch counts, limit their starting pitcher to approximately 100 pitches a game, claiming this will protect a pitcher's arm (and the club's investment) and will extend the pitcher's career. However, that theory is open to debate. There seem to be more injuries to pitchers' arms today than ever before.

This book is a study of the evolution of baseball pitching from its primitive beginnings in games called rounders, the Massachusetts Game, and the New York Game, into baseball as we know it. It will investigate the numerous modifications that have been made to the rules governing the strike zone and the height of the pitching mound, as well as the decline in the number of complete games thrown by starting pitchers; the value of pitch counts and the pitch count limit; the rise of the relief pitcher; the emergence of the closer; and the effect of trainers, conditioning, weight training, and pitching coaches on the welfare of pitchers.

All the parameters affecting the pitching game will be examined in detail, and conclusions will be drawn regarding the state of major league pitching. Is it better than ever? Or is it in decline? This study will answer those questions. But first, to better understand the state of pitching in the major leagues, it is necessary to go back to the development of the modern game of baseball and to trace the evolution of the game and the changes that have been made in the pitching department over the past 170 years.

PART I.
THE EVOLUTION OF PITCHING

1

In the Beginning: Up to 1844

Beer was invented in Mesopotamia, in present-day Iraq, over 5,000 years ago. Writing was invented about the same time in the same area. Thirteen hundred miles away, in ancient Egypt, according to Bowman and Zoss, the first recorded instance of batting contests took place "with Egyptian priests engaged in mock combat with bats. Fertility of crops and people were undoubtedly the goal, and balls, which sometimes represented such symbols of springtime potency as the sun, or the mummified head of Osiris, eventually found their way into the game." A sculpture on the temple of a twelfth dynasty pharaoh Beni Hasan, built prior to 2000 B.C., depicts figures throwing and catching balls. Five hundred years later, an inscription in the tomb of Thutmose III represented a bat and ball ceremony, according to Robert W. Henderson in *Ball, Bat and Bishop*. The pharaoh is pictured holding a ball in his left hand, and a wavy olive-wood stick, ready to hit the ball, in his right hand. Two priests, standing in front of Thutmose, appear to be catching balls. Albert G. Spalding reported seeing a similar ball in 1874. "A leather-covered ball used in games played on the Nile forty centuries ago, has a place among the many archaeological specimens in the British Museum, in London. It has a sewed cover and is still in a remarkable state of preservation." Spalding apparently visited the museum and saw the ball during a visit to England with a touring major league baseball team in 1874. Another game involving a ball, bowling, was also a popular activity with the ruling classes in the Egypt of the twelfth dynasty.

Ball games, in various forms, were enjoyed around the globe during this period, as attested to by the ball courts unearthed in dozens of Mayan cities throughout Mexico and Central America, as well as by references to the sport in ancient journals in China and Japan. Ancient Chinese references describe a game called *tsu chu*, an ancestor of soccer, that was played as part of the emperor's birthday celebration as early as 2500 B.C. In *tsu chu*, balls made of animal skin were kicked through a gap in a net stretched between poles 30 feet high. The Mayan ball games were strikingly similar. The playing fields in Mexico were about 50 feet long, with vertical walls stretching up 15 feet on either side. Small stone rings mounted halfway up each wall were the goals, and the object was to send the world's first rubber ball through the ring using only the hips, head, legs, or feet. Soccer may have

Club ball, a game similar to baseball, was played in England as early as A.D. 1344 (AUTHOR'S COLLECTION).

been introduced into England during this same period, or shortly after, by the marauding Celts. There are reports of a soccerlike game being played in the villages around the island, the skulls of defeated Romans being used as balls. One story, recalled in "World Soccer History" at www.soccernova.com, tells of a soccer game played between English villagers and Roman soldiers. After defeating the pride of the Roman army, the villages drove the soldiers out of the town. The date was A.D. 217.

Spalding noted,

> The game of ball was prized by the Greeks as giving grace and elasticity to the human figure, and they erected a statue to one Aristonicus for his proficiency at it. We are told by Horace that Maecenas amused himself during his journeys by playing ball. In the Greek gymnasia and in the Roman baths, there were special compartments for ball-playing, called Sphaeristerii, where certain rules and gradations of exercise were observed, according to the health of the player. The balls used were of various materials, the most common being of leather, filled with hair, while others were stuffed with feathers. Ancient medical practitioners were wont to prescribe a course of ball-playing where the modern doctor would order a diet of pills.

Another favorite game in ancient Rome was a game called Paganica, as reported in "Maui Croquet Club History" on the club's website. The game was played in the fields around the town. The players hit a small leather ball with a curved stick, trying to hit specific trees with the ball. The player who hit all the trees in the fewest number of shots was the winner. Over the years, the sport developed in two ways:

> In country areas where there was adequate space, courses were laid out and the target became a hole. Thus the game of golf was created. In towns, where space was limited, the game of Paille-Maille (ball-mallet) became popular. In this game, a box-wood ball, a foot in circumference, was played down an alley, passing through a number of arches or hoops on the way. The winner was the person achieving this in the fewest number of shots. Peasants from southern France played Paille-Maille around 1300, using shepherd's crooks to hit balls through bent willow branches.

This game eventually evolved into croquet.

Games using a ball continued to be played in all civilized societies, and many of the games grew in popularity over the centuries. Bowman and Zoss noted that "in Europe, ballgames were rapidly incorporated into Christian ceremonies from Austria to France. During the Middle Ages, the Cathedral of Rheims wound up Easter services with a ball game in which contending teams either kicked or swatted a ball with a stick." Many of the games became favorite pastimes of the ruling classes. In France, as far back as 1100, two of the more favored ball games were tennis and croquet, which could be played on the spacious lawns around the castle by men and women alike. Another game, called ground billiards, which might have been a form of bowling, was enjoyed by French nobles in 1351, as recorded in royal pardons. These activities and others made their way across the English Channel in short order.

Once England emerged from the Dark Ages about the time of William the Conqueror and began to establish herself as one of the leading nations in the world, written histories and other works of literature became more plentiful and popular, and eventually included such subjects as the diversionary activities of the people. And, of course, after Johannes Gutenberg invented the printing press around the year 1450, books became accessible to a much larger portion of the population, although still restricted to the upper classes. One of the earliest documented bat and ball games is described in a book titled *Sports and Pastimes of the People of England*, published in London in 1832 by Joseph Strutt. The game, called club ball, is portrayed in a drawing copied from a Bodleian manuscript dated to 1344. It shows a woman about to pitch a ball to a man, who stands with a bat in his hand, ready to hit the ball. The original drawing also showed several players of both sexes standing behind the pitcher or bowler, ready to catch the ball after it was hit. An even earlier game, shown in the same book and dated to the reign of Henry II, 1207 to 1272, shows a man holding a ball and a bat in his hands. He appears ready to throw the ball into the air, to attempt to hit it with his bat; while another man, standing in front of him, is ready to catch the batted ball. A similar game, called trap ball, consisted of a trap, a devise like a catapult, that propelled a ball into the air which a man with a bat then tried to hit to defensive players standing in front of him.

The English sport of cricket dates to this same period, and may have descended from a game called stool ball that was described in England's Domesday Book in the year 1085. Stool ball, as described by Strutt,

> consists simply of setting a stool upon the ground, and one of the players takes his place before it, while his antagonist, standing at a distance, tosses a ball with the intention of striking the stool, and thus it is the business of the former to prevent by beating it away with the hand, reckoning one to the game for every stroke of the ball; if, on the contrary, it should be missed by the hand and touch the stool, the players change places; the conqueror at this game is he who strikes the ball most times before it touches the stool.

The first mention of the game of modern cricket can be traced to the year 1598, when J. Strutt's book on the town of Guildford noted that several students from the free school of Guildford "did run and play there at cricket."

Another game that was popular with the people of England was a game called football, known as soccer in America. It became savagely popular with the lower classes by the twelfth century, and was called "a violent mob sport with no rules and any sort of behavior condoned," according to the "World Soccer History" site. Broken bones were common and fatalities were an accepted result of the aggressive play. Several times during the

Middle Ages, football was banned by royal decree, for one reason or another. During the reign of King Edward II, around 1369, it was banned because it interfered with archery. Two hundred years later, all sports were banned by Queen Elizabeth I, who considered them to be too exhausting for her subjects. She feared the people would not have the energy to carry out their daily chores if they were allowed to participate in sports.

British royalty, however, were not banned from playing sports. They enjoyed most sports, with the possible exception of football, and they played them on a regular basis. One sport that became a particular favorite of the royal court was tennis, a game that had its roots in fifth century Tuscany, where villagers were reported to hit balls up and down the streets with their bare hands. In the eleventh century, the game was enjoyed by French monks in the courtyards of monasteries, using balls made of wood, and later of leather stuffed with wool or hair. As monks traveled to other monasteries around Europe, they brought the game with them. At that time, it was called *Jes de Paume* or "game of the palm," since the hand was used to hit the ball. Over a period of 300 years, racquets gradually replaced hands, making tennis the oldest of all racquet games. At one point, the game became so popular and time consuming that the pope actually forbade monks to play it. Across the channel in England, when Henry VIII ascended the throne in 1509, tennis became one of his great passions, and he played it as often as possible, even having an indoor court built in Hampton Court Palace in 1530. He was considered to be an accomplished tennis player by his peers, often challenging visiting kings to matches, with large sums of money being wagered on the outcome.

Many of the sports that were developed over the 2,500 years since the first leather sphere was constructed on the banks of the Nile have become extraordinarily popular with people around the world. Some of the more successful ball games include football (or soccer), rugby, American football, bowling, volleyball, and basketball. Favorite ball and bat games include tennis, cricket, golf, lacrosse, baseball, and croquet. Cricket has become the sport of choice for the upper classes in England and is still popular in some of the countries that were part of the British Empire, such as India and Australia. But one sport that was developed in England traveled over the ocean to America, and eventually became the national pastime of the United States. It was called club-ball in the year 1300, but over a period of 400 years, the game was modified to accommodate a growing number of people who were attracted to it, and a set of rules was established that determined the number of players on a side and the layout of the playing field, including the number of bases to be used, the scoring, and numerous other details governing how the game should be played. By the eighteenth century, it had become one of the favorite outdoor activities in England, for children and adults alike. It was called rounders then. Some sources claim that baseball evolved from a combination of cricket and rounders, but it is unlikely that cricket played any part in the development of baseball since it and rounders developed simultaneously during the Middle Ages. In fact, as noted earlier, Strutt stated that cricket descended from the eleventh century game of stool-ball. Rounders, on the other hand, was most certainly an immediate precursor of baseball. Club-ball, the prototype for both games, had several similarities to baseball. It had a thrower or pitcher, a striker or batter, and several defensive players who stood behind the pitcher. The rules of club-ball have been lost to antiquity so it is not certain exactly how the game was played. But it was played and enjoyed by many people, both men and women, in England from the fourteenth century on, as diagrammed in the Bodleian manuscript.

The first documented mention of the game of rounders was in Newbury's *Little Pretty Pocket Book*, published in London in 1744. More importantly, a game called baseball was diagrammed in the same book, followed by this verse:

> The ball once struck off
> Away flies the boy
> To the next destin'd Post
> And then Home with joy.

Four years later, the game of baseball was mentioned in a letter from Lady Hervey (Mary Leppell), describing the family of Frederick, Prince of Wales, "diverting themselves with baseball, a play all who are or have been schoolboys are well acquainted with."

William Clarke described the rules for rounders, reviewed in his *Boy's Own Book*, originally published in London in 1829:

In the west of England, this is one of the most favorite sports with bat and ball. The players divide into two equal parties and chance decides who shall have first innings. Four stones or posts are placed from twelve to twenty yards asunder, as a, b, c, d, in the margin; another is put at e; one of the party which is out, who is called the pecker or feeder, places himself at e. He tosses the ball gently toward a, on the right of which, one of the in-party places himself, and strikes the ball, if possible, with his bat.

From the diagram shown below, which was copied from the *Boy's Own Book*, it is readily apparent that the shape of the playing field closely resembled a baseball diamond as we know it.

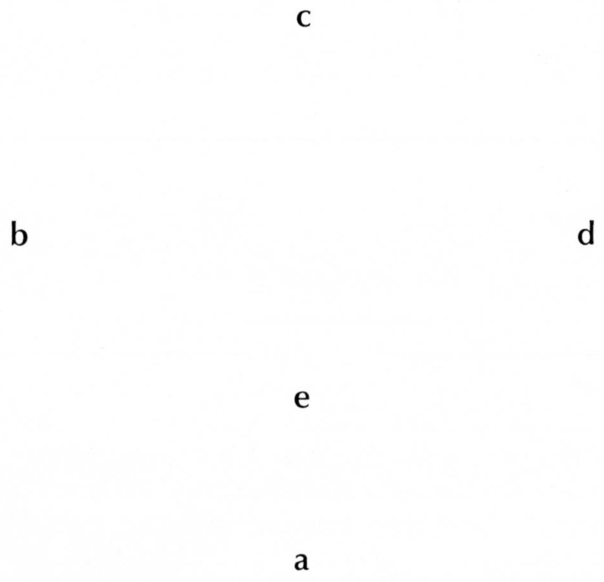

c

b   d

e

a

The description of the rules of rounders continued:

If he misses three times, or if the ball when struck, fall behind a, or be caught by any of the players, who are all scattered about the field except one who stands behind a (the catcher), he is out and another takes his place. If none of these events takes place, on striking the ball he drops the bat, and runs toward b, or, if he can, to c, d, or even to a again.

One of the major differences between rounders and baseball is that the runner runs clockwise around the bases in rounders and counterclockwise in baseball. Also, in rounders, the team at bat continues to bat until all their players have been retired, which ends their inning. An American version of the book, published in Boston in 1834, substituted the names "base" or "goal ball" for "rounders" in the title of the section because, as author Robin Carver noted, "This game is known under a variety of names. It is sometimes called 'round ball,' but I believe that 'base' or 'goal ball' are the names generally adopted in our country."

Rounders made the trip across the Atlantic Ocean on the *Mayflower*, and was first played in the Plymouth Plantation in 1620. William Bradford, governor of the plantation, in his memoirs, chastised the men in the town for "frolicking in ye street, at play openly; some at pitching ye ball, some at stoole-ball and shuch-like sport," on Christmas day in 1621. Many different types of bat and ball games, variations of rounders, were played in the American colonies in the seventeenth, eighteenth, and nineteenth centuries. Rules were changed from town to town, to accommodate the space available for play and the number of players who wanted to participate. The game was variously called rounders, baseball, or town ball.

Thomas L. Altherr, author of "A Place Leavel Enough to Play Ball," a description of baseball-type games that were played in the eighteenth century, reported, "About mid-century, however, the frequency of references to baseball and baseball-type games, increased. Three groups, in particular, book writers, soldiers, and students, were apparently enthusiasts for ball." There were numerous entries in the diaries of Revolutionary War soldiers referring to ball games they played in camp. Simeon Lyman, a soldier from Sharon, Connecticut, noted in his diary for September 1775, "Wednesday the 6. We played ball all day." On April 30, 1778, private Benjamin Gilbert, bivouacked in the lower Hudson River valley, noted, "In the morning I went down the hill to play ball and was called up immediately to gather watch coats." That same year, at Valley Forge, George Ewing wrote, "Attested to my Muster Rolls and delivered them to the Muster Master, exercised in the afternoon, in the intervals playd at base." One entry even noted that George Washington "sometimes throws and catches a ball for whole hours with his aides-de-camp." These entries however, did not identify the game well enough to know if they were referring to baseball, as there was no mention of a bat.

The first references to ball games using a bat originated in colleges in the New England–New Jersey corridor, as reported by Altherr. Sidney Willard, a Harvard professor, recalled playing baseball as a student. "Referring to the campus Buttery (dispensary) of the 1760's, Willard wrote, 'Besides eatables, everything necessary for a student was there sold, and articles used in the playgrounds, such as bats, balls, etc.' Then, recalling the campus play fields of the last decade of the century, he noted, 'Here it was that we wrestled and ran, played at quoits and cricket, and various games of bat and ball.'" Another reference to bat and ball games was found in the diary of John Rhea Smith, who noted, in an entry for March 1786, while at Princeton College, "A fine day, play baste ball in the campus but am beaten for I miss both catching and striking the ball." Oliver Wendell Holmes, man of letters and the father of the legendary jurist, played baseball at Harvard in the 1820s. And according to Altherr, even the Indians got into the act. "Farther north, in Scarborough, Maine, and in later decades, indigenous people played against Euro-americans, according to town historian, William Southgate: 'The game of 'base' was a peculiar favorite with our young townsmen, and the friendly Indians, and the hard beach of Garrison Cove afforded a fine ground for it.'"

The first official documented reference specifically to the game of baseball in the American colonies was recently discovered in a town bylaw in Pittsfield, Massachusetts, dated September 5, 1791. It said, in part, "The following bye-law, for the preservation of the windows in the new Meeting House in said town — viz,

> Be it ordained by the said inhabitants, that no person, an inhabitant of said town, shall be permitted to play at any game called wicket, cricket, baseball, batball, football, cat, fives, or any other game or games with balls within eighty yards from said Meeting House."
>
> The fine for ignoring the bylaw was five shillings. The existence of this document makes it obvious that baseball had been played in the Pittsfield area for some time prior to 1791, long enough that its popularity required it to be mentioned in a town bylaw.

Somewhere along the line, the playing field changed from the diamond-shape of the early rounders game to a square shape, as shown below.

C   D

                                              F

B   A   E

Where B, C, D, and E, represent the four bases, F is the pitcher or feeder, and A is the batter or striker. The teams usually consisted of 8 to 15 players per side, although they were flexible to accommodate all players who wished to participate. At least one game had two 50-man teams. The batter, after hitting the ball, ran around the bases in a counterclockwise direction. In addition to being put out in the normal manner, he could also be put out by hitting him with the ball while he was running between bases, a maneuver called "soaking" or "plugging."

Another Massachusetts town, Worcester, also defended itself against ball-playing in the streets by passing an ordinance forbidding it, in 1816.

Curiously, there is further evidence that baseball existed back into the early to mid 1700s, in a book on sports published in Germany in 1796. A game called "ball with free station" or "English base ball" matched the American game to perfection. The bases were 10 to 15 paces apart, the distance from the pitcher's box to home plate was 5 or 6 paces, the batter ran the bases in a counterclockwise direction, "plugging" was no longer allowed, and the bat used in the game was a short bat with a flat face similar to a cricket bat. The bats used in America were also similar to cricket bats until the early 1800s, when less expensive round bats were introduced.

From this point on, there are frequent references to the game of baseball being played

A 1791 Pittsfield, Massachusetts, bylaw forbad the playing of baseball within 80 yards of the new meeting house to protect the windows (AUTHOR'S COLLECTION).

up and down the East Coast. A SABR Web page for "1791 Baseball in Pittsfield, MASS." noted several instances of this passion. A writer in the *National Advocate* of April 25, 1823, reported,

> I was last Saturday much pleased in witnessing a company of active young men playing the manly and athletic game of "baseball" at the (Jones') Retreat in Broadway (on the west side of Broadway between what nowadays is Washington Place and Eighth Street). I am informed they are an organized association and that a very interesting game will be played on Saturday next at the above place, to commence at half past 3 o'clock PM. Any person fond of witnessing this game may avail himself of seeing it played with consummate skill and wonderful dexterity. It is surprising, and to be regretted that the young men of our city do not engage more in this manual sport; it is innocent amusement, and healthy exercise, attended with but little expense, and has no demoralizing tendency.

Two years later, the SABR site noted, Thurlow Weed, a noted journalist and politician of New York State, told of playing baseball as a young man in Mumford's Meadow (now part of Rochester). "A base-ball club, numbering nearly fifty members, met every afternoon during the playing season." SABR noted that, in 1831, "A group of Philadelphians form the Olympic Town Ball Club and cross over to Camden, New Jersey, on the Market Street ferry to escape restrictive ordinances prohibiting games within the boundaries of Philadelphia." The following year, the first baseball teams were formed in New York City, one from lower Manhattan and one from upper Manhattan. The two teams would eventually evolve into the Knickerbockers, New Yorks, and Gothams.

Robin Carver, in the *Book of Sports*, published in London in 1827, listed the first rules for baseball. They were very similar to the rules for rounders: three strikes was out, a caught fly ball was out, a runner who was "soaked" was out, and a batter who got a hit and made it around all four bases was credited with an ace or a run. The game, also known as town ball in New England because it was played on the town commons, grew in popularity all along the East Coast from Maryland to Maine. Organized baseball clubs popped up in Baltimore, Philadelphia, New York, Brooklyn, and Boston. In 1838, two teams met on Boston Common, using a fixed set of rules for a game that would become known as the Massachusetts Game. Initially, the rules established the shape of the field as a rectangle, with the distances between home and first base, and second and third base, being 45 feet, and the distance between first and second, and third and home, being 60 feet. There were eight players on a side, including the pitcher (or thrower as he was then called), two catchers, and five fielders, three of them manning the bases and the other two playing outfield. One out constituted an inning, and 21 tallies or runs constituted a victory. Subsequent rule changes fixed the distance between all bases at 60 feet, and the distance from the mound to home plate at 45 feet. The batter, or striker, was positioned halfway between home and first base and, after hitting the ball, he ran around the bases in a counterclockwise direction. The pitcher had to throw the ball overhand to the batter. Most of the rules were similar to rounders, such as three strikes was an out, a ball caught on a fly was an out, and "plugging" or "soaking" a player was an out. A run was called a tally, and the teams were limited to from 10 to 14 players per side. The biggest drawback to the Massachusetts Game was the 1858 rule specifying that 100 tallies were required to win the game. That rule resulted in some games lasting several days.

In 1840, another version of baseball was created in New York, and became known as the New York Game. According to Hickocksports.com, "The four bases were usually posts set in the ground, though shallow holes were used in less formal play, and the layout was asymmetrical. The batter, called the 'striker,' was stationed about 36 feet to the right of the fourth post; he had to run, at an angle, 45 feet to the first post, then 60 feet to the second, 72 feet to the third, and another 72 feet to the fourth, or home." There could be anywhere from 8 to 15 players on a side, and the batter circled the bases in a counterclockwise direction. Unlike the Massachusetts Game, the pitcher was called the "feeder" in the New York game, and he was required to toss the ball underhand, over the center of the plate, to the batter, making it a "hitters' game." There were usually three outs per inning, although occasionally there was only one, and 100 runs constituted a victory.

Three years later, the New York Club was formed by a group of men who had been playing baseball at Madison Square since the 1830s. When that field became unavailable, they moved their games across the river, to the Elysian Fields in Hoboken, New Jersey, a popular summer resort with picnic grounds and a bandstand. During this same period, another group of men, who had been playing baseball in Manhattan for several years, founded the Knickerbocker Base Ball Club of New York City. The game of baseball was about to leave the arena of prehistory and enter the arena of history.

2

The Early Days of the Game:
1845 to 1875

In 1845 a group of 28 middle-class professional men in New York City organized the Knickerbocker Base Ball Club with the express purpose of forming a baseball team that would play challenge matches with other baseball teams around the metropolitan area. One of the founders, Alexander Joy Cartwright, had been a clerk at the Union Bank of New York until the bank burned down, following which he opened a book and stationery store. Addictsports.com reported that "a four-man committee was appointed to draft a constitution and by-laws. Cartwright and the Committee President, Daniel L. 'Doc' Adams, a physician from New Hampshire, did most of the work on the by-laws, which became baseball's first formal rules." There were 20 rules in all, and they were adopted on September 13, the most important rules being these:

- "The ball must be pitched, and not thrown for the bat." The word "pitch," when used in a cricket or baseball sense, meant to toss the ball underhand.
- The pitching plate was 45 feet from home plate.
- The field was diamond-shaped, with the bases 90 feet apart. The diamond-shaped field was copied from the field described in the rules of another rounders offshoot, the Philadelphia Game.
- Three strikes was an out.
- Three outs ended an inning.
- The game ended when one team scored 21 aces (runs). If the visiting team scored the 21 aces, the home team still had their at-bats to try to match it or surpass it.

The bases were canvas bags, not posts or stones such as had been used previously.

Cartwright didn't see the sport he helped develop blossom into the professional game it would become over the next 25 years. He left the New York area in 1849 to join the gold rush in California, but poor health drove him further west, to Hawaii, where he lived until his death in 1892.

Prior to the formation of the Knickerbocker Base Ball Club, baseball was still considered to be primarily a child's sport, although it was popular with soldiers and with college students. But Cartwright's rules, which more than doubled the distance between bases, gave baseball an adult flavor. Initially, it was a gentleman's game, designed by Manhattan bankers, physicians, and merchants for leisurely recreation. According to Henderson, "They were wont to gather on a plot of ground at the corner of Twenty-Seventh Street and Madison Avenue on sunny days, in search of exercise, which took the form of primitive ball games of the time. It was customary for two or three of them to round up enough players to make a match." Baseball was not a competitive sport in the early days. It was more of a social function and a form of recreation. It also brought back pleasant memories of youthful endeavors to older men, as reported by John P. Rossi:

> Baseball's appeal initially was to an older generation of Americans and was largely nostalgic. Because most men had played some form of it as children, they could identify with baseball and enjoy playing or watching. It gave the businessmen in cities and towns a way to relive their youth. One of them, Frank Pigeon of the Brooklyn Eckford Club, summed up this aspect of the new game. He saw baseball as a way for he and his friends to "forget business and everything else, go out on the green fields, don our ball suits, and go at it with a rush. At such times we were boys again."

The typical blue-collar workingman didn't have the time to engage in this type of activity, which he still considered to be a child's game. He often worked until dark, six days a week, leaving him only Sunday for rest and recreation. Once the sport became professional, however, and the players were paid for their efforts, that situation changed dramatically. Laborers flocked to the sport like ducks to water, looking for an easy way to make a buck. And, for a period of time, from the 1870s through the end of the century, baseball gained a reputation as a low-class sport that attracted vulgar, uncouth ruffians. For many years, women were forbidden by their guardians to attend professional baseball games, for fear of their safety.

But in 1845, the game was a gentleman's sport, and according to SABR, the New York Nine met the Brooklyn Baseball Club on Elysian Fields on October 21 of that year. The highly talented New York Nine defeated their cross-river rivals by the score of 24–4 in four innings. Four days later, the two teams met again, this time on the Brooklyn's home grounds at the Star Cricket Club on Myrtle Avenue. The New Yorkers won again, this time 37–19 in another four-inning game. The box score for that game, shown below, may be the first known baseball box score ever printed in a newspaper. It appeared in the *New York Herald*.

NEW YORK BALL CLUB

	Hands Out	Runs
Davis	2	4
Murphy	0	6
Vail	2	4
Kline	1	4
Miller	2	5
Case	2	4
Tucker	2	4
Winslow	1	6
Total	12	37

BROOKLYN CLUB

	Hands Out	Runs
Hunt	1	3
Hines	2	2
Gilmore	3	2
Hardy	2	2
Sharp	2	2
Meyers	0	3
Whaley	2	2
Forman	1	3
Total	12	19

Eight months later, on June 19, 1846, the New York Nine hosted the Knickerbocker Base Ball Club in a match game, using the new rules the Knickerbockers had drawn up the previous September, including playing the game on a diamond-shaped field. The teams fielded nine players each; this number of players was subsequently added to the rules. Alexander Joy Cartwright, although generally recognized as the Knickerbockers' best player, did not participate in the game, preferring instead to umpire. The game was played on the Elysian Fields, with the New York Nine winning easily by a count of 21–1 in four innings. This was a historic game because it was the first scheduled baseball game between two organized baseball clubs to use the rules that became the foundation of the modern game.

The Knickerbockers didn't play another match game for five years, choosing to concentrate on intrasquad games instead, but there was a beehive of activity in other baseball clubs around the metropolitan area and throughout the northeast sector of the country after 1846. It was a veritable baseball explosion, with the country's largest cities leading the way. New York, with a population of 516,000, Philadelphia with a population of 340,000, Brooklyn with a population of 200,000, and Boston with a population of 137,000, were in the forefront of this explosion, as dozens of baseball clubs were formed in their cities. Chicago, with just 30,000 inhabitants, was still in its infancy. Finally, on June 3, 1851, the Knickerbocker Base Ball Club played their second match game, traveling to Yorkville to do battle with the Washington Club on Washington's home field, the Old Red House Grounds. The Knickerbockers created quite a stir when they took the field decked out in fancy uniforms consisting of blue trousers, white shirts, and straw hats, and their play lived up to their looks; they won the game 21–11 in eight innings.

Three years later, John H. Suydam and a few friends, members of the Jolly Young Bachelors Baseball Club, founded the Excelsior Baseball Club in Brooklyn. They played their games in South Brooklyn, at Smith and DeGraw Streets, before moving to a field near what is now Brooklyn Borough Hall. The following year the Eckford Baseball Club was organized, playing their games in the Greenpoint section of Brooklyn, near the waterfront. As Richard Goldstein noted,

> Two other Brooklyn clubs that would thrive — the Putnams and the Atlantics — were also formed about this time....
>
> Baseball was a gentleman's game at its dawn, with good fellowship much prized. Wining and dining after the game was as important as winning....
>
> One autumn evening in 1856, the Putnams, after defeating the Excelsiors, played host to them at Trenor's Dancing Academy in the Williamsburg section. There was some serious eating along with a few light speeches, and toasts were offered to the Knickerbockers, as baseball's pioneers, and to the press, which presumably had yet to misquote a ballplayer. To conclude the happy evening, the Putnams escorted the Excelsiors to the horse cars taking them back to their homes in South Brooklyn.

The "City of Churches," with a population of 200,000, was now America's third largest city.

In December 1856, the *New York Mercury* called baseball "The National Pastime." There were more than 50 baseball clubs in New York and neighboring Brooklyn by that time, and that figure increased to 200 within five years. Another of baseball's pioneers appeared on the scene in the late 1850s, and he would spend his entire newspaper career publicizing the grand old sport, so much so that he was given the title of "Father of Baseball." Henry Chadwick was born in England in 1824 and moved to Brooklyn with his family when he was 13 years old. He had played rounders and cricket as a child in England, but he was soon converted to baseball in Brooklyn during the 1840s. As a young man, he worked for several metropolitan newspapers, including the *New York Times*, the *New York Clipper*, the *Herald-Tribune*, and the *Brooklyn Eagle*. He began by reporting cricket matches, but from 1856 on he concentrated on baseball, and he spent the last 52 years of his life promoting the sport. His achievements are duly reported in Mike Shatzkin's *Ballplayers*:

> By the time the last New York newspaper began reporting baseball in 1862, Chadwick had taken on his next task: promoting changes through his writing and his membership on an early baseball rules committee — that would move the game toward a more balanced offense and defense. He expanded the box score (to include a batter's runs, hits, and outs), and developed a scoring system that enabled reporters to record every play, allowing them to describe games in greater detail. A modified version of his system is standard today.

He also introduced the first baseball scorecard, and provided fans with most of the basic statistics of the game, including batting averages and pitcher's earned run averages. He was one of the most prominent chroniclers of the game: "In 1860, Chadwick prepared baseball's first guide; he edited one or more annually until his death, including the famous and respected Spalding Guide, from 1881–1908." He was the official scorekeeper for many of the early baseball games including the historic 1870 meeting between the Cincinnati Red Stockings and the Brooklyn Atlantics. And he was a lifelong crusader against the evils of gambling and of alcoholism. Chadwick's career spanned the baseball scene from the initial development of the game to the introduction of the modern game. He saw the famous Knickerbockers of the 1840s cavort around the newly-designed diamond at the Elysian Fields, and he was still around to witness the first World Series between the Pittsburgh Pirates and the Boston Pilgrims (now the Red Sox) at the old Huntington Grounds in Boston in 1903.

On March 10, 1858, representatives from 22 amateur baseball clubs around the New York and Brooklyn area met to establish a ruling body for the game of baseball. They formed the National Association of Base Ball Players (NABBP), and they drew up a set of rules to govern the conduct of the game throughout the country. The rules were similar to the Knickerbocker rules with the exception that a game would be nine innings long, instead of being called after one team had scored 21 runs. One of their most important rules stated that baseball would remain an amateur sport, and that no one could be paid for his services. That particular rule would be violated in less than two years, and would be repealed in 1868.

Once the game of baseball became deeply rooted in both New York and Brooklyn, it was only natural that a fervid rivalry would emerge between the two cities, one that would last almost 100 years. In the spring of 1858, representatives of the four Brooklyn teams— the Eckfords, Atlantics, Excelsiors, and Putnams—challenged the teams from Hoboken and New York to a three-game series for the national championship, to be played at the Fashion Race Course on Long Island. All-star teams were selected to represent the cities and, as noted in this author's *Dodgers Encyclopedia*,

> The first game was held on July 20, amid a genuine World Series atmosphere. Fans from both cities flocked to the ballpark, decked out in their Sunday finery. The ferries from Manhattan were packed to the gunwales with exuberant New Yorkers. The Flushing railroad had to add extra cars to their trains to accommodate the hordes of people headed for Long Island. Large, horse-drawn buses, decorated with colorful banners, flags, and streamers, converged on the

Fashion Race Course from all directions. Even the respective baseball clubs arrived in style. The Excelsior Club entered the grounds in a gaily decorated bus pulled by 14 smartly groomed horses with fancy feather headdresses.

The series was hotly contested before crowds of 5,000–10,000 people, who paid a 50¢ admission fee, the first time admission was charged to see a baseball game. The New Yorkers won two of the three games, the scores being 22–18, 8–29, and 29–18. The series established a pattern of New York dominance over Brooklyn teams that would last for 97 years. Johnny Podres finally put the ghost to rest once and for all on a comfortable fall day in 1955.

It was obvious from the intense baseball rivalries that sprang up around the northeast section of the country in the late 1850s, not only in New York and Brooklyn but in Boston, Philadelphia, and points west, that the day of the "feeder," a pitcher who casually tossed the ball over the plate so the hitter could attack it with abandon, was nearing an end. The pitchers in the New York–Brooklyn national championship series pitched with a determination not seen in the old Knickerbocker days. The New York and Brooklyn pitchers were the sworn enemy of the batter, and their objective was to retire the batter before he could make a base hit.

Baseball, as noted in chapter 1, was popular in many eastern colleges as early as the mid–1700s. It was only fitting that the first college baseball game was played in Pittsfield, Massachusetts, where the first mention of the game appeared in a town bylaw dated to 1791. Williams College and Amherst College crossed bats in the Berkshire County town on Friday, July 1, 1859, using the rules of the Massachusetts Game. There were 13 players on each side, chosen by ballot from the student body. Williams College had a large cheering section at the game, as everyone at the school, students as well as faculty, was encouraged to attend. Amherst College allowed only the players to go. Spalding reported the scene in *America's National Game*:

> On Thursday afternoon, Amherst's seventeen picked men started for Pittsfield. They arrived in Pittsfield eager for battle. Soon the Williams boys began pouring into town until it seemed as if Williams must be deserted. Old men and women, young men and maidens, proprietors of female schools with their pupils—the great square of the ball ground was surrounded five or six deep.
>
> The appearance of the teams on the field must have been very amusing although there was some attempt at uniformity of dress, as "the Williams team were all dressed alike and wore belts marked Williams, but the appearance of the Amherst team was decidedly undress. The only attempt at a uniform was the blue ribbon which each man had pinned on his breast."
>
> It seems that the question of professionalism entered even into the first game, as it was "rumored that the Amherst thrower was the professional blacksmith who had been hired for the occasion." A bystander remarked that "the story must be true, as nobody but a blacksmith could possibly throw for three and a half hours as he did."
>
> The Amherst ball weighed two and one-half ounces and was about six inches in circumference. It was made by Henry Hebard of North Brookfield, and was considered a work of art at the time.
>
> The Williams ball was about seven inches in circumference, weighed about two ounces, and was covered with light colored leather, so as to make it seen with difficulty by the batters.

The Williams College boys jumped out to a 9–1 lead after two innings, but Amherst took the lead in the fourth inning and held it the rest of the game. After four hours and 26 innings, the game was called with Amherst on top by the score of 66 to 32. Amherst kept both balls, which are still displayed at the college with the notation, "The veritable balls used in the first intercollegiate game of Base Ball ever played."

The game of baseball was firmly entrenched in the northeast by 1859, entertaining thousands of fans from Boston to Philadelphia, but until that time there were no well-known players, especially pitchers. In most eastern cities, baseball was still a hitter's game, and had been for more than 500 years. The pitcher, or feeder, was one of the least appreciated players on the team. He had only one responsibility, to gently toss the ball over the center of the plate, underhand with a stiff arm, so the batter could take a good whack at it. He could not bend his elbow or snap his wrist. He was probably his team's weakest defensive player, as very few balls were hit to the pitcher, so he was assigned the demeaning task of serving the ball to the batter. But all that changed during the 1850s when teams in general, and pitchers in particular, began to reevaluate the game. This might have begun with the formation of Brooklyn's blue-collar teams, like the Atlantics and the Eckfords, who were organized in 1856.

Jimmy Creighton was baseball's first superstar as well as the game's first celebrity (JAY SANFORD).

Unlike their genteel counterparts, who considered the game to be primarily a form of exercise, followed by an evening of social graces, the blue-collar boys approached the game as a war, with winning the number one priority. It was during that period that some unknown feeder decided he should challenge the batter instead of giving him a fat pitch to hit, so he began putting a little more mustard on the ball to intimidate and confuse the batter. From the description of the Amherst-Williams match, the Amherst feeder must have been firing the ball with serious intentions.

The pitching revolution was carried one step further by a young man by the name of James "Jimmy" Creighton, who appeared on the scene in 1858. Born in New York in 1841 and raised in Brooklyn, Creighton was a star cricket player as well as an outstanding baseball player during his youth. The slightly built pitcher, who began his baseball career with a boy's team called the Niagaras, did not adhere to the idea that the game was basically a recreational pastime. He pitched to win, as noted in All-Baseball.com: "Creighton thought the game could be something more ... a competition. What's more, he acted on his supposition, and started the most basic paradigm shift in the game's history, transforming what was then base ball into a sport from a leisurely pastime where the pitcher and batter actually worked in together to initiate the play." Standing only 5' 7" tall, and weighing about 145 pounds soaking wet, the feisty right-hander was not about to be a serving boy for opposing batters. He developed a blazing fastball, and he used an imperceptible, and illegal, snap to his wrist as he released the ball, causing it to move at an incredible velocity. As a result, he was almost unhittable at the official pitching distance of 45 feet. The 17-year-old phenomenon originally played second base, third base, and outfield for the Niagara Club, but also took a turn on the mound, as a "change" or relief pitcher. One of the rules that had been enacted in 1857 stated that no player could be replaced after the game had started unless he was ill or injured. If a starting pitcher was being hit hard, the manager could not bring in a fresh arm from the bench. He had to use someone who was already in the game. The pitcher and the other player, usually a strong-armed outfielder with decent control, changed positions, giving birth to the term "change pitcher." During a game against Brooklyn's strong junior team, the Stars, a trade card gave this account, as reported by Tiemann and Rucker:

> On the final inning of the game, when the Stars were a number of runs ahead, the Niagaras changed pitchers, and Jimmy took that position. Peter O'Brien (Capt. of the Atlantics of Brooklyn), witnessed this game, and when Creighton got to work, something new was seen in base ball — the low swift delivery, the ball rising from the ground past the shoulder to the catcher. The Stars soon saw they could not cope with such pitching.

Creighton's career progressed rapidly. He joined the Stars for the 1858 season, but was recruited by the Excelsiors the following year, turning a good team into a great one. Two years later, the Excelsiors made a historic tour of the northeast, bringing the romance and excitement of baseball to outlying regions of the area. John P. Rossi commented on it:

> A clear sign of baseball's popularity occurred on the eve of the Civil War. In 1860 the Excelsior Club of Brooklyn undertook the first tour of a baseball nine, traveling by train throughout New York State and down to Pennsylvania, Maryland, and Delaware, playing before large crowds that were already deeply informed about baseball. The success of this tour showed the possibility of spreading the game throughout the nation now that a railway network was near completion.

The first stop on the Excelsiors' tour was Albany, New York, where, on July 2, they defeated the Champion Club by a score of 24–6. The next day, they beat the Victory Club of Troy 13–7 in a rare pitchers' duel. Continuing west, the Brooklynites walloped the Niagaras of Buffalo 50–19. They followed that drubbing by defeating the Flour City Club of Rochester 21–1, the Live Oak Club of the same city 27–9, and the Hudson River Club of Newburgh 59–14, before returning home with a perfect 6–0 slate. Back in Brooklyn, they knocked off the Atlantics 23–4, as Jimmy Creighton kept the Atlantic batters back on their heels with his vicious speedball. Next, the Excelsiors went back on the road, traveling to Pennsylvania, Maryland, and Delaware. Their first stop was Baltimore, where they easily defeated a city all-star team by the count of 51–6, after which the locals feted the Brooklyn boys at a fine banquet at Guy's Hotel. Two days later, on July 24, the Excelsiors defeated the Athletics of Philadelphia by the score of 15–4 before a crowd of 3,000 who cheered in vain for the home team. In all, they won 15 consecutive games, including the games in New York, and they returned home undefeated. And, along the way, a superstar was born. In a game where teams routinely scored 20 to 30 runs a game, and more, Jimmy Creighton held the opposition to less than nine runs a game, a virtually unheard-of achievement in that day and age. Addictsports.com quoted one reporter's observation that "the ball Creighton tosses looks as though it had been launched from a cannon." And they added, "Armed with his speedball, Creighton would mix in normal slow pitches, he dubbed 'dewdrops' to further baffle early batsmen." The Genesee Country Village & Museum website reported that a New York newspaper called him "the pitcher par excellence" and said, "his forte was great speed and thorough command of the ball." The 19-year-old youngster had suddenly become more than just a pitcher. He was a celebrity and the game's first matinee idol. Young women flocked to the ballpark to see the handsome Excelsior pitcher do his stuff. Along the way, the boy prodigy also became baseball's first professional player, as the Excelsiors, ignoring the NABBP's amateur rule, secretly paid him a salary.

On their return home, the Excelsiors played a return match with the Atlantics on the Atlantics' home field at the corner of Marcy and Gates avenues, but this time their luck deserted them. Creighton did not have his "A" game with him, and the Atlantics prevailed by a count of 15–14. The Excelsiors held a comfortable 12–6 lead at the end of the sixth inning, but Creighton hit the wall in the seventh, and the Atlantics lit up the scoreboard, pushing over nine big runs, spearheaded by doubles off the bats of McMahon and Peter O'Brien and a booming triple by John Oliver. On August 10, 1860, the *New York Times* commented, "Creighton's pitching was very good for the first few innings, but it became manifest in the seventh inning that he was not in condition." He was replaced by Russell in the eighth. Having split the two games played, the managers agreed to a rubber match, to be played on a neutral field, to determine an unofficial national champion. The game was played on August 23 on the Putnam's field at Gates and Lafayette avenues, with an enormous gathering of 20,000 fans surrounding the field. The game was chaotic from start to end, as recounted by Richard Goldstein:

> The potential for trouble was there before a pitch was thrown. Gambling, having become common at games, could always inflame things. Beyond that, there was social-class antagonism: the Atlantics' fans were mostly Irish immigrant workingmen while the Excelsiors' backers were mainly from the old Anglo-Saxon stock, in white-collar positions and the professions. When the Atlantics began bickering with the umpire in the early going, their supporters were quick to anger. After each close play, the Atlantic fans showered abuse on the umpire and the Excelsior players. Things got even uglier when the Atlantics' McMahon was called out for overrunning third base in the fourth inning. Despite pleas for calm by the Atlantic players, the 100 policemen at the game were hard-pressed to keep the crowd under control. With the Excelsiors leading, 8–6, in the sixth inning, their captain, Joseph Leggett, finally pulled them off the field. Leggett supposedly handed the baseball to Matty O'Brien, the Atlantics' captain, and declared "Here, O'Brien, the ball, you can keep it." O'Brien reciprocating the sporting gesture, is said to have replied: "Will you call it a draw?" "As you please," Leggett icily responded. The Excelsiors then departed in their horse-drawn omnibus, pursued by Atlantic fans hurling stones at them. The uproar was not forgotten. Never again would the Excelsiors and the Atlantics face each other.

Jimmy Creighton was not only a great pitcher; he was also a batter without equal. It was reported that he was retired only four times one season, while averaging 4.2 runs per game. Tragically for the sensational young hurler, his time was running out. Just two years later, on October 14, 1862, in a game against the Unions, he slugged a ball to the deepest reaches of the field and circled the bases with a home run. The cheers of the crowd suddenly turned to gasps of anguish when Creighton, on crossing the plate, collapsed with an internal injury, possibly a ruptured bladder. He was carried to his father's home at 307 Henry Street, where he died four days later. The *New York Times* obituary noted, "he was known extensively as an expert base ball player." He was buried in Greenwood Cemetery, his grave marked by a large, gaudy, granite tombstone crowned with a granite baseball, erected by his teammates. The stone contained carvings of several baseball articles, including two crossed bats, a base, a baseball cap, and a scorebook. Above all was the single word "Excelsior." Jimmy Creighton was just 21 years old.

Although his career was short, Creighton was one of the most important players in baseball history. He single-handedly took the position of pitcher, which had previously been one of serving soft pitches to the batter so the batter could hit the ball with abandon, and elevated it to perhaps the most important position on the team. The pitcher, thanks to Creighton, became the sworn enemy of the batter. It was his job to prevent the batter from reaching base. He revolutionized the pitching position, transforming it from one of servitude to one of dominance. He was the Father of Pitchers.

The Civil War interrupted baseball's progress in the early 1860s, but over the last half of the decade, Brooklyn was the center of the baseball universe, the Atlantics capturing the national championship three successive times between 1864 and 1866, although they were hard pressed to take two out of three from the powerful Athletics of Philadelphia in '66 by scores of 27–13, 12–31, and 34–24. It was during this period that another innovator made a significant contribution to the game, one that would further strengthen the pitcher's role in the game. A 14-year-old boy named William Arthur "Candy" Cummings, while throwing clamshells on the beach at Ware, Massachusetts, near Boston, noted with interest how the wind caused the shells to curve, first one way, and then the other. The youngster became obsessed with achieving the same results with a baseball, and he worked on developing his delivery for more than three years. Finally, in 1867, the 5' 9", 120-pound hurler, while pitching for the Excelsiors against the Harvard University baseball team, unveiled his new pitch to the delight of the fans. Even though the haughty physics professors at the elite school ridiculed his declaration that he could make a baseball curve, Cummings just laughed it off and said, "I curveballed them to death," according to Frederick Ivor-Campbell. Over the next few years, he kept perfecting his execution and improving his control of the pitch. By 1870, he was considered by many baseball men to be the best pitcher in the country. It was during this time that he acquired the nickname "Candy," nineteenth century slang for "the best."

Then, in 1868, the game took another turn that had serious ramifications for the sport. A Cincinnati businessman named Aaron Champion, convinced that baseball could be a profitable business, not only for himself but for the city of Cincinnati, decided to form a professional baseball team. He built a new ballpark, hired Harry Wright as manager, and set out to hire the best players in the country, offering them a generous salary to play for his Red Stockings full time. By the time the 1869 season opened, baseball's first professional team was ready to take the field. Shortstop George Wright had joined the team from the

Unions, third baseman Fred Waterman came from the Mutuals, and right fielder Cal McVey came from the Actives of Indianapolis. George Wright was the star of the team, and its highest paid player, at a salary of $1,400 for the season. Pitcher Asa Brainard, who had starred for the Excelsiors for seven years, was regarded as one of the best pitchers in the country. The Red Stockings embarked on a grand tour in 1869, traveling 11,877 miles by train and engaging the best teams from San Francisco to Baltimore. They drew an estimated 200,000 people to their games, an average of 3,500 spectators per game, and they heavily outscored their opponents, achieving an average score of 43–10. The Red Stockings ran off 39 consecutive victories before being tied by the Troy (New York) Haymakers 17–17. They completed their first season with a record of 56–0–1. And George Wright earned his exorbitant salary by lacing the ball at a .518 clip with 59 home runs.

The following year, the Cincinnati steamroller hit the road again, sweeping through the South and demolishing everyone in its path. The Red Stockings massacred the Louisville, Kentucky, team by the count of 94–7, whipped the Southerns of New Orleans 80–6, and embarrassed the Orientals of Memphis 100–2. Moving up through the Midwest, they knocked over the Unions of Urbana, Illinois, 108–3 and treated Dayton just as roughly, 104–9. They then turned their attention to the East, where the toughest teams in the country were located, and they were slowed down somewhat, but never put to the test. They beat Flour City of Rochester, New York, 56–13, took the measure of Old Elm of Pittsfield, Massachusetts, 66–9, and humbled Tri-Mountain of Boston 30–6. Marching boldly into Brooklyn, New York, they defeated the Mutuals 16–3, running their record for the season to 23–0. On June 14, 1870, Harry Wright's proud Red Stockings paraded into the Capitoline Grounds in Brooklyn, the country's first enclosed ballpark, decked out in dazzling white uniforms, with knee-length trousers and bright red stockings. Their opponents, the Atlantics, wore long, blue trousers and white shirts. The opposing pitchers, George Zettlein of the Atlantics and Asa Brainard of the Cincinnati Red Stockings, were arguably the two greatest pitchers of their era. They were also old adversaries, having faced each other several times over the previous four years, while Brainard was pitching for the Excelsiors and Zettlein was on the mound for the Eckfords and the Atlantics. The estimated 20,000 fans who pushed their way into the Atlantics' home field witnessed the greatest baseball game of the nineteenth century.

George "the Charmer" Zettlein, the Atlantics starting pitcher, was a hometown boy, having been born in Brooklyn in 1844. He had enlisted in the Union army at the outbreak of the Civil War, later transferring to the navy, where he participated in the Battle of Mobile Bay under Admiral Farragut. Returning to Brooklyn after the war, Zettlein began his professional baseball career with the Eckfords in 1865. He went on to play for the Atlantics from 1866 through 1870, compiling a win-loss record of 77–36 in Brooklyn, including a 31–5 season in 1868. The Brooklyn pitcher would subsequently play in the National Association from 1871 to its demise in 1875, going 125–91. And he would end his professional career with the Philadelphia Athletics in the National League's inaugural season in 1876, winning four games against 20 losses. The 5' 9", 160-pound right-handed pitcher was a one-pitch pitcher, who got by with an overpowering fastball.

Zettlein's opponent in the big game, Asa Brainard, was born in Albany, New York, in 1841, joining the Excelsiors of Brooklyn in 1860, where he played right field behind the pitching of Jimmy Creighton. Eventually, Brainard took to the mound himself. He reportedly owned one of the best fastballs in the game, and he may have added Creighton's illegal wrist-snap to his repertoire, but he also kept the hitters off balance by changing speeds and location. The 5' 8", 150-pound right-hander starred for the Excelsiors for seven years and the Nationals for one year before signing with the Cincinnati Red Stockings for $1,100 a season. In 1869, as the Red Stockings went 56–0–1, Brainard pitched most, if not all, of the games. He did the same in 1870, achieving a 79–0–1 record over the two-year period, on entering the game with the Atlantics.

The Cincinnati Red Stockings were heavily favored to make the Brooklyn team their eightieth consecutive victim. The odds were 5–1 according to the New York betting line, and the Red Stockings started off as if the game would be another rout. George Wright led off with a single, and scored the first run of the game on subsequent singles by Doug Allison and Harry Wright, with Allison continuing across the plate on a throwing error by right fielder Dan McDonald. They added a single run in the third to up the count to 3–0, but the Atlantics pushed over two in the fourth, and two more in the sixth for a 4–3 lead. Brooklyn's joy was short-lived, however, as the Red Stockings put a two-spot on the board in the top of the seventh to regain the lead once again. Charlie Smith got the Atlantics back even when he smashed a triple to deep left field in the bottom of the eighth and carried home the tying run on a sacrifice fly by Joe Start. The game remained tied into the eleventh when Cincinnati appeared to put the game away with a two-run rally off a rapidly tiring Zettlein. But the Atlantics weren't through. Brainard, who was also running out of gas, was touched up for a single by Smith leading off the bottom of the eleventh. "Old Reliable," Joe Start, plated Smith with a whistling triple down the right-field line, sending the big Brooklyn crowd into a frenzy. The next batter, left fielder John Chapman, grounded out with Start holding third, but Bob Ferguson singled sharply past second to tie the game at 7–7. George Zettlein then stepped to the plate and smashed a ball off Gould's glove at first base. Gould, rushing his throw in an attempt to nail Ferguson at second, threw wildly, with the ball sailing into left field. The speedy Atlantic catcher picked himself up, raced around third, and slid home with the winning run, as the Capitoline Grounds exploded with a deafening roar, celebrating the impossible. The mighty Cincinnati Red Stockings had tasted defeat for the first time in their two-year existence.

CINCINNATI RED STOCKINGS

Name	Pos	AB	R	H
G. Wright	SS	6	2	4
C. Gould	1B	6	0	0
F. Waterman	3B	5	0	1
D. Allison	C	5	1	3
H. Wright	CF	5	0	1
A. Leonard	LF	5	0	0
A. Brainard	P	5	2	2
C. Sweasy	2B	5	2	3
C. McVey	RF	5	0	0
Totals		47	7	14

ATLANTICS OF BROOKLYN

Name	Pos	AB	R	H
D. Pearce	SS	5	2	2
C. Smith	3B	5	2	2
J. Start	1B	6	3	3
J. Chapman	LF	5	0	1
B. Ferguson	C	5	1	2
G. Zettlein	P	5	0	0
G. Hall	CF	5	0	1
L. Pike	2B	5	0	1
D. McDonald	RF	4	0	0
		45	8	12

Cincinnati Red Stockings 2 0 1 0 0 0 2 0 0 0 2 — 7 — 14 — 12

Brooklyn Atlantics   0 0 0 2 0 2 0 1 0 0 3 — 8 — 12 — 11

The number of errors in the game were not unusual for that period. The players did not wear gloves, the fields were ragged, and players were charged with an error if they touched a ball, even if it was a difficult chance. That defeat spelled the end of the line for the nineteenth century version of the Big Red Machine. They lost several more games before the season ended, five by one count, and the team was then disbanded, supposedly because of salary disputes.

Professionalism, however, was here to stay. A group of ballplayers, representing ten professional baseball teams, met in Collier's Café on Broadway and 13th Street in New York City on St. Patrick's Day, 1871, and formed the National Association of Professional Base Ball Players (NA), a nine-club league run by the players. The new league was perhaps doomed from the start, according to Rossi: "Consequently the league suffered from the kind of chaos one would expect when the inmates run the asylum: sloppy scheduling, poor management, incompetent business practices and constant 'revolving,' a plethora of gambling scandals, and, with the emergence of professionalism, a number of unsavory players." Several rule changes over the next few years affected the competitive balance between the pitcher and the batter. The first rule change, in 1871, allowed the batter to call for either a high pitch or a low pitch, the high pitch crossing the plate between the batter's shoulders and his waist, and the low pitch crossing the plate between the batters waist and his knees. The lower limit of the low pitch was changed the next year to "one foot from the ground." Also in 1872, the rule governing the pitching motion was changed, legalizing the jerk, wrist snap, and bent elbow deliveries. This change permitted pitchers to throw a curveball legally for the first time. Two years later, yet another rule change instructed the umpire to tighten the reins on the pitcher's unfair deliveries. He was instructed to call every third unfair pitch a ball, and awarding the batter first base after three balls, a total of nine pitches. Overall, the various changes seemed to help the batter more than the pitcher. He could now demand either a high pitch or a low pitch, and he could take a base on balls after nine errant pitches. On the other hand, the pitcher, who already had the advantage of throwing to the batter from a cozy 45-foot distance, now had the advantage of being allowed to legally curve the ball.

Over the course of its existence, the National Association encountered growing pains that it could not overcome. Many of the teams had financial problems and were unable to wait very long to generate a profit. As a result, there was considerable turnover of the member teams. The Fort Wayne Kekiongas won the first professional baseball game ever played as Bobby Mathews tossed the first major league shutout, blanking Forest City of Cleveland by the score of 2–0 on May 4, 1871. That was the high point of the Kekiongas' season, as they dropped out of the league after playing just 19 games. As Rossi noted, the clubs had no set schedule. The plans called for each team to play five three-game series with each other team, with the champion being the team with the best winning percentage. The *Baseball Encyclopedia* added, "Of course, not everyone played all the requisite series. Teams with little to gain and longer to travel didn't make every road trip — and the NA wasn't big on discipline for those who strayed." The Philadelphia Athletics won the first National Association pennant, with a record of 21–7, for a winning percentage of .750. Dick McBride of the A's was the top pitcher, with a record of 18–5, although Al Spalding of the Boston Red Stockings led the league in victories with 19, against 10 losses. The league was, not surprisingly, a hitter's league, with 10.5 runs being scored per game thanks to a .287 league batting average. The extra-base hit averages were very similar to the 2003 National League averages, in total. The NA averaged 6.1 XBH per game compared to 5.7 XBH per game for the 2003 NL, but the NA's were primarily doubles and triples while the NL's were mostly home runs. The NA averaged 3.4 doubles, 1.9 triples, and 0.4 home runs, per game, while the 2003 NL averaged 3.6 doubles, 0.4 triples, and 2.1 home runs. The NA league ERA of 4.22 was almost equal to the 2003 NL ERA of 4.28. The rosters were kept to a minimum in order to keep expenses down. The A's, for instance, carried only ten men, with George Bechtel, the utility player, dividing his time between right field and "change" pitcher.

The Boston Red Stockings, who finished in second place — two games behind the A's — in the National Association's inaugural season, won the next four pennants by increasingly larger margins,

Candy Cummings claimed to have invented the curveball in the late 1860s (JAY SANFORD).

removing most of the competitiveness from the league and hurting the attendance figures. The biggest change in the league over the years was in the pitching department, where the league earned run average dropped from 4.22 in 1871, to 3.65, 3.40, 2.19, and 2.23 over the ensuing four years. Since most teams carried only one pitcher, the change pitcher had to come in from his position in the field to provide relief in case of injury or illness to the starting pitcher, or to relieve the starting pitcher if the game was one sided. In those days, all the players including the pitcher were expected to play the entire game. The moundsmen who compiled the best completion records included McBride, Spalding, George Zettlein, and Candy Cummings. The league's pitchers, in total, completed 90 percent of their starts. Candy Cummings led the way with a 97 percent completion rate while compiling a sensational record. In 1872, he went 33–20, completing 53 of 55 starts. The next year he won 28 games against 14 losses, and completed all 42 of his starts. In '74, he was 28–26, with 52 complete games in 54 starts. And in '75, he went 35–12 with 47 complete games in 48 starts. The game's two greatest pitchers in 1869 fared much differently in the National Association. George Zettlein compiled a record of 125–92 during five years in the NA, while his opponent in the famous game between the Cincinnati Red Stockings and the Atlantics of Brooklyn, Asa Brainard, could do no better than 24–53 in four years.

Joseph Borden of the Athletics of Philadelphia recorded the first no-hitter in major league history on July 28, 1875, when he defeated the Chicago White Stockings 4–0. The 21-year-old Borden completed all seven of his starts that year, finishing the season with a 2–2 record. After going 11–12 with the Boston Red Stockings in the National League's inaugural season in 1876, Borden never pitched another major league game.

The National Association lasted only five years with teams coming and going. From a nine-team league in 1871, the NA had 11 teams in 1872, 9 teams in '73, 8 teams in '74, and 13 teams in '75. In all, a total of 24 different teams played in the NA during its five-year existence. There were many reasons for the collapse of the NA, the most important of which was the failure of the clubs to generate a profit. And in the final year, there was essentially no competition in the league. The Boston Red Stockings, whose roster had been stocked with many of the old Cincinnati Red Stockings players, raced off to a big lead, winning their first 22 games. They also won their final 24 games, finishing the season with a record of 71 and 8, giving them a healthy 18½-game bulge over the second place Hartford Dark Blues. At the other end of the spectrum, the Brooklyn Atlantics went 2 and 42 for a winning percentage of .042, finishing 51½ games off the pace. But the financial problems and lack of competition weren't the only problems plaguing the new league. Gamblers roamed the stands betting on the outcome of the game, and often conspired with players to throw important games. And whiskey was sold on the premises, resulting in drunken rowdiness and frequent fights. There were reports of fans spilling onto the field in New York on more than one occasion, disrupting play.

The National Association folded after the 1875 season, to be replaced by the more financially responsible National League. It did, however, bring several "firsts" to the professional game. The Union Grounds in Brooklyn introduced box seats, which for a premium of 25 cents offered a spectator protection and privacy. And Joseph Borden of the Philadelphia Athletics tossed the first major league no-hitter, blanking the Chicago White Stockings 4–0. The NA also introduced some of the game's greatest players to baseball fans from the Mississippi River to the Atlantic Ocean, including Al Spalding, Cap Anson, Dickey Pearce, George Wright, Pud Galvin, George Zettlein, Asa Brainard, and Bobby Mathews.

Perhaps the greatest player to come out of the National Association was Albert Goodwill Spalding, a tall, lanky right-handed pitcher from Byron, Illinois. As William Curran noted, "In some ways, Spalding established a model for pitchers. Tall, handsome, confident, and dignified. A.G., as he was widely known, added luster to the popular image of the pitcher, as he compiled 207 wins against just 56 losses, and led the Red Stockings to four consecutive pennants and one second place finish." His pitching delivery was described in the *New York Star*:

> On receiving the ball, he raises it in both hands until it is on a level with his left eye. Striking an attitude he gazes at it two or three minutes in a contemplative way, and then turns it around once or twice to be sure that it is not an orange or coconut. Assured that he has the genuine article, and after a scowl at the shortstop, and a glance at home plate, [he] finally delivers the ball with the precision and rapidity of a cannon shot.

The 6' 1", 170-pound underhand hurler, using a fastball and a change of pace, led the National Association in victories all five years of the league's existence. He also led the league in winning percentage four times, games pitched three times, and innings pitched twice. Although he put together win-loss records of 19–10, 38–8, 41–14, 52–16, and 54–5, he was not a one-dimensional player. He also wielded a potent bat, compiling a career batting average of .323, with a high of .354 in 1872. And to top off his versatility, he twice led the league in fielding percentage. The 25-year-old Spalding joined the Chicago White Stockings as manager and pitcher for the National League's inaugural season in 1876. He led the league in pitching that year with 47 victories and paced the Chicagos to the league pennant by six games over the St. Louis Brown Stockings. A.G. played 60 games in '77, all but four of them in the infield. He concluded his major league career the following season, playing one game at second base. His association with baseball continued long after his playing days, however. He opened a sporting goods company in 1876, which eventually became the country's largest manufacturer of sporting goods. He also served as president of the White Stockings from 1882 to 1891, and was baseball's most famous goodwill ambassador around the world.

James "Pud" Galvin was another player who got his feet wet in the National Association, winning four games against two losses as an 18-year-old pitcher for the St. Louis Brown Stockings in 1875. He would go on to fame and fortune with the Buffalo Bisons and Pittsburgh Alleghenies of the National League from 1876 through 1894.

Bobby Mathews was a tiny 5' 5", 140-pound submarine right-hander who played major league baseball from 1871 to 1887, spending five years in the National Association, five years in the National League, and five years in the American Association. After compiling a brilliant 42–22 record for the New York Mutuals in 1874, he dropped to 29–28 the following season, then had a letdown midway through his career with four losing seasons and one year where he was out of the game. But, at the age of 30, Mathews came back strong, with five good seasons, including three consecutive 30-win seasons. He retired in 1887 with a major league career record of 297–248 over 15 years. His success can be attributed to his command of three pitches: a good fastball, and the raise-curve and spitball, both of which he has been credited with inventing.

Jack Manning, a right-handed pitcher from Braintree, Massachusetts, may have been the game's first relief pitcher, according to John Thorn. Manning spent two years in the National Association, going 16–2 with six saves in 1875, starting 18 games and relieving in nine. The previous year, as strictly a starting pitcher, he compiled an embarrassing 4–16 mark. After the NA folded, Harry Wright, the manager of Boston in the newly formed National League, signed the 22-year-old Manning to play right field for the Red Caps and to double as the change pitcher. Manning played in all 70 of Boston's games in 1876, batting .264 and pitching in 34 games, 20 as a starter and 14 as the change pitcher. John Thorn reported that the Boston press dubbed him the "saver," after he pitched 40 innings in relief, posting a perfect 4–0 record, with a league-leading five saves and a miniscule 0.68 earned run average. His five saves remained the high-water mark for relief pitchers for 29 years. Overall, including his starts, Manning compiled an excellent 18–5 record over 197 innings, with a 2.14 ERA. For some unknown reason, his pitching career essentially ended after the 1876 season. He pitched in just 13 games combined in 1877 and '78, with a 1–4 record and one save. He continued to play in the National League through the 1886 season, but he was primarily an outfielder, with some time as shortstop and at first base. He batted .257 in 682 games over his 12-year career.

The period from 1845 to 1876 was a time of development and growth for the game of baseball. One Web article titled "Baseball in the Nineteenth Century" noted,

The game ... more closely resembled a modern softball game played by men not thoroughly familiar with its rules. The ball was oversized. It was delivered underhand to the bat. Occasionally the ball was so full of rubber that it bounced way over a man's head when it hit the outfield. But sometimes it was so mushy that a hitter could hardly get it out of the infield. Bats were hardly uniform in size, some thin as a broomstick, others longer than a man's leg.

John P. Rossi reported on changes to the baseball:

By the 1870's, the baseball began to take on the look of a modern ball, shrinking to its present size ... from the softer, larger ball used earlier in the century. The 1870's baseball consisted of a small core of hard rubber, surrounded with tightly wrapped wool and covered with two carefully stitched figure-eight pieces of horsehide, which gave the ball its distinctive look. Earlier baseballs had been stitched with a cover that looked like a peeled orange.

The construction of the baseball was continually modified during the 1860s and 1870s, a practice that continues to the present day. After decades of high-scoring games, the baseball was intentionally deadened to reduce the scores to a more modest level. William Curran reported, "By 1876, Kelley Brothers of New York was able to boast in its ads, 'Our Professional Dead Balls ... are the deadest balls made.'"

Other changes to the game and its equipment in the years leading up to the formation of the National League included the introduction of gloves, although these were limited to the pitcher and the catcher. The gloves offered only a minimum of protection since they were skin-tight leather gloves that covered only the palm of the hand. Fielders still caught the ball bare-handed. There were also some significant rules changes between 1845 and 1876, many of them involving the evolving responsibilities of the pitcher. These are some of the more important rules established by the ruling bodies over the years that defined the role of the pitcher:

• In 1845 the distance from the pitcher's box to home base was set at 45 feet. Also, three balls struck at and missed was an out.
• In 1854, the ball had to weigh 5½ to 6 oz. and be 2¾ to 3½ inches in diameter. These specifications were adjusted several times over the years, finally settling in at 5–5¼ oz. in weight and 9–9¼ inches in circumference, in 1872.
• In 1857, the pitcher had to deliver the ball as near as possible over the center of the plate. The pitcher's position was designated by a line 4 yards in length, with a fixed iron plate in the center, 15 yards from home plate. Also in 1857, no changes or substitution were allowed after the game had commenced unless for reason of illness or injury.
• In 1858, if a batter stood at the plate and didn't offer at a fair pitch, the umpire was ordered to call a strike.
• In 1863, if a pitcher did not throw a fair ball, he was given a warning. The second time he did it, a ball was called. Three balls constituted a walk. In the same year, the pitcher's box was introduced. It measured 12' wide by 3' deep. The pitcher's box was modified several times between 1863 and 1893, when the pitcher's plate replaced it.
• In 1867, the pitcher had to deliver the ball with a straight arm, swinging perpendicularly and free from the body. Also, pitches striking the ground in front of home base, over the head of the batter, or outside the batter's reach, were considered unfair balls.
• In 1870, there was no warning before calling balls and strikes. But the umpire only called every third ball, so it took nine pitches for a walk. This rule was changed several times before settling at four balls, in 1889.

• In 1871, the batter was allowed to call for either a high pitch (between the waist and the shoulder) or a low pitch (no higher than the waist and at least one foot from the ground). That rule was rescinded in 1887. The strike zone was redefined the same year as being between the shoulder and the knee. It has been modified several times over the years, the most recent time being in 1995.
• In 1872, the jerk, wrist-snap, and bent elbow deliveries were legalized, giving pitchers additional weapons, such as curveballs, in their war against batters.

Games of bat and ball had evolved from primitive games of catch along the banks of the Nile 4,000 years ago, to club ball and rounders in medieval England, to town ball, and finally baseball, in the American colonies. Along the way, several important pioneers helped to mold the game into its current form. Alexander Joy Cartwright helped to develop the first formal rules and the standard diamond-shaped field. Henry Chadwick produced the detailed box score, the first scorecard, and the first set of statistics such as the batting average and the fielding average. Jimmy Creighton elevated the position of pitcher from that of second-class citizen to one of the most important members of the team. Candy Cummings' invention of the curveball significantly increased the pitcher's stature. The evolution of pitching began the day the Knickerbockers formulated the first rules for the game of baseball, but the strategy for the position, utilizing relief pitchers, would not be realized until 1891. Since free substitution was illegal until that date, and relief pitchers had to come from the ranks of the position players who were already on the field, the game was in the hands of the starting pitcher. Change pitchers only replaced the starting pitcher in the event of an injury or illness, or if the game was out of hand. The Cincinnati Red Stockings gave the fans of the country their first professional baseball team. Asa Brainard of the Red Stockings made pitching a thinking man's sport, by constantly changing speed and location, to keep the batter off balance. And the National Association of Professional Base Ball Players, albeit a short five-year experiment, proved that a professional baseball league could exist and could prosper in America. The stage had been set. It was time for the game of professional baseball, as we know it, to begin.

3

The Professional Game:
1876 to 1892

The period from 1876 to 1892 was one of the most important periods in American baseball history. It was the time when the National League was formed, the beginning of major league baseball, and it was a transition between the bat and ball games of centuries past to the modern game that can be seen daily in ballparks all across the United States between April and October. With the collapse of the National Association after the 1875 season, it looked as though baseball would be without a professional league once again. But such was not the case. William Hulbert, the owner of Chicago White Stockings of the defunct NA, along with other interested owners, met at the Grand Central Hotel in New York and created the National League. It was designed to be a league of management-controlled teams, as opposed to the player-controlled teams that spelled the downfall of the National Association. The primary objectives of the new professional baseball establishment were to recruit the best players possible, provide paid umpires for the games, and eliminate gambling and drunkenness from the ballparks, making it a family oriented sport.

Rosters were small out of necessity, since owners didn't have the money to pay for substitutes. The Chicago entry in the National League in 1876 carried only nine players, including one pitcher and one catcher. No team had more than 11 players, so complete games by the pitcher were the order of the day. It was a time in baseball history when pitchers finished what they started. It was also a time when versatility was in demand, even among pitchers. John Montgomery Ward, for instance, was equally at home at second base, shortstop, outfield, or on the mound. He began his major league career as a pitcher, going 22–13 with the Providence Grays in 1878. The following year, he unlimbered his pitching arm in earnest, confusing hitters with a baffling array of curveballs, to run up a league-leading 47–19 win-loss record, on his way to a career mark of 164–103. His 291 career games pitched included 30 games pitched in relief, where he compiled an 11–5 record with three saves. He led the league in relief wins twice, with five in 1879 and four in 1883. Over one two-year period, according to Thorn, Ward yielded only four earned runs in 65 innings of relief pitching. When his pitching arm gave out in 1884, Monte Ward deftly moved to shortstop, where he became the top shortstop in the National League. In 1887 the 5' 9", 160-pound infielder led the league in fielding, batted a scorching .338, scored 114 runs, and stole 111 bases. He went on to produce a .275 lifetime batting average over a 17-year career, with 2,107 base hits, 1,410 runs scored, and 540 stolen bases. During his pitching period, Ward was credited with being the first pitcher to build an elevated mound. In 1879, the pitcher's box was a six-by-six flat square area, but Ward choose to pitch from a mound to obtain better leverage and more speed. From that time until the baseball establishment defined the limits of a mound in the rule book, the pitcher's box varied from a flat area to a mound that sometimes reached as high as 20", as estimated from photographs of the period. The 1903 rule limited the mound height to a maximum of 15".

Albert Spalding, called "the organizational genius of baseball's pioneer days" by the National Baseball Hall of Fame, as quoted in Shatzkin, managed the Chicago White Stockings to the National League pennant in 1876, and he paced the league's pitchers with a record of 47–12, tossing 60 complete games in 61 starts. He also played ten games in the outfield and one game at third base, while compiling a fine .312 batting average. First baseman Cal McVey, doubling as Spalding's change pitcher, finished at 5–2. George Bradley of the St. Louis Brown Stockings completed all his 64 starts, pitching all but four of his team's 577 innings. His 45–19 win-loss record included 16 shutouts, which is still the major league record, although it was tied by Grover Cleveland Alexander in 1916. And the 5' 10", 175-pound right-handed hurler had the honor of throwing the first no-hitter in National League history, when he blanked the Hartford Dark Blues without a hit on July 15, 1876, winning 2–0. He also played a respectable third base, holding down the hot corner in 170 of his 507 major league appearances. Bobby Mathews of the New York Mutuals pitched 516 of his team's 530 innings, completing every one of his 56 starts. And Jim Devlin of Louisville pitched 68 of his team's 69 games, all complete-game efforts.

Candy Cummings joined the National League in 1876, but pitched only two years, going 16–8 with Hartford in the inaugural season and falling to 5–14 with Cincinnati in 1877. He left the National League that year to assume the presidency of baseball's first minor league, the International Association, but before he put his glove away for good, he established one additional major league record that will probably never be broken. On September 9, 1876, he pitched two complete games in one day, becoming baseball's first Iron Man.

Tommy Bond was one of the top pitchers in the early days of the National League. After spending two years in the National Association, where he went 22–32 and 19–16 for the Brooklyn Atlantics and Hartford Dark Blues respectively, the 5' 8", 160-pound hurler compiled a sparkling 31–13 record for Hartford in the National League's inaugural season. Moving to the Boston Red Stockings in 1877, he became major league baseball's first "triple crown" winner, going 40–17 in 1877 with 170 strikeouts and a 2.11 earned run average. He also led the league with a .702 winning percentage and 6 shutouts. And he started 58 of his team's 61 games, completing every one of them. He followed that with two more 40+ victory seasons, going 40–19 and 43–19 in 1878 and '79, becoming the only pitcher in major league history to win 40 or more games three years in succession. But that was the end of the trail for the slender right-hander. The 2,866 innings he had pitched over a six-year period, an average of 478 innings a year, took its toll. He was washed up at the age of 25. Bond, who was called the "premier fastball pitcher of his day" in Curran, throwing from a cozy distance of 45 feet from home plate, intimidated batters with an 85-mile-per-hour "cannonball," which would be equivalent to a 100-mph pitch at today's pitching distance.

Over his eight-year major league career, he won 193 games, lost 113, and completed 294 of his 314 starts, a 94 percent completion rate. His career 2.25 ERA is still the ninth-best ERA in baseball history.

On June 12, 1880, a tall, skinny southpaw named Lee Richmond, while still a student at Brown University, pitched the first perfect game in major league history. As a member of the Worcester Brown Stockings, he blanked the Cleveland Blues 1–0. Richmond was quoted by James and Neyer as saying, "I did have a fast jump ball that was hard to hit when it was working right.... It is a singular thing that of that first no-man-reach-first-base game in 1880 I can remember almost nothing except that my jump ball and my half stride ball were working splendidly and that Bennett and the boys behind me gave me perfect support." Five days after Richmond's historic feat, Monte Ward of the Providence Grays tossed another perfect game, stopping the Buffalo Bisons 5–0. Two other no-hitters were recorded that year, with Larry Corcoran of Chicago beating Boston by a count of 6–0, and Pud Galvin taking the measure of Worcester by a count of 1–0.

Pitchers in the 1870s and '80s routinely pitched from 300 to 600 innings a year. Will White of the Cincinnati Red Stockings set the record for the most innings pitched in a season, with 680 innings pitched in 1879. Five years later, Charles "Old Hoss" Radbourne pitched 678⅔ innings. When the league schedule was increased from 63 games in 1876 to 84 games in 1880, and to 98 games in 1882, it became imperative for teams to provide more pitching help, so the typical 10- and 11-man rosters of 1876 were begrudgingly increased to 11- and 12-man rosters, which included two pitchers. Detroit's 13-man roster included four pitchers. The schedule reached 134 games in 1887. It finally peaked at 154 games in 1904, and remained there until 1961 when it was increased to 162 games.

In 1881, the batters were given a brief respite from the heat that was being thrown at them by a cordon of 6' tall, 200-pound fireball pitchers from a distance of just 45 feet. The rules committee declared that the pitcher's box should be located 50 feet from home plate, giving the batter another fraction of a second to prepare to swing at the ball or to hit the dirt to avoid an errant pitch. This change raised the league's batting averages by 15 points and decreased strikeouts by 10 percent.

One of the most significant events in the history of professional baseball was the formation of the American Association, to compete with the National League as a major league. The AA came into existence in 1882 and closed its doors after the 1891 season following a truce with the National League, which absorbed four Association teams. The American Association developed some of the outstanding players of the era, including pitchers "Old Hoss" Radbourne, Tim Keefe, Adonis Terry, Bob Caruthers, Jack Stivetts, and Tony "the Count" Mullane. During the ten years that the two leagues existed side by side, they met in a postseason World Series seven times, with the National League capturing four championships, the American Association winning one, and two series ending in ties. In 1884, the Providence Grays, led by Radbourne, defeated the New York Mets, three games to none, with "Old Hoss" pitching and winning all three; and that after his fantastic 60-win regular season.

There were other rule changes that affected pitching during the early years of major league baseball, as summarized below.

• In 1883, the pitcher was allowed to pitch sidearm, as long as his hand did not pass above the line of his shoulder. The change wasn't as dramatic as it might have seemed, because many pitchers had been cheating for years, and were already pitching from a near-sidearm position.

- The following year, another rule change in the pitcher's delivery created temporary havoc in professional baseball and would change the face of the game forever. In 1884, overhand pitching was legalized and, from a distance of only 50 feet from the pitcher's box to home plate, the power pitchers overwhelmed and intimidated the batters with their blinding speed. National League strikeouts increased from 2,877 in 1883 to 4,335 in 1884. After adjusting for the difference in the number of league games played, that was still an increase of 31 percent. In the American Association, meanwhile, strikeouts went from 2,417 to 5,672, which, after the necessary adjustments, represented an increase of 40 percent. Six of the top ten major league single season strikeout records were established in 1884, and two others were set in 1886. Nolan Ryan with 383 strikeouts in 1973 and Sandy Koufax with 382 strikeouts in 1965 were the only modern pitchers to break into the top ten. Twenty-year-old Matt Kilroy, a husky 5' 9", 175-pound southpaw, set the all-time major league single season strikeout record when he fanned 513 batters in 583 innings in 1886, his rookie season in the AA. Toad Ramsey, the number two man on the strikeout list, set his mark the same year, sending 499 batters back to the bench dragging their bats behind them. The big southpaw, at 6' 1" tall and 190 pounds, towered over the average major league player, who was about 5' 7" tall and weighed in the neighborhood of 150 pounds. Both men experienced short careers, however. Kilroy injured his arm in a base running collision and retired after just four full seasons. Ramsey, after compiling a record of 38–27 in 1886, went 37–27 the next year, but then fell to 8–30, and 1–16, in '88 and '89. He bounced back in 1890 to go 24–17 for St. Louis, but he was released late in the season because of a drinking problem. He never pitched in the major leagues again.

The 1884 strikeout leaders were Hugh "One Arm" Daily, Dupee Shaw, Old Hoss Radbourne, Charlie Buffinton, Guy Hecker, and Bill Sweeney. Radbourne enjoyed the best overall season of the group. Not only did he increase his strikeouts from 315 to 441; he also set the major league record for most victories in a season, when he put together a win-loss record of 59–12 while pitching 678.2 innings, the number-two all-time record. Guy Hecker used his drop pitch to go 52–20 during the season, while increasing his strikeouts by 60 percent based on games played. And Charlie Buffinton, another pitcher with a hard drop, increased his strikeouts by 26 percent.

- In 1884, a base on balls was awarded to the batter after six balls were issued, a decrease from the previous rule awarding a base on balls after seven balls were issued.
- In 1885 the National League sanctioned the use of flat-sided bats.
- In 1887, a batter could no longer call for a high pitch or a low pitch. The strike zone was defined as the area between the top of the shoulder and the bottom of the knee. That was a decided advantage for the pitcher, and gave him a target that was twice as big as today's strike zone. A base on balls was awarded to the batter after five balls were issued. And the pitcher's box was decreased to 5½ × 4 feet.
- In 1888, a batter was out after three strikes were called by the umpire.
- In 1889, a base on balls was awarded to the batter after four balls were issued.
- In 1891, a new rule noted that each team was required to have one or more substitutes available. This was a major modification to the rules, and it led to the first actual relief pitchers. The first saves by a substitute relief pitcher were achieved, although they were not identified and recorded for almost 100 years. The new rule required that each team

have an area near the field where relief pitchers could warm up. It was usually along the first or third base foul lines. Eventually this area became known as the bullpen, a name that derived from an incident that occurred in 1877, as noted by John Thorn in *The Relief Pitcher*:

> The term bullpen, signifying the foul areas in back of first and third bases, was in use as early as 1877. On May 4 of that year, the Cincinnati Enquirer frowned on the practice some clubs followed of admitting latecomers to the park for less than the league's standard admission of fifty cents—"for ten cents or three for a quarter, herding them in like bulls within a rope area in foul territory, adjoining the outfield."

During the period from 1885 to 1888, starting pitchers completed 97.8 percent of the games they started. The total number of saves recorded during that period was 48, according to Thorn. After overhand pitching was legalized, strikeouts increased from 2–3 strikeouts per game to 5–6 strikeouts per game.

NATIONAL LEAGUE BATTING AND PITCHING STATISTICS

Year	Teams	Games	R/T/Y	HR/T/Y	BA	ERA
1876	8	65	908	12	.265	2.31
1877	6	60	873	10	.271	2.81
1878	6	60	814	10	.259	2.30
1879	8	80	820	14	.255	2.50
1880	8	85	723	14	.245	2.37
1881	8	84	785	17	.260	2.77
1882	8	85	828	29	.251	2.88
1883	8	99	888	24	.262	3.13
1884	8	114	849	54	.247	2.98
1885	8	111	764	30	.241	2.82
1886	8	124	805	39	.251	3.29
1887	8	127	937	58	.269	4.05
1888	8	136	699	47	.239	2.83
1889	8	133	898	54	.266	4.02
1890	8	135	857	37	.254	3.56
1891	8	138	853	41	.252	3.34
1892	12	154	782	35	.245	3.28

KEY:

R/T/Y = Runs per team per year, based on a 154-game season.
HR/T/Y = Home runs per team per year, based on a 154-game season.

In 1884, home runs in the National League went crazy in spite of the legalization of overhand pitching, but the culprit was a baseball park, not the ball. The Chicago White Stockings played their games in cozy Lake Front Park II during 1883 and 1884. The park had a left field fence that was just 180 feet from home plate and a right field fence that hovered over the first baseman, just 106 feet behind first base. In 1883, a ball hit over the left field fence was ruled a double, but in '84 it was deemed a home run. The White Sox home run totals exploded from 13 home runs in 1883 to 142 home runs the following year.

The National League continued to increase the playing schedule over the ensuing years, the number of games finally stabilizing at 154 in 1904. The number of teams in the league fluctuated between 6 and 12 from 1876 to 1892, before settling at 8 teams in 1900. Those conditions did not change again until major league expansion was initiated in 1961.

In 1887, four strikes were required to record a strikeout. Also, pitchers were not allowed to hide the ball during their delivery, and they were not allowed to take a running start before releasing the ball. Only five balls were required for a walk. Home runs jumped up by 19 per team, batting averages increased by 18 points, and ERAs went from 3.29 to 4.05.

In 1888, the strikeout rule was changed again, this time requiring only three strikes for a strikeout. Strikeouts immediately increased by 32 percent, batting averages dropped by 30 points, home runs decreased by 11 homers per team per year, and ERAs plummeted from 4.05 to 2.83. By this date, nearly all catchers were using the new, padded catcher's mitt, which became a necessity after overhand pitching was legalized.

Baseball gloves had been in a state of development since 1860 when a Mr. Delaverage, a catcher for the Troy Victory Club, introduced one to prevent injury to his hands from fast pitches, according to Jonathon F. Light. Gradually, over the next two decades, gloves became normal everyday equipment for all players, with the possible exception of Bid McPhee. The Hall-of-Fame second baseman continued to field the ball bare-handed until 1897. After he finally surrendered and began using a glove he set a fielding record that stood for several decades. The first padded glove was worn by Providence Grays shortstop Art Irwin in 1882. Harry Decker of the Philadelphia Phillies developed the first padded catcher's mitt in 1884, permitting catchers to hold the fiery slants of pitchers such as Old Hoss Radbourne, Kid Nichols, and Amos Rusie, "the Hoosier Thunderbolt." The catcher's mask was developed in 1877 by Fred Thayer, captain of the Harvard baseball team; the first chest protector was worn secretly underneath the uniform shirt by Jack Clements in 1884; and the first outside protector was used in Dallas of the minor leagues in 1903. Roger Bresnahan was credited with wearing the first shin guards in 1907.

Once overhand pitching was legalized, power pitching became the name of the game. Big, strong, pitchers, many of them standing over 6' tall and weighing more than 200 pounds, were in demand by major league teams. James Francis "Pud" Galvin was a former steam fitter with the body of a weightlifter. The stocky, 5' 9", 190-pound pitcher, who has been recognized as one of baseball's first overhand pitchers, had a blazing fastball that put fear into the hearts of opposing batters, especially from the pitching distance of 45 feet. The batters were lucky in one respect. Galvin was a good-natured Irishman with excellent control. The St. Louis native received his major league baseball baptism with the St. Louis Red Stockings of the National Association in 1875, winning four games and losing two. He joined the National League with the Buffalo Bisons in 1879, and had an outstanding rookie season, going 37–27 while pitching 593 innings in 66 games. From 1880 through 1883 he recorded seasons of 20–35, 28–24, 28–23, and 46–29, while pitching in more than 80 percent of his team's games. He threw a no-hitter at Worcester on August 20, 1880, and tossed one at Detroit on August 4, 1884. He also pitched two no-hitters for the St. Louis Red Sox in 1876 and one for Buffalo in an exhibition game in 1881. The conversion to overhand pitching didn't have a major effect on Galvin except that his strikeout total increased from 293 in 1883 to 373 in '84. He went 46–22 pitching overhand, while leading the National League in shutouts with 12. On September 9 of that year, he stopped Providence's 20-game winning streak and Hoss Radbourne's personal 18-game winning streak with a 2–0 victory. When he retired after the 1894 season, he had accumulated 361 victories against 308 losses. Pud Galvin was a great pitcher when he was limited to pitching sidearm and was even more imposing when he was allowed to pitch overhand. He was a successful pitcher when the pitching distance was 45 feet, and also when it was 50 feet.

Charles Gardner Radbourne, better known as "Old Hoss" because of his endurance, starred in the National League for 12 years between 1881 and 1891. The 5' 9", 168-pound pitcher quickly developed into the Grays' leading pitcher, winning 25 games against 11 losses in his rookie season, thanks to a fastball that

Old Hoss Radbourne won an amazing 59 games in 1884 when he started 40 of his team's last 43 games (AUTHOR'S COLLECTION).

moved, a good curve, a changeup, and a drop. He had a bewildering assortment of pitches and arm angles that befuddled batters, and he could spot any pitch in any location with his pinpoint control. In 1882, alternating with John Montgomery Ward, Old Hoss rolled to a 33–20 record, and the following year, with Charlie Sweeney serving as backup, he pitched in 76 of the Grays' 98 games, going 49–25, with 66 complete games in 68 starts. On July 25 of that year, Radbourne tossed a no-hitter at the Cleveland Spiders, winning 8–0.

In 1884, he once again shared mound duties with Sweeney, until the alcoholic Sweeney was expelled from the team and the league for disciplinary reasons. It was during that period that Old Hoss earned his sobriquet, starting 40 of the 51 games remaining in the season. Overall, he appeared in 75 games, completed every one of his 73 starts, and racked up the phenomenal total of 59 victories, a record that, in all probability, will never be broken. And for good measure, he ran up a personal 18-game winning streak and tossed 11 shutouts. But the season was not an easy one for the Providence ace. According to his manager, Frank Bancroft, Radbourne suffered from a sore arm all season. He could not raise his arm high enough to brush his hair in the morning, but after continually stretching it by playing long toss at the ballpark, he was always ready to go by game time. At the end of the season, the Grays met the New York Mets, champions of the American Association, in the equivalent of the World Series. Behind Old Hoss, who won all three games, the Grays swept the Mets in convincing fashion. When he retired in 1891, he had accumulated a total of 309 victories against 195 losses. Radbourne was considered to be a marvel, even in that time. He began his career pitching underhand, but after overhand pitching was legalized in 1884, there is some evidence that he pitched, at least some of the time, with a three-quarter overhand motion. John Thorn said, "Radbourne was never a pure underhand pitcher. Sidearm and from-the-shoulder pitching had been legalized earlier, and while I can't recall a source for this, my impression is that Radbourne employed a variety of delivery styles." Charles Radbourne, who was known as the King of Pitchers in his day, and is considered by many historians to be the greatest pitcher of the nineteenth century, died at his home on February 5, 1897, at the age of 42.

One of the first fastball pitchers to arrive on the scene after the legalization of overhand pitching was John Clarkson, a tall, slender right-hander from Cambridge, Massachusetts. The 5' 10", 155-pounder was the complete pitcher. His repertoire included a good fastball, a drop, and a change of pace, all of which he sent plateward with a deceptive motion. His delivery was similar to the deliveries used by Luis Tiant and Hideo Nomo, giving the batter a good look at his back before twisting around to unleash his throw. Clarkson debuted with the Chicago White Stockings in 1884, winning ten games against just three losses, after going 34–9 with Saginaw of the Northwestern League earlier in the season. In 1885, the 24-year-old hurler pitched in 70 of Chicago's 112 games, completing 68 of them and winning 53 against 16 losses, as the White Stockings won the league title by two games over the New York Metropolitans. He was practically a one-man pitching staff, leading the league in games pitched, games started, complete games, victories, shutouts (10), innings pitched (623), and strikeouts (308). He was sold to the Boston Beaneaters for $10,000 in 1888, and went 49–19 the following year. He teamed with Kid Nichols to win the National League pennant in 1891, but was traded to Cleveland four years later where he retired after two so-so seasons. His 11-year major league career included a sensational 328–178 win-loss record and three league pennants.

Amos Rusie was probably the most terrifying pitcher of the late 1880s and early 1890s since his overpowering fastball, thrown from a distance of 50 feet, was equivalent to a 100-mph heater at today's pitching distance. He was not only the fastest pitcher of his time; he was the wildest, setting bases-on-balls records that still stand today. His 289 walks in 1890 are still the National League record, even though his team played only 131 games. His career will be reviewed in chapter 4.

"Happy Jack" Stivetts was another fireballing right-hander whose career straddled the end of the early era and the beginning of the modern era. The 6' 2", 185-pound Pennsylvanian, whose career will also be reviewed in chapter 4, played in the major leagues from 1889 to 1899. During his three years in the American Association and his first year in the National League, between 1889 and 1892, he played 53 games in the outfield, in addition to pitching, to keep his big bat in the lineup. In 1890, Stivetts batted .288 and ripped 7 home runs in 226 at-bats, equivalent to 17 homers for every 550 at-bats, a prodigious feat in those dead-ball days. The next year, he hit .305 with 7 homers in 302 at-bats. And his pitching record during those two years was 27–20 and 33–22.

Kid Nichols, whose major league career spanned the years from 1890 to 1906, was probably the Boston Beaneaters' (later the Braves) greatest pitcher. Since most of his career fell into the modern era after 1893, his career will be reviewed in chapter 4. He did, however, have several sensational years prior to that time. In his debut season of 1890, the 20-year-old power pitcher won 27 games against 19 losses for Frank Selee's fourth-place club. He followed that up with seasons of 30–17 and 35–16, leading up to the modern era.

The game wasn't all power pitching in the years from 1884 to 1892, however. Some of the most outstanding pitchers of the era relied on finesse rather than speed to quiet enemy bats. Michael Francis Welch, nicknamed Smiling Mickey because of his pleasant disposition and captivating smile, was one of the finesse pitchers. Welch, who was born in Brooklyn,

New York, on July 4, 1859, was a slender 5' 8", 160-pound, right-handed pitcher who had to outwit opposing batters, as he noted in Frederick Ivor-Campbell's *Baseball's First Stars*: "I was a little fellow, and I had to use my head. I studied the hitters and I knew how to pitch to all of them, and I worked hard to perfect my control. I had a pretty good fastball, but I depended chiefly on change of pace and an assortment of curveballs." The future Hall-of-Famer made his professional debut in 1878 with Auburn and Holyoke in the National Association, and later was signed by the New York Gothams, where he spent the bulk of his major league career. Welch had been an outstanding pitcher between 1880 and 1883, but after overhand pitching was legalized, he became one of the National League's most dominating pitchers. He went 39–21 in 1884, while striking out 349 batters, an average of six strikeouts per game, compared to three strikeouts per game prior to '84. His next two years were just as impressive. He went 44–11 with 256 strikeouts in '85, and 33–22 with 269 strikeouts in '86. Smiling Mickey enjoyed ten 20-victory seasons over his 13-year career, winning more than 30 games three times, and topping out at 44–11 in 1885. In all, he won 307 games against 210 losses, for a fine .594 winning percentage. The durable pitching star completed 525 of his 549 career starts, with 41 shutouts and a 2.71 earned run average.

Timothy John Keefe's career could have been included with the fastball pitchers, but his repertoire consisted of three outstanding pitches. Although he was a hefty 185 pounds, he relished putting batters away with a tantalizing change of pace that had batters screwing themselves into the ground in a vain attempt to make contact. Keefe had a memorable 14-year major league career, beginning with the Troy Trojans in 1880 and ending with the Philadelphia Phillies in 1892. In between, he pitched for the New York Metropolitans of the American Association for two years, and then went to the New York Giants of the National League where he starred for six years. While with the Giants, he teamed with Mickey Welch to give his team one of the best pitching duos in major league history. He twice won more than 40 games, with a high of 42 in 1886, and passed the 30-victory mark four other times. The Giants appeared in two World Series during the Welch-Keefe era, with Keefe throwing four complete-game victories with a barely-visible 0.51 ERA in the 1888 series, as the Giants humbled the St. Louis Browns, six games to four. Sir Timothy retired after the 1893 season at the age of 36, with 342 victories against 225 defeats, and 554 complete games in 594 starts, a 93 percent completion rate.

Great strides were made in fine-tuning the game of baseball over the two decades prior to 1893. It was a time when a primitive game of bat and ball was molded into the exciting game that is played today on baseball diamonds all across the United States. Most of the rules and specifications that identify the game were established during that period, including the definition of three strikes as an out and four balls as a walk. Overhand pitching was legalized, gloves were worn by all the players, and protective equipment for catchers was evaluated. But perhaps the most significant change, and one that has been generally overlooked by many historians, was the rule that allowed teams to make substitutions while the game was in progress. That rule was the beginning of relief pitching as we know it today, a strategy that has risen to be the determining factor in the game in the twenty-first century. During the 17-year period prior to 1892, when change pitchers were in vogue, there were just 155 saves recorded, and most of them were recorded by starting pitchers. Over the next 102 years, the total number of saves would run into the thousands, 1,230 in the year 2004 alone.

Jack Manning may have been the only bona fide relief pitcher of the change era, coming in from his regular right field position to rescue a harried teammate. Although he played in the National League from 1876 through 1886, his pitching career was limited to one full season with the Boston Red Stockings in 1876. He relieved in 14 games that year, leading the league in relief wins with four and saves with five. He also started 20 games, posting a 14–5 record. Strangely enough, he pitched in only ten games the following season and three games in 1878, before becoming a full time outfielder.

Jack Stivetts of Boston started 170 games between 1889 and 1892, compiling an 88–60 record. The big slugger, who carried a .298 career batting average and who played 213 games at other positions, also relieved in 27 games, recording a 12–5 win-loss record with four saves. Stivetts led the National League in relief wins four times. Old Hoss Radbourne relieved in 25 games in 11 years, with an 8–5 record and two saves. Amos Rusie relieved in 22 games in four years, winning five, losing four, and saving two. Kid Nichols, while posting a 30–17 record in 1891, relieved in four games and led the league in saves with three. Tony "the Count" Mullane, a matinee idol during the 1880s, started 447 games between 1881 and 1892, compiling a 257–182 record. He also relieved in 35 games, with a 12–3 record and nine saves. In 1893 and '94, after the substitution rule was passed, Mullane led the league in saves both years, with two and four saves respectively. And Bob Caruthers, a two-time 40-game winner, relieved in 30 games in nine years, winning 11, losing two, and saving three.

Relief was on the way, but in 1893 it was still the property of the starting pitcher.

4

The Modern Game Begins:
1893 to 1919

The year 1893 marked the beginning of the modern era of major league baseball. As noted in the previous chapter, all the players wore gloves, and protective equipment for the catcher was being evaluated and would soon become part of his standard equipment, including shin guards and a chest protector. Many pitchers unofficially pitched from a mound that, in at least one case, was 20" high. The strike zone was from the batter's shoulders to his knees. And relief pitchers could be brought into the game from the bench, to relieve a troubled starting pitcher. There were still two major changes to be made after 1893 to bring the game completely into agreement with today's game. In 1903, the pitcher's mound was legalized, with a maximum height of 15". And, in 1920, trick pitches like the spitball and the emery ball were banned, as was the practice of putting foreign substances on the baseball. It was also the year that the lively ball was introduced. In addition to all the rule changes, the philosophy of the game also changed around the turn of the century. The big, powerful sluggers such as Dan Brouthers, Sam Thompson, and Roger Connor, were no longer in demand. The owners became convinced that big sluggers were bad for the game, that the extra base hits they produced were more than offset by their deficiencies in other areas. The big men were generally slow and lacked agility. On defense, they had limited range. And on the bases they frequently clogged up the base paths. The player of the early 1900s was small and fast. He was an excellent fielder with outstanding range. He was an expert at handling a bat, and could lay down a sacrifice bunt, bunt for a base hit, hit and run, or steal a base, as required.

Most of the rule changes had a significant effect on the pitcher-batter confrontation. The first change, in 1893, was to replace the pitcher's box with a rubber plate measuring 12 inches long by 4 inches wide. Two years later, it was increased to its present size of 24" × 6". The introduction of a pitching rubber meant that pitchers could no longer get a running start before pitching the ball. They had to stand with at least one foot in contact with the rubber at all times until they released the pitch. The first pitching rubber was positioned level with home plate, at a distance of 60' 6" from the plate. One popular theory held that the distance from the mound to the plate was increased to protect batters from Amos Rusie's fastballs. The big 6' 2", 200-pound Hoosier Thunderbolt was baseball's foremost power pitcher during the 1890s, a hard-throwing wild man who intimidated batters but had no idea where the pitch was going. Over his career, Rusie fanned five men a game, a high number in those days, walked an equal number, and hit more than a few. He was the scourge of the league, feared by most batters with some justification, since he had sent several players to the hospital with enormous headaches. In fact, Hughie Jennings, the feisty field leader of the Baltimore Orioles, lay unconscious in a hospital bed for three days after running into one of Rusie's blazers. After 1892, the increased pitching distance had a significant effect on the pitcher-batter relationship because it gave the batter additional time to react to the pitch. Rusie's hit-batter rate fell from 0.32 hit batters per nine innings to 0.22 hit batters. He still led the league in strikeouts, but his strikeout rate was reduced by one-third. During his ten-year career, the Hoosier Thunderbolt won 246 games against 174 losses. His total of 1,707 bases on balls is still the seventh highest in major league history.

The batter, with more time to see the pitch before committing himself to a swing, benefited greatly from the increased pitching distance. Batting averages jumped up 35 points in '93, while home runs increased by 10 percent. Strikeouts, however, didn't decrease as expected, remaining at 3–4 strikeouts per game. One year after the changes were made, the league batting average reached .309 and home runs were up another 37 percent. The Boston Red Sox were the first major league team to hit more than 100 home runs in a season, topping out at 103 in just 132 games. It seems that it took a couple of years for pitchers to become accustomed to the new pitching distance, because in 1895 the batting and slugging statistics began to stabilize. Batting averages gradually settled out in the .270 range, and home runs returned from the 1894 high of 61 home runs per team per 154 games to a normal level of 30 home runs per team.

Overall, most of the changes that were made between 1900 and 1903 worked to the advantage of the pitcher. In 1900, the shape of home plate was changed from a 12-inch square to a five-sided plate, 17 inches wide, increasing the strike zone by 42 percent. The next year, the pitcher received another benefit when the rules committee declared that any foul that was hit and not caught was a strike unless two strikes had already been called. Previously, a batter could hit foul balls all day without any strikes being called. Those advantages for the pitcher were increased even more by the legalization of a pitching mound. In the last decade of the nineteenth century, the pitcher had been required to pitch from a rubber that was at the same level as home plate, although some clubs had secretly been building mounds since the late 1870s. Photographs taken at different ballparks at different times over the years show mounds that varied in height from 4" to 20". In 1903, the mound height was set at a maximum of 15", giving pitchers tremendous leverage in the delivery of the pitch, while increasing the speed and the angle of the pitch. There was no minimum, however, so teams still had the ability to vary the height of the mound depending on what team they were playing, who was pitching for the other team, and what height their own pitchers preferred.

The strike zone remained at the level set in 1887, being not lower than the batsmen's knee or higher than his shoulder. The bat, which previously could have one flat side, now had to be round, not more than 2½" in diameter, and not more than 42" in length. All players were now wearing fielder's gloves, and these too were soon regulated. In 1895, the catcher and first baseman were permitted to wear gloves of any size, but the other players were restricted to the use of a glove weighing not over 10 ounces and measuring not more than 14" in circumference.

In 1901 the major leagues took on a new and different look when Ban Johnson, the president of the Western League, a longtime minor league, renamed his league the American League and declared it to be a major league. The announcement didn't sit well with National League owners, and open warfare broke out between the two leagues, with the American League pirating players from the other league. Established stars such as Cy Young, Nap Lajoie, and "Wee Willie" Keeler joined the upstart league, lured away by salaries that were more than double their National League pay. The American League prospered in its new identity, reaching an equal status with its rivals in less than two years. In 1903, the two leagues finally sat down at the conference table and negotiated a peace settlement that, among other things, protected each league's players from outside interference. Additionally, the two leagues scheduled a postseason series between the league champions to determine a world champion. A nine-game series between the American League pennant winners, the Boston Pilgrims, and the National League pennant winners, the Pittsburgh Pirates, resulted in an eight-game victory for the upstart Pilgrims behind the pitching brilliance of Bill Dineen and Cy Young. The World Series went on sabbatical in 1904 after New York Giants manager John McGraw and owner John T. Brush refused to entertain a series between the Giants and the Boston Pilgrims. Brush was angered because the American League had put a team in New York, diluting his fan base. The public outcry over the cancellation of the series was so heated that Brush was forced to reconsider his position. A new peace agreement reached between the two leagues included an annual seven-game World Series that, in 1905, saw McGraw's Giants dismantle the Philadelphia Athletics in five games. The highlight of the series, and one of the great individual performances in World Series history, was Christy Mathewson's three complete-game shutout victories, achieved over a six-day period. Mathewson was touched up for just 14 base hits in 27 innings, striking out 18 batters and issuing a single base on balls.

The two leagues increased their schedules from 140 games to 154 games in 1904, which necessitated an increase in the pitching staff. The four-man pitching staff was increased to five and sometimes six pitchers. Most starting pitchers were throwing 250 or more innings, while the aces of the staffs were still occasionally throwing in excess of 400 innings. Amos Rusie pitched 482 innings in 1893, which is still the record for the modern era, but Jack Chesbro checked in with 455 innings pitched in 1904, and Ed Walsh, the last 400-inning pitcher in baseball history, tossed 422 innings in 1907 and 464 innings in 1908. The pitchers still ruled the roost between 1903 and 1909, thanks to the rule changes. Home runs decreased from 23 per year per team to 16, and batting averages plummeted 18 points.

In 1911, the situation changed somewhat as major league baseball replaced the rubber-core baseball with a ball having a cork center. That change resulted in a livelier ball that seemed to work to the advantage of the batter, as home runs jumped up from 23 per team to 32 per team, and batting averages increased by 17 points. Pitchers didn't take the change to the cork-center ball kindly. They responded by increasing the number of trick pitches they threw, including the emery ball, spitball, mud ball, and shine ball.

World War I interrupted the country's national pastime during this hectic period, as the United States was eventually drawn into the war against Germany. The U.S. entered the war in April 1917 and, one year later, baseball was declared a nonessential industry, threatening its future. With many of its players volunteering for military service, including Grover Cleveland Alexander and Rube Marquard, and other players leaving the game to work in defense industries, the leagues began recruiting older, retired players, and players too young for military service. Finally, they decided to shut the season down completely. The last game was played on Labor Day, after playing just 127 games. In 1919, the major leagues were back in operation again, but with a reduced schedule of 140 games.

The American and National League statistics for the period from 1893 through 1919 are shown below.

Year	Teams	Games	R/T/Y	HR/T/Y	BA	ERA
1893	12	131	1011	45	.280	4.66
1894	12	133	1138	61	.309	5.33
1895	12	133	1015	47	.296	4.77
1896	12	132	929	39	.290	4.36
1897	12	135	907	35	.292	4.30
1898	12	154	761	25	.271	3.60
1899	12	154	806	29	.282	3.85
1900	8	142	804	34	.279	3.69
1901	8	139	766	32	.272	3.49
1902	8	140	681	24	.267	3.18
1903	8	139	685	23	.262	3.10
1904	8	154	582	21	.247	2.67
1905	8	154	602	21	.248	2.82
1906	8	154	555	16	.247	2.66
1907	8	154	544	15	.245	2.50
1908	8	154	526	17	.239	2.37
1909	8	154	551	16	.244	2.53
1910	8	154	599	23	.250	2.77
1911	8	154	698	32	.267	3.37
1912	8	154	697	28	.269	3.37
1913	8	154	623	29	.259	3.07
1914	8	154	588	26	.250	2.76
1915	8	154	590	24	.248	2.84
1916	8	154	556	24	.248	2.72
1917	8	154	559	21	.249	2.68
1918	8	127	560	18	.254	2.77
1919	8	140	595	28	.263	3.07

KEY:

R/T/Y = Runs per team per year based on a 154-game season.
HR/T/Y = Home runs per team per year based on a 154-game season.

In 1920, the game changed dramatically, producing some of the most electrifying slugging feats baseball fans had ever seen. But before that time, pitching was the name of the game, and fastball pitchers were the heroes of baseball. The first and most notorious flamethrower was the aforementioned Amos Rusie.

Other legendary pitchers who lived and died by the fastball during the last decade of the nineteenth century included Jack Stivetts, Kid Nichols, Clark Griffith, and Cy Young. Early twentieth century fireballers included Walter Johnson, Rube Waddell, and Rube Marquard. Jack Stivetts was a big man for his time, standing 5' 8" tall and weighing a husky 185 pounds. He was a selfless player who was nicknamed Happy Jack because of his easygoing demeanor. Stivetts teamed with Kid Nichols to give the Boston Beaneaters a formidable pitching duo during the 1890s. Together they pitched the Bostons to three National League pennants and one World Championship, a five-game sweep of the Cleveland Spiders in 1892, with Stivetts winning two games and battling Cy Young to a 0–0 eleven-inning tie. The hard-throwing right-hander won 20 or more games four times during his six years in Boston, before sustaining an arm injury that brought the curtain down on his career. He retired with a career record of 203–132 and a 3.16 ERA. In addition to starting 333 games in 11 years, he also relieved in 55 games with 5 saves. And when not pitching he could be found playing elsewhere in the field, thanks to his fearsome bat. He was credited with playing 141 games in the outfield and 44 games in the infield during his career. His offensive contributions included a .297 batting average, with 23 doubles, 13 triples, and 10 home runs for every 550 at-bats. In today's game, he could be expected to average 25 home runs a year, with 35–40 home runs a distinct possibility in any particular year. Stivetts batted over

.300 four times with a high of .367 in 1897, and three times he hit two home runs in a game, including on June 10, 1890, when he put two balls into orbit, one a grand slam, in a 9–8 St. Louis Browns victory. But his most memorable days occurred in Brooklyn in 1892. He played left field in the opener of a two-game series, and broke up a scoreless game with a home run in the twelfth inning. The next day, he tossed an 11–0 no-hitter at the Bridegrooms, and helped his own cause with a triple and a double. Then, on Labor Day, he tossed both ends of a doubleheader, defeating the Louisville Colonels 2–1 in 11 innings in the morning game, and coming back in the afternoon to win again, 5–2.

Charles "Kid" Nichols was another fireballing right-hander who burst upon the major league scene in 1890 at the tender age of 20, after spending three years perfecting his trade in such places as

Cy Young is baseball's all-time victory leader, winning 511 games over a 22-year career (AUTHOR'S COLLECTION).

Kansas City, Memphis, and Omaha. The precocious kid from Wisconsin burned up the National League in his rookie season, winning 27 games against 19 losses. The next year, teaming up with John Clarkson, he helped carry the Boston Beaneaters to the National League pennant, compiling a 30–17 record. During his 12 years in the country's hub, Nichols won 30 or more games seven times, and Boston won five league pennants. When he retired in 1906, completing a memorable 15-year career, he had accumulated 361 victories, the sixth highest total in major league history, against just 207 losses. He also relieved 59 times, and was credited with 17 saves. Nichols had only one pitch, an overhand fastball, but he was recognized as the first pitcher whose fastball had a hop on it. The 5' 11", 175-pound power pitcher had excellent command of his pitches. Unlike Rusie and Stivetts, Nichols walked only two men a game and relied on a changeup to throw batters off balance, inducing them to hit weak groundballs or pop-ups.

The next world-class pitcher to appear on the major league scene was a husky right-handed pitcher from the farms of Gilmore, Ohio. Denton True Young, pitching for Canton in the Tri-State League in 1890, was tabbed with the nickname Cyclone because of the blinding speed that accounted for 201 strikeouts in 260 innings, an average of 7 strikeouts a game in an age when it was humiliating for a batter to strike out. He was also blessed with two curveballs, a sharp-breaking curve thrown at the same speed as his fastball and a wide curve thrown slower. Young joined the Cleveland Spiders the same year, beginning a 22-year odyssey that would result in a total of 511 victories against 316 losses, the most victories compiled by any pitcher in professional baseball history. In fact, he racked up 94 more wins than the number-two man, Walter Johnson. The 6' 2", 210-pound Ohioan threw three no-hitters during his career, including a perfect game. Four days prior to his perfect game, Young threw seven perfect innings in relief against Washington, giving him 16 consecutive perfect innings. He later added another 9⅓ hitless innings to his string, giving him a major league record of 25⅓ consecutive no-hit innings. In addition to starting, he relieved in a total of 91 games during his career, compiling a record of 28–18 with 17 saves, twice leading the league in saves. He credited his long career to his physical condition, the result of his youth on the farm and his off-season farm routine of clearing and tilling the fields, reaping, and chopping wood.

The period from 1903 to 1920 has been called the Golden Age of Pitching, with good reason. The top four pitchers in career victories, Cy Young, Walter Johnson, Grover Cleveland Alexander, and Christy Mathewson, all pitched in this era. Young was in the twilight of his career when the twentieth century began, but he still won 244 games between 1900 and 1911. The other three pitchers, as well as many other outstanding pitchers, reached their prime in the first two decades of the new century. One of the most colorful characters in the early days of major league baseball was George Edward "Rube" Waddell. One time he walked off the field in the middle of a game to chase a fire engine, one of his favorite hobbies. Another time, he delayed the start of a game while he played marbles with the kids outside the park. And inside the park, he occasionally held up the game to watch a flock of birds fly over. He even wrestled alligators during spring training in Florida. But whatever his personal quirks, the man could throw a baseball with authority. He was a power pitcher who threw smoke. But, as his manager, Connie Mack, once reported, "His curveball, which is a fast as his fastball, and breaks sharply, down and away from a right-handed batter, is his best pitch." And Mack should know. Waddell pitched for him on the Philadelphia Athletics for six years, helping the A's win two American League titles. The eccentric

Pennsylvanian always played to the fans, but his antics annoyed his manager and alienated his teammates. By 1908, Connie Mack had run out of patience with his erratic pitcher, and he traded him to the St. Louis Browns where he finished out his major league career. Rube Waddell was one of the great pitchers in major league history, compiling a record of 193–143 over a 13-year career. He led the league in strikeouts for six consecutive years, averaging seven strikeouts a game, more than double the league average. His relief record shows 67 games pitched, 19 wins, 9 losses, and 10 saves. The big lefty, whose fastball was said to be the equal of Walter Johnson's, still holds the American League record for most strikeouts in a season by a left-handed pitcher, with 349.

Walter Johnson, who is generally considered to be the greatest pitcher in baseball history, was a big, rawboned kid from the farmlands of Kansas. The 6' 1", 200-pound right-hander had long arms and a smooth sidearm motion that sent the baseball plateward as though it was shot from a cannon. Today, 97 years after his major league debut, Johnson is still considered to be the fastest pitcher who ever toed the rubber. His 5.3 strikeouts for every nine innings pitched pales in comparison to the 9.5 strikeouts racked up by Nolan Ryan or the 9.3 strikeouts credited to Sandy Koufax, but his totals were accumulated during a time when a batter would do anything to keep from striking out because it was considered to be a stain on his manhood if he couldn't make contact with the ball. Today, batters swing from the heels on every pitch, showing compete disdain for the strikeout. The modern mentality is reflected in the major league average of 86 strikeouts per man per 154 games in 1974 and 112 strikeouts per man in 2003, compared to 64 strikeouts per man in 1913. That year Johnson went 36–7 on the mound for the second-place Washington Senators with a brilliant 1.09 ERA. The following year he led the American League in games pitched (51), games started (40), complete games (33), shutouts (9), victories (28), innings pitched (372), and strikeouts (225). During his 21-year career, the Big Train, as he was called, won 417 games against 279 losses, with a major league record 110 shutouts, 20 more shutouts than the next highest man. He led the American League in victories six times, complete games seven times, shutouts seven times, innings pitched five times, and strikeouts 12 times—a major league record.

Walter Johnson could beat a team any number of ways. In addition to pitching, he could also run, field, and hit. He led the league in fielding percentage five times. And he had a career batting average of .236 with 22 doubles, 10 triples, 6 home runs, 3 stolen bases, and 60 runs batted in, for every 550 at-bats. The Big Train often stepped in as a relief pitcher between starting assignments, relieving in 136 games in his career, and compiling a 42–25 win-loss record with 34 saves.

Smokey Joe Wood was another hard-throwing farm boy who came out of the Midwest with a blazing fastball and a genuine love for the game of baseball. Standing 5' 10" tall and weighing a solid 180 pounds, he mixed in a curveball and a mediocre changeup with his fastball, but it was his heat that dominated his pitching arsenal. He threw it 90 percent of the time, but he spotted it effectively to keep batters off balance. Smokey Joe was quoted by Neyer and James as saying, "I sometimes use a curve ball, but the occasions are rare indeed, and it is effective only for the reason that I have established a reputation as a pitcher of a fast ball.... Perhaps I throw a curve ball once in ten times." Wood reached the major leagues with the Boston Red Sox in 1908 at the tender age of 18, and three years later he had a season that most pitchers can only dream of, compiling a record of 34–5 for the pennant-winning Bostonians, with 35 complete games, 10 shutouts, and a brilliant 1.91

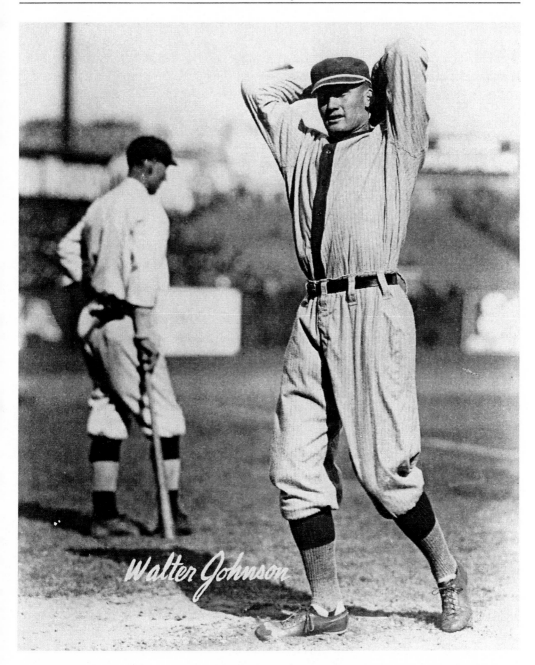

Walter Johnson is still regarded as baseball's most intimidating strikeout artist (AUTHOR'S COLLECTION).

ERA. Included in his achievements were 16 consecutive victories, tying the major league record, and a much-publicized 1–0 victory over Walter Johnson before an overflow crowd in Fenway Park on September 6. Smokey Joe's magical season carried over into the World Series where he sparked the Red Sox to a world championship, winning three games as the Sox defeated the New York Giants in eight games. Unfortunately, a spring training injury the next year essentially ended his career. He pitched with pain in his right shoulder for three more years before hanging his glove up for good. An article in a 1916 *Baseball* magazine, reprinted in James and Neyer, quoted Walter Johnson as saying, "It made my own shoulders ache to watch his delivery. That pitching with the arm alone, that wrenching of the muscles in the shoulder, would wear out my arm." In answer to a question as to whether or not he threw faster than Smokey Joe Wood, Johnson said, "No man alive threw harder the Smokey Joe Wood."

Richard W. "Rube" Marquard was born in Cleveland, Ohio, on October 9, 1889, just 16 days before Joe Wood was born. He joined the New York Giants in 1909, beginning a notable 18-year career. The husky 6' 3" pitcher relied on his heater to get batters out during his first few years in New York, but he eventually developed an effective curve, a screwball, and a change of pace that kept him in the Big Show until 1925. As he said, quoted in Shatzkin, "Any hitter can hit a fast one. But not many can hit slow ones." One of the highlights of his career occurred on July 17, 1914, when he defeated Babe Adams and the Pittsburgh Pirates 3–1 in 21 innings. Pittsburgh touched up the Giants southpaw for a run in the first inning and New York countered with a run in the third. For the next 17 innings the two baseball legends tossed goose eggs at each other before John McGraw's troops pushed over the game-winner in the twenty-first inning. Marquard and Adams were typical of the pitchers who toed the rubber during the first two or three decades on the century. They were control pitchers who specialized in making the hitter hit their pitch rather than trying to overpower the hitter with strikeouts. Over the course of his career Marquard struck out four men for every nine innings pitched and walked only two. His 19-year career showed 201 victories against 177 losses, and a 3.13 ERA. He also worked in 132 games out of the bullpen, where he accounted for 28 of his victories and 12 of his losses. He saved 13 games.

The previous group of pitchers represented the power pitchers of the period, but there was a group of finesse pitchers who were just as good. Clark Griffith, one of the first finesse pitchers in the major leagues, did most of his pitching prior to the Golden Age. The slightly built right-hander, who stood only 5' 6" tall and weighed a wispy 155 pounds, was taught the rudiments of the pitching game by Old Hoss Radbourne. Griffith was subsequently nicknamed the Old Fox because of his wide pitching repertoire, which included a sharp-breaking curveball, an average fastball, a screwball, a spitball, and a scuff ball that he rubbed against his spikes to roughen up the surface. He also fast-pitched the batter whenever possible. Griffith put together six consecutive 20-win seasons beginning in 1894, with a high of 26–14 in 1895. He joined the new American League movement in 1901 as manager and star pitcher for the Chicago White Stockings, and guided his team to the first American League pennant while going 24–7 on the mound. Two years later, he was recruited to manage the fledgling New York Highlanders, to compete with John McGraw's Giants for the huge metropolitan market. As a pitcher, the Old Fox compiled a record of 242–131 over a successful 21-year career, 24–10 in relief, with 9 saves in 81 games.

Another of the early finesse pitchers was Mordecai "Three-Finger" Brown, a former coal miner from Nyesville, Indiana. An industrial accident left him with just three good fingers on his throwing hand, a situation that led to his unique arsenal of curveballs, including a sharp-breaking overhand hook and a sidearm curve. He also threw a moving fastball and a change of pace. As the ace of the Chicago Cubs staff, the husky right-hander pitched his team to four National League pennants and two world championships between 1906 and 1910, going 5–4 in the four series, with a 2.81 ERA. In regular season play, the 5' 10",

175-pound pitcher won between 20 and 29 games every season from 1906 to 1911. And he faced Christy Matheson many times over the seasons, running up a nine-game winning streak against Big Six between 1905 and 1908.

Three-Finger Brown was noted for his durability and, as reported in Shatzkin's *Ballplayers*, "admired for his fitness. In 1914, 'American Monthly,' a national magazine, published photos of his exercise program, a rugged series of body building routines." The indefatigable Hoosier led the league in games pitched with 53 in 1911 and 50 in 1909. He also led the league in innings pitched (343) and victories (27) in the latter year. During his 14-year major league career, Brown pitched 250 or more innings five times, twice exceeding 300 innings. In addition to starting 332 games, and completing 271 of them for an 81 percent completion rate, he was also one of the top relief pitchers of his era, coming to the rescue of his teammates 149 times. He won 30 games in relief, lost 20, and saved 49 in his career, leading the league in saves four consecutive years, from 1908 to 1911. His total of 13 saves in 1911 was the major league record until Firpo Marberry of the Washington Senators broke it in 1924. Jack Quinn of the Brooklyn Dodgers broke his National League mark in 1931.

Ed Walsh was baseball's first notable spitball pitcher. He threw the spitball up to 90 percent of the time, as does Tim Wakefield of the Boston Red Sox. F.C. Lane quoted Walsh as saying he only threw two curveballs in seven years. The sidearm pitcher also had a respectable fastball, which he used occasionally to fool batters. Walsh, affectionately known as Big Ed, began his major league career with the Chicago White Sox in 1904. Four years later, he put up a brilliant 40–15 mark, becoming the last pitcher in baseball history to win 40 games in a season. He led the American League in most pitching categories that year, including number of games (66), games started (49), complete games (42), shutouts (11), victories (40), winning percentage (.727), innings pitched (464), strikeouts (269), relief appearances (17), and saves (6), while his 1.42 ERA was third behind Addie Joss and Cy Young. His 464 innings pitched, the modern major league record, represented 34 percent of his team's innings. And he also became the first major league pitcher to record 100 relief appearances. The husky, 6' 1", 193-pound spitballer, in a desperate effort to win the pennant for his team, pitched 41⅓ innings over the last eight days of the 1908 season, but it all went for naught as the White Sox finished third, 1½ games behind the pennant-winning Detroit Tigers. Walsh, like Three-Finger Brown, was a two-way pitcher, starting and relieving. He started 315 games in 14 years, and relieved in another 115. His career numbers showed a 195–126 win-loss record, including a 16–15 record in relief with 35 saves.

Christy Mathewson is often called the greatest pitcher in baseball history. If he wasn't number one, he was certainly one of the top five, along with contenders Young, Johnson, and Alexander. Lefty Grove, Bob Feller, Warren Spahn, and Sandy Koufax, of later eras, could also challenge for spots in the top five. The handsome, 6' 1½", 195-pound right-handed pitcher put together a sensational 20–2 season with Norfolk in the Virginia League in 1900, leading to his purchase by the big-city Giants, managed by John McGraw. In his rookie season of 1901, Matty compiled a 20–17 record, with 215 strikeouts. Although he had an excellent fastball, he also possessed a devastating curveball and a fadeaway or screwball. He considered his curve to be his best pitch but he was famous for his fadeaway, which he said he only threw about six times a game. In fact, his greatest weapon may have been his control. He could spot any of his pitches anywhere around the plate on any count for a strike. His 1.6 bases on balls for every nine innings pitched attests to his pinpoint

Christy Mathewson hurled three shutouts in six days in the 1905 World Series (AUTHOR'S COL-
LECTION).

control. He may also have been baseball's greatest thinking-man's pitcher. Unlike many
other great pitchers, including the mild mannered Walter Johnson, who occasionally
plunked batters intentionally, Mathewson never threw at a batter. He never intimidated
them. He out-thought them.

Mathewson's greatest all-around season was probably 1905. He pitched the Giants to
a pennant, winning 31 games against 9 losses and leading the league in victories, shutouts

with 8, and strikeouts with 206. But it was his overpowering World Series performance that will be remembered the longest. It may never be equaled. Big Six, as he was called after the era's most famous fire truck, pitched his team to a five-game victory over the Philadelphia Athletics by shutting the A's out three times in six days. He out-pitched Eddie Plank 3–0 in the series opener, blanked them 9–0 in game three, and closed out the mismatch with a 2–0 win over Chief Bender in game five. He held Connie Mack's hard-hitting team to just 14 hits in 27 innings, 10 of them singles, with 18 strikeouts and one walk. Matty enjoyed three other 30-win seasons, including a 37–11 season in 1908, but all things considered, 1905 had to be his best. His 17-year career produced a total of 373 victories and 188 losses. And Big Six was devastating out of the bullpen as well. Over his career, he came on in relief 84 times, registering a 26–9 record with 30 saves.

Grover Cleveland Alexander, known as Pete to his teammates, starred in the National League for 20 years, from 1911 to 1930. Along with Christy Mathewson, he was one of the greatest finesse pitchers in the annals of the game, and another of the big, strong farm boys who gravitated to professional baseball around the turn of the last century. Born in St. Paul, Nebraska, on February 26, 1887, Pete began his baseball career with Galesburg in the Illinois-Missouri League in 1909, racking up an excellent 15–8 mark. Even at the young age of 22, he was already a control artist, walking only 42 batters in 219 innings. Over his memorable 20-year major league career, he walked an average of just 1.6 batters for every nine innings pitched. Alexander joined the Philadelphia Phillies in 1911 and immediately demonstrated his exceptional ability to the National League teams by leading the league in victories with 28, and innings pitched with 366. The easy-throwing right-handed pitcher dazzled major league batters with a smooth, no-windup, sidearm delivery. His repertoire, consisting of a hard curveball, the league's best change of pace, and a devastating sinking fastball, coupled with pinpoint control, kept opposing batters guessing all day long. And disdaining the upper part of the plate and the center of the plate, he pinpointed most of his pitches to the lower outside corner of the plate. His workload, which averaged 377 innings a year from 1914 to 1917, is mind-boggling to modern baseball enthusiasts, who believe that pitching more than 200 innings a year puts an undue strain on a pitcher's arm and shortens his career. Grover Cleveland Alexander is best remembered for his performance in the 1926 World Series against the New York Yankees, when he trudged in from the St. Louis Cardinals bullpen in the seventh inning of game seven to strike out Tony Lazzeri with the bases loaded, and then blanked the Yankees over the last two innings to bring the city of St. Louis a world championship. When he retired after the 1930 season, he had compiled a 373–208 win-loss record with 90 shutouts. He was also on call, out of the bullpen when needed. He relieved in 98 games during his career, going 23–17 with three saves.

The major leagues lost one of its most outstanding pitchers in 1918 when Babe Ruth traded in his toe plate for an outfielder's glove. The Sultan of Swat joined the Boston Red Sox as a talented southpaw pitcher in 1914 after recording a mark of 22–9 in the International League. In his rookie season in Boston, Ruth went 18–8 in 32 games. The next year, he came into his own, winning 23 games against 12 losses, and leading the American League with 41 games started, 9 shutouts, and a sizzling 1.75 ERA. He went 24–13 in 1917 before tailing off to 13–7 and 9–5 during his transition to an everyday outfielder. And the Bambino was at his best in the World Series. He went 3–0 in two Fall Classics, and set a World Series record of 29⅔ consecutive scoreless innings, finally broken by Whitey Ford in 1960. Ruth and Walter Johnson met on the field of battle ten times, with Ruth holding a 6–4 advantage. His brief pitching career covering just 4½ full seasons, resulted in a 94–46 win-loss record. His .671 winning percentage has been exceeded by only four men in the history of the game, and his 2.28 ERA is the number-ten all-time record.

With the new rule changes, particularly the rule that permitted teams to substitute players during the game, and the rule that lengthened the distance from the pitching rubber to home plate, relief pitching gained in popularity in the major leagues. In 1892, starting pitchers completed 88 percent of the games they started. By 1910, perhaps assisted by the introduction of the new cork-centered baseball, but more probably the result of a general drop-off in runs scored, which had plummeted from 1,011 runs per team per 154 games in 1893 to 685 in 1903 and to 588 in 1914, the number of complete games had tumbled to 56 percent in the National League and 68 percent in the American League. Five years later, the American League complete-game percentage stood at 53 percent. More teams, it seems, were pinch-hitting for the pitcher in the late innings in an effort to win the low-scoring games that were common at the time.

Although the use of relief pitchers became more commonplace after 1892, they were still not generally used in a "save" situation. If a starting pitcher had a lead, he usually stayed in the game. If he was tied or trailing late in the game, he might be lifted for a pinch hitter and, if his team regained the lead, a relief pitcher would be called in to save the game. In those cases, the responsibility usually fell on one of the starting pitchers. In the 1890s Kid Nichols was one of the busiest relief pitchers, coming in from the bullpen 59 times. Jack Stivetts answered the call 55 times and Brickyard Kennedy relieved teammates 52 times. The second-line relief pitchers were used in mop-up situations, when the team was far behind and the manager wanted to save his starting pitcher's arm.

During the first two decades of the twentieth century, the trend continued. Starting pitchers were used in game situations and second-line relief pitchers were used only after the game got out of hand. The second-line pitchers were not held in high esteem by the baseball establishment. They generally fell into three categories: a young kid trying to break into the starting rotation, a starting pitcher whose career was on the decline, or a pitcher who didn't have the stamina to pitch nine full innings. Some of the most popular starting pitchers who were used in relief in tight game situations are listed below.

Pitcher	G	W	L	Saves
Slim Sallee	171	24	25	35
Three-Finger Brown	149	30	20	49
Eddie Cicotte	143	25	12	22
Walter Johnson	136	42	25	35
Rube Marquard	132	28	12	13
Hooks Wiltse	131	20	13	33
Chief Bender	124	20	14	36
Ed Walsh	115	16	15	40
Ed Reulbach	100	18	7	11

In 1913, Chief Bender started 21 games and relieved in 27, going 15 and 6 as a starter and 6 and 4 as a reliever, for a total record of 21–10. He also led the league in saves with 13. That same year, Larry Cheney of the Chicago Cubs started 36 games and relieved in 18, going 17–14 as a starter and 4–0 as reliever, with 11 saves. Three-Finger Brown was another popular multiduty pitcher in the early days. Between 1903 and 1916, the 5' 10," 175-pound right-hander trudged in from the bullpen 149 times, passing the 100 mark in 1913. He also started 332 games, mostly with the Chicago Cubs, winning 239 times against 130 losses, and saving 49. Slim Sallee, a member of the St. Louis Cardinals for nine years between 1908 and 1916, started 305 games during his career and relieved in 171 others. His career record shows 174 victories, 143 losses, and 36 saves. Hooks Wiltse started 226 games during his 12-year career, and relieved in 131 others, compiling a career record of 139 wins, 90 losses, and 33 saves. And there was Tom Hughes, who pitched in the major leagues for nine years, with the Yankees and the Red Sox. He was groomed to be a double-duty pitcher, but he was more successful as a relief pitcher than he was as a starting pitcher. He did have two career highlights as a starting pitcher, however. He once pitched nine no-hit innings against Cleveland only to lose 5–0 in the eleventh. He finally got his no-hitter on June 16, 1916, beating Pittsburgh 2–0. For the year, he went 16–3 with 13 starts and 37 relief appearances. His bullpen statistics included a 9–2 record with five saves. The previous year, he started 25 games and relieved in the same number, going 10–14 as a starter, and 10–0 with a league-leading five saves out of the pen. Hughes pitched only 14 games over the next two years, and then was gone.

Clark Griffith, the manager of the New York Highlanders, whose team had the highest earned run average in the American League in 1905, continually shuffled pitchers in and out of the lineup in an attempt to find a winning combination. As a result of the pitching staff's ineptness, the Highlanders were the first major league team to have less than 100 complete games pitched over a 154 game schedule. Their 88 complete games amounted to 57 percent of their games played, compared to a league average of 80 percent. New York finished the season in sixth place, with a 71–78 record, 21½ games behind first-place Philadelphia.

New York Giants manager John McGraw was one of the pioneers in the use of full time relief pitchers, but he used them to win or save games, not to mop up games that had gotten out of hand. McGraw initiated the practice in the early 1900s with Claude Elliott, a tall right-hander from Wisconsin, who joined the team in 1904; Elliott pitched in ten games the following year, relieving in eight of them and leading the league with six saves. Elliott's major league career ended the following year, however, and McGraw had to look around for another reliever. George Ferguson was next on McGraw's list. He pitched in 22 games in 1906, relieving in 21 of them, recording a league-leading seven saves to go along with a 2–0 win-loss mark. The next year he appeared in just 15 games, ten in relief, with one save. He was traded to Boston in 1908.

The persistent Giants manager finally found his ideal relief pitcher in the person of James Otis Crandall, a laid-back Hoosier who was never flustered by any situation. In fact, he once said he didn't feel comfortable unless there were men on base. One day, when an enemy crowd was hooting and hollering at him, Christy Mathewson, as he recalled in his book, remarked to him, "That crowd was making some noise," to which Crandall calmly replied, "Was it? I didn't notice." Crandall, nicknamed Doc by Damon Runyon, who also called him "the physician of the pitching emergency," as noted in Thorn's *Relief Pitcher*, started and relieved for the Giants from 1908 through 1913. He jumped to the Federal League in 1914 after a disagreement with New York management, pitched for the Feds for two years, and then came back to the majors, where he finished his career in 1918. Crandall went on to pitch in the Pacific Coast League for 13 more years, where he won 230 games against

Doc Crandall of the New York Giants is considered to be baseball's first bona fide relief pitcher (GEORGE E. OUTLAND).

151 losses, mostly as a starting pitcher. He finally hung his glove up for good in 1929 at the age of 41. During his tenure with the Giants, Crandall was one of the most valuable players on the team, starting 134 games, relieving in 168, and serving as John McGraw's number one pinch hitter, batting a steady .285 in 887 at-bats. He also filled in at second base and in the outfield in an emergency. He was the first of the double-duty pitchers, alternating between starting and relieving, who relieved in more games than he started. He was also one of the first pitchers to relieve in 100 career games, reaching that level in 1912, two weeks after Ed Walsh broke the barrier. In 1909, he pitched in 30 games, 22 of them in relief, going 6–4 with six saves. He followed that up with four more sensational years:

• In 1910, he started 18 games, relieved in 24, and compiled a 17–4 record with five saves.
• In 1911, he started 15 games, relieved in 26, and compiled a 15–5 record with five saves.
• In 1912, he started ten games, relieved in 27, and compiled a 13–7 record with two saves.
• In 1913, he started two games, relieved in 33, and compiled a 4–4 record, with six saves.

Doc Crandall was baseball's first true relief pitcher.

Dave Danforth, known as Dauntless Dave because he constantly pitched with a sore arm, was another early relief pitcher. He pitched for a total of ten years between 1911 and 1925, starting 112 games and relieving in 174 games. His best year was 1917, when he went 11–6, while leading the league with six saves and 50 games pitched. His 41 relief appearances were a record, broken by Firpo Marberry eight years later. Danforth was followed to the majors by Allan Russell, who pitched for the New York Yankees, Boston Red Sox, and Washington Senators. Russell, who was called Rubberarm because of his ability to toe the rubber often, pitched in the major leagues from 1915 until 1925, starting 112 games and relieving in 233. He was one of 17 spitball pitchers who were grandfathered after the pitch was banned in 1920, and he continued to throw it throughout his career. He led the league in saves twice, with five saves in 1919 and nine saves in 1923. He retired in 1925 with a record of 70 victories, 76 losses, and 42 saves.

Two of the more memorable relief appearances in the early days involved pitchers for the Boston Red Sox. The first of these games was played on July 20, 1914, with Fritz Coumbe pitching against the Detroit Tigers. The lanky southpaw carried a 2–0 lead into the ninth inning, but the powerful Tigers pushed across the tying runs before a batter could be recorded. Manager Bill Carrigan rushed Dutch Leonard, his most dependable reliever, into the game to stem the tide. The 22-year-old Leonard, in just his second year in the major leagues, retired the side without further scoring and went on to pitch eight innings of no-hit relief, until the Red Sox could plate the winning run in the sixteenth inning. Leonard went on to record an excellent 19–5 mark for the year, while leading the league with four saves and a 0.96 ERA, still the lowest in modern baseball history. The second memorable game involved a game started by Babe Ruth. In the first game of a June 23, 1917, double-header in Fenway Park, Ruth walked the Washington Senators lead-off batter and then was tossed out of the game by the umpire for arguing the call. He was relieved by Ernie Shore, who proceeded to retire 27 men in a row, fanning just two in a 4–0 victory. The base runner was thrown out trying to steal second base, and Shore got the next 26 batters for a perfect game.

Some of the game's greatest pitchers gave memorable performances pitching in relief of their beleaguered teammates. Three-Finger Brown, who had many memorable confrontations with Christy Mathewson, faced Big Six in a one-game playoff after the conclusion

of the regular season on October 8, 1908, to determine the National League champion. Jack Pfiester actually started the game for the Chicago Cubs but was kayoed in the first inning after retiring only one of the five batters he faced. After two runners had scored, Brown came to the rescue and blanked John McGraw's troops the rest of the way, the Cubs winning 4–2. On May 13, 1911, Grover Cleveland Alexander, a 24-year-old rookie with the Philadelphia Phillies, came on in relief in the ninth inning against the Cincinnati Reds and tossed eight no-hit innings, to win 5–4 in the sixteenth. Two of Walter Johnson's relief appearances bear repeating. On July 5, 1912, he came on in relief against the New York Highlanders in the fourth inning, pitched 12⅔ scoreless innings, yielding only four hits while fanning five and walking three. He won the game in the sixteenth inning, 6–5. The next year, the Big Train was called into a game on July 24, 1913, and pitched 11⅓ innings for a victory, fanning 16 men along the way.

The most outstanding pitchers of the era included starting pitchers such as Walter Johnson, Christy Mathewson, Grover Cleveland Alexander, Mordecai "Three-Finger" Brown, and Eddie Plank. Doc Crandall represented the new breed of pitcher, the full-time relief specialist.

STARTING PITCHER STATISTICS: AVERAGES PER 154 GAMES

Pitcher	GS	CG	IP	W	L	GR	SV
Mordecai "3-Finger" Brown	26	21	244	18	10	11	4
Ed Walsh	26	21	247	16	11	10	3
Christy Mathewson	32	26	282	22	11	5	2
Walter Johnson	32	25	282	20	13	6	2
Eddie Plank	33	26	281	20	12	6	6
Grover Cleveland Alexander	33	24	288	21	12	2	5

RELIEF PITCHER STATISTICS: AVERAGES PER 154 GAMES

Pitcher	GR	W	L	SV
Doc Crandall	21	5	2	3

KEY:

GS = Games Started
GR = Games Relieved
SV = Saves

The six starting pitchers listed above were giants in their profession, averaging 30 starts, 24 complete games, 277 innings pitched, 19 victories, 12 losses, nine relief appearances, and four saves a year. They averaged 328 victories in their careers. They were paid to pitch, and pitch they did, posting a sensational 80 percent completion rate. In addition, they were available for bullpen duty whenever they were needed. Never again would major league baseball be represented by such an illustrious array of durable, strong-armed pitchers.

Opposite: **Babe Ruth was baseball's greatest southpaw pitcher before he emerged as the game's greatest slugger** (AUTHOR'S COLLECTION).

Doc Crandall was a pioneer in his field. He was the first bona fide relief pitcher, and the ancestor of great firemen and closers like Johnny Murphy, Bruce Sutter, and Mariano Rivera.

The Golden Age of Pitching was drawing to an end in 1919, but a few of the legends of the game, such as Walter Johnson and Grover Cleveland Alexander, continued to pitch well into the 1920s. And, except for the likes of Doc Crandall and Claude Elliott, most starting pitchers still handled the relief chores. While relief pitching was just gaining a toehold in the mentality of the major league baseball establishment, other changes were also shaping the future of the pitching fraternity, notably the introduction of the lively ball. The Black Sox scandal of 1919 almost destroyed major league baseball, but a big, homely slugger by the name of George Herman Ruth brought the crowds back to the ballparks with his towering home run blasts. He almost single-handedly saved the game.

5

The Lively Ball Era: 1920 to 1946

From the advent of the modern game of baseball in 1893, the grand old sport became a pitcher's game for the better part of three decades. They were in command, even after the introduction of the cork-center baseball in 1910. The 15" high pitcher's mound, the foul strike rule, and the wider home plate all worked to the pitcher's advantage. The most outstanding pitchers also benefited from the 1903 expansion that brought the American League into the fold, from the increase in the playing schedule from 140 games to 154 games, and from the increased use of trick pitches like the shine ball and the spitball. Teams averaged just 26 home runs per year between 1910 and 1919, so pitchers could pace themselves over a nine-inning stretch without having to worry about some big lout hitting a ball over the fence.

But all that changed in 1920 when Babe Ruth revised the dynamics of the sport forever. From the game's best left-handed pitcher, he became the game's greatest slugger. He revolutionized the game of baseball with his awesome hitting, and the credit for his history-making performance should be given to the man himself. He was without a doubt the greatest offensive force ever to play the game. He was big and strong, and his hand-eye coordination and quick wrists terrorized opposing pitchers. Even before the lively ball was introduced into the game, the Sultan of Swat was in a league of his own. His compact swing, quick wrists, and uppercut sent balls into orbit all over the American League. His professional growth as a slugger really began in 1918 when he was just 23 years old. He was penalized by the enormous size of his home park, which measured 380 feet to right-center field and 488 feet to deep center, but his 11 home runs on the road in 172 at-bats equated to 35 homers for every 550 at-bats. The next year, he led the league with 29 homers, 20 of them on the road. Tilly Walker, the number-two man, had ten homers. Ruth's road totals averaged 47 homers for every 550 at-bats, and overall he out-homered four other teams— and that was in the dead ball era. The advent of the lively ball just increased his advantage.

The early years of the 1920s brought about several rule changes that served to penalize pitchers and further aid the sluggers. There were two major changes, in particular, that changed the game forever, and one of them created havoc in the major leagues throughout the decade. The first change, to the ball, may have been the result of the world war. According to TheDeadballEra.com, when the U.S. entered World War I,

As with all wars, there is always a shortage of materials. When it came to baseball, this was no exception. Since the standard yarn that was used for baseball winding was now being put to use to help the "Doughboys keep the world safe for democracy," baseball manufacturers had no choice but to use inferior, cheaper yarn for the standard National and American League spheres. It was found that the inferior yarn made the baseballs even more loosely wound than before. To make up the difference, the machines that wound the baseballs were set so that the yarn would be wound tighter making up the difference. Here's where it starts to get interesting. The Great War ended on November 11, 1918, but the flow of high quality raw material back into the private sector was a slow process. High quality yarn was not made available for the 1919 season. When the baseballs made with the old, high quality yarn were finally manufactured again, there was a noticeable difference in the feel of the ball. The baseball winding machines continued to wind the yarn with the new, tighter settings. Why no one ever decided to go back to the old settings remains a mystery! But when the new "lively" ball first was shown at the end of the '19 season, many pitchers became nervous at the thought of serving up the new product. Cy Young commented, "When I had a chance to take a gander at that lively ball before the '20 season began, my first thoughts were that I was sure glad I was retired."

Perhaps the baseball establishment became so enamored with the exploits of the Sultan of Swat, and the excitement generated around the American League in 1919 when he slammed 29 home runs, that they were happy with the juiced-up ball, and they decided to keep it in hopes the increased home run production would attract more fans to the ballparks. One source claimed the manufacturer of the American League baseball, A.S. Reach Co., began using an Australian yarn that was stronger than the American yarn they had been using. This permitted them to wind the ball more tightly and resulted in a livelier ball. Roger Kahn also referred to that change in *The Head Game*. He went on to say, "Spalding juiced the National League baseball in its Massachusetts factory in 1922, and Rogers Hornsby hit 42 home runs." It is possible that there was more than one change to the windings on the baseball in the early 1920s that led to the lively ball. Whatever the real story was, the new baseball introduced in the 1920–22 period was, without a doubt, much livelier than its predecessor. And the loose specifications of the major league baseballs allow significant variability in the performance of the ball.

The other changes that affected the game were the abolition of trick pitches and the banning of administering foreign substances to the ball. Some of these changes came about as a result of an on-field tragedy. Ray Chapman, the shortstop of the Cleveland Indians, was killed by a pitch thrown by submarine pitcher Carl Mays of the New York Yankees, in the Polo Grounds on August 16, 1920. The pitch was reportedly a strike on the inside corner of the plate, and Chapman, who was notorious for crowding the plate, lost sight of the ball as it approached the plate, and was unable to get out of the way in time. The major league owners took immediate action to prevent that type of accident in the future. As TheDeadballEra.com notes,

> The era before 1919 was known as The Dead Ball Era. It was definitely a time that favored the pitcher. Most games started and finished with the same ball, unless the ball was hit out of the park for a home run. Even foul balls were returned and used! A ball had to be literally in tatters for an ump to heave it out. By the middle innings of a game, the ball took on a black look. Covered in tobacco juice and dirt! The ball became soft and round. To make things even tougher for batters, baseballs of that time were wound very loosely by the manufacturers. The batters were also at a major disadvantage because of the many "illegal" pitches that hurlers were serving up like the spitball, the Emory ball and the shine ball. In an interview, Frank "Home Run" Baker said, "And we didn't have a white ball to hit either, we had a black ball.

First of all, it's a whole lot different hitting that black ball on a dark evening than hitting a white ball. And we had a spitball to go up against. And the Emory ball such as Russ Ford used to throw. And another number of pitches that you don't have today."

The major league owners banned trick pitches, including the infamous spitball, over the winter of 1919–1920. However, 17 major league pitchers who were designated as spitball pitchers were grandfathered; in other words, permitted to continue to throw the spitball throughout their careers. Burleigh Grimes, who retired in 1934, was the last official spitball pitcher. Owners also banned the use of any foreign substance on the ball, including dirt and rosin. And one year later, as a result of the Chapman tragedy, umpires were directed to remove any ball from the game that was discolored or misshapen. That last move created havoc around the major leagues for nine years. New balls were put into service as they were received from the manufacturer, meaning they were white, shiny, and slippery. Prior to 1920, new balls could be rubbed up by the pitcher, using rosin or dirt, to take the sheen off the ball. After 1920, that action was illegal. And pitchers suffered. Instead of using only one ball in a game, a pitcher had to contend with several new balls over a nine-inning contest. And a new, slippery ball was difficult to grip properly. As a result, fastballs lost most of their hop, and curveballs didn't break as much as they had previously. And the batters happily flailed away at pitches that didn't break. Wild Bill Donovan was quoted by Roger Kahn in *The Head Game* as stating in 1923, "The trouble with pitchers nowadays is that they can not curve the ball."

The period from 1920 through 1946 was a particularly difficult time for major league pitchers. The introduction of the lively ball turned their lives into a nightmare, and a number of other changes to the game during that period just added to their frustration. The emergence of Babe Ruth as the game's premier slugger, and the frenzy his long wallops generated around the American League, created an army of Babe Ruth wannabees who gripped the bat down at the end and swung for the fences. During the decade after 1920, major league home runs more than doubled their pre–1920 totals and, from 1930 to 1946, with a new generation of sluggers coming up, they increased by another 73 percent. Other changes involving the baseball also aided and abetted the sluggers and penalized the pitchers.

In 1920, Babe Ruth crushed the fantastic total of 59 home runs, almost double his record-breaking 1919 total. Suspicions about the liveliness of the ball surfaced immediately and, as they have done every time the question has arisen over the past 85 years, the baseball establishment denied any changes had been made to the ball. Billy Evans, writing in the *Sporting News* on December 23, 1920, reported that critics claimed the American League ball was more lively than the National League ball. Evans said, "I thought it might be true even though earlier in the season I had watched the manufacture of both major league balls and knew they were identical. To satisfy my curiosity, I, with the umpire who was working with me, procured an American and a National League ball, and performed an autopsy. We found the composition to be identical, just as I had observed it in the factory. That killed one reason offered for Ruth's marvelous swat ability."

In spite of Evans' testimony, and other observations like it, the lively-ball debate continued throughout the decade, and with good reason. When the cork-centered baseball was introduced in 1910, home runs increased from 21 home runs per team per 154 games between 1901 and 1910 to 26 home runs from 1911 to 1919, an increase of 24 percent. And, as noted earlier, during the first decade of the Babe Ruth era, home runs jumped up to 66 home runs per team per year.

John McGraw, the venerable manager of the New York Giants, complained about the lively ball for several years during the mid '20s, but his exhortations fell on deaf ears. In 1925, the major leagues began using a new cushioned-cork baseball, the nucleus of which was a mixture of cork and rubber. Needless to say, it was even livelier than the 1920 ball, and pitching continued to deteriorate until, in 1930 — a year that has come down in history as the Year of the Hitter — the situation came to a head. Another change in the construction of the baseball, probably inadvertent, resulted in a ball with recessed seams, which had a disastrous effect on pitchers. The pitchers, already hampered by the slippery surface of the ball, had even more difficulty gripping the ball and making it curve, and the batters had a field day. The change actually became noticeable in 1929 when the new balls were probably being worked into the system, and reached a peak in 1930. Happy hitters teed off on the deliveries of the hapless pitchers, resulting in a 43 percent increase in home runs and a 15-point rise in batting averages. The National League, as a whole, averaged .303 with 112 home runs per team in 1930.

There was another culprit that crept into the baseball equation during the 1920s and that contributed to the Year of the Hitter episode, and that was the changing size of the ballparks. Avaricious owners, intent on promoting the romance of the home run to the baseball public, kept shortening the fences in an attempt to increase the home run output of their sluggers. Although Connie Mack shortened the left field fence in Shibe Park from 380 feet in 1921 to a cozy 312 feet in 1926, most of the changes occurred in the National League, where severe shrinkages in the playing area were witnessed in Forbes Field in Pittsburgh, Braves Field in Boston, Sportsman's Park in St. Louis, Ebbets Field in Brooklyn, Crosley Field in Cincinnati, and Wrigley Field in Chicago. In Pittsburgh, for example, the right field fence was shortened from 376 feet in 1922 to just 300 feet in 1925. Wrigley Field's right field fence shrank from 356 feet in 1914 to 318 feet in 1923. Ebbets Field's left field wall was shortened from 419 feet in 1921 to 384 feet in 1926. And Crosley Field's fences were shortened by 22 feet all around the perimeter of the outfield in 1927. The result of all these National League shenanigans was that the home run totals for the league jumped from 60 to 76 in 1927, to 94 in 1929, and to 112 in 1930. The American League saw a smaller increase, with the league home runs going from 60 to 74 in 1929, and to 84 in 1930.

During the winter of 1931, the two leagues took steps to address the problem, according to the *Los Angeles Times*:

> Definite steps to curb the home-run barrage in the National and American Leagues have been taken, it was revealed today with the announcement that a new and "slower" ball will be used during the 1931 season.
>
> The National League naming more drastic changes than its younger brother, the American, announced at New York that the 1931 ball would have a thicker cover and heavier stitch.
>
> The American League through President Ernest S. Barnard at Chicago announced that the American League would retain the same weight cover but that stitches would be heavier.

The Sporting News also reported on the lively ball discussions at the winter meetings:

> In the past two years there has been a growing appreciation in the National League that the pitcher is not receiving a fair deal in the rules and in the implements that are provided to play the game of baseball. The theory of a lively ball was suggested several times by John J. McGraw and he kept it up.
>
> Despite the fact that the makers of the ball told McGraw and others interested in baseball that no change had been made, McGraw clung to his idea after others had abandoned it.

John A. Heydler, the president of the National League, added,

We have been trying for a long time to keep our games from dragging along and taking more than two hours to play. One of the delaying factors was the necessity of bringing in relief pitchers. If the new ball is as helpful to pitchers as we hope, more of them may be able to pitch complete games. There should be fewer replacements. As a result, the games should be played more quickly.

Heydler's comments regarding relief pitchers reinforced the low esteem that relief pitchers were still held in at that time. In spite of the success of Firpo Marberry, the great relief ace of the Washington Senators, and others like him, the game was still in the hands of the starting pitcher, with relievers only being used in a dire emergency or in mop-up situations. It would be well into the 1940s before such bullpen specialists as Johnny Murphy, Joe Page, and Hugh Casey brought the relief pitcher the respect he deserved. The changes did seem to stabilize the complete-game situation however, but only temporarily. The two leagues, which saw their complete games drop from 50 percent in 1923 to 44 percent in 1930, realized a slight, 4 percent increase in 1931. The percentage held relatively stable between 44 percent and 46 percent for the next 15 years, until after World War II. Then, with returning servicemen manhandling the wartime replacement pitchers, the admittance of Negro league players into organized baseball, the acceptance of firemen such as Page and Casey, and the introduction of the Kiner Syndrome, complete games began to tumble again, on a decline that continues to this day. John B. Foster noted in the *Sporting News* on February 12, 1931,

One of the greatest handicaps to pitchers who were using the old ball was its smoothness. The gloss was so well attached that the pitchers complained of their inability to grip the ball as they would like to grip it. Thus it was roughened by the umpires before the game began. In addition to that, the pitchers of the National League were permitted to use the rosin bag.

The use of dirt to rough up the baseball was discontinued in 1938, and was replaced by the use of a special mud taken from Pennsauken Creek, a tributary of the Delaware River. The mud, which the umpires applied to the game balls over a 20-minute period, dulled the gloss of the ball without changing its color. Rubbing the balls with dirt is now against the rules.

The changes had the desired effects. The National League saw home runs decrease by 45 percent, batting averages decrease by 26 points, and earned run averages plummet from 4.97 to 3.86 in 1931. The American League, with less drastic measures, experienced a 14 percent decrease in home runs and a 10-point drop in batting averages, with a modest reduction in ERA from 4.65 to 4.38. John B. Foster commented in the *Sporting News* on the reduced playing field dimensions:

Many stands had been built so close to the diamond in some cities that the normal distance of a batted home run hit, which really should be never less than 360 feet, had been brought down as low as 255 feet. It does not mean much to hit a ball 255 feet. Almost all hits of that length would be easily caught in any ball field.

In 1934, the National League began using the same ball as the American League, bringing their statistics more in line with each other. Using the ball with the thinner cover, the National League's batting averages rose by 13 points, home runs increased from 58 per team to 82 per team, and ERAs soared from 3.34 to 4.06. By 1936, the batting and slugging statistics were on the rise again, and the leagues once again took corrective action, voting to use a new "dead" ball. But there was a slight problem. As the *Los Angeles Times* reported on December 11, 1936,

> The major league baseball, voted "dead" yesterday, came to life again today in the league meetings when manufacturers advised club owners they have almost a season's supply of "the fast balls" in stock.
>
> The club officials directed the manufacturers to turn out "several new balls varying between the 1933 season National League ball and the present ball." These will be clearly marked, the players will be asked to experiment with them in batting practice, and the owners will consider changing the ball again at the end of the 1937 season.

The baseball situation didn't change during the 1937 season, and the issue was reviewed again at the winter meetings in December. The *L.A. Times* covered the meetings:

> The National and American Leagues, which used the "rabbit" baseball through their "boom" 1937 campaigns, split wide open today on the kind of ball they will use in 1938.
>
> The National circuit voted unanimously to use a slower, more heavily covered ball next season, and less than an hour later, the American League decided to retain the faster pellet which it has used many seasons and which the Nationals had used four years.
>
> The junior circuit decision in favor of the faster ball was seen as the possible beginning of a "feud" between the majors over types of balls to be used. Previously, it was reported, the American League had stood at 6–2 in favor of the slower ball.
>
> The new National League ball, technically known as the No. 4 ball with five strands in the seam instead of four, is expected to result in a year of improved pitching and tighter games in the senior circuit and another of long distance blasting and wide open tilts in the American League. The powerful world champion New York Yankees led the movement for retention of the livelier sphere.
>
> The last time both circuits used different balls was in 1933, when the National clubs performed with a No. 5 ball, even slower than the one they will use next season. The ball the American clubs will continue to use is known as the No. 3 type.
>
> "The new ball will give the pitchers a better grip," said Ford Frick, National League president, "but it will not impair the possibility of long hits if the ball is hit right."
>
> It was learned senior circuit officials, in deciding on the slower ball, were hopeful of reducing the number of "cheap" homers and scratchy hits off good pitches made with the lively sphere. In the 1938 World Series, the ball used by the home park team will be used.

The results of the 1938 series confirmed the difference in the construction of the baseballs. In games played in the National League park, the two teams combined for two home runs and 13 runs, while in the American League park, they scored 18 runs, while smashing five homers.

The controversy over the use of two different baseballs in the major leagues disappeared with the announcement that the two leagues would use the same ball in 1939. As reported in the *Sporting News* on January 5, "Batting averages in the American League probably will shrink but there will be little difference in the slugging figures as the result of the introduction of a uniform ball in the majors next season." The general consensus was that the delivered ball would have more of an effect on the free swingers than on those who poke the ball. The effect, however, would only be on the batting averages of the free swingers, not on their home runs. American League home runs were expected to remain at the 1938 level. In fact, the American League didn't experience changes in any batting, slugging, or pitching statistics in 1939. They did see an increase in home runs from 1935 through 1937, which may have been the result of continued tweaking of the size of the playing fields. There were significant reductions along the foul lines in Fenway Park, Navin (Briggs) Stadium, and Comiskey Park, and in center field in Fenway Park, which was cut from 468 feet to 389 feet.

Many baseball historians claim the period from 1920 to 1946 was a hitters' era, devoid of good pitching. It may be true that the bullpen brigade was not up to the standards expected of major league pitchers, but there were still many world-class pitchers in the American and National Leagues in the 1920s and 1930s. It was still the domain of the starting pitcher, and particularly the fastball pitcher who didn't rely so heavily on the slipperiness of the ball as the curveball pitchers did. The starting pitchers on all teams were the best pitchers available, and they were also the pitchers of choice whenever a relief pitcher was needed in a tight situation. According to John Thorn, "The school of thought was still, if you had a lead late in the game, why put your fate into the hands of a second-rater? If the starter was too pooped to pitch any further, bring in another starter." Still, starting pitchers were not used indiscriminately. They were not used in games where the outcome was not in doubt. The regular denizens of the bullpen were used in those situations. Starting pitchers were normally used in relief only when the original starter was removed for a pinch hitter in a close game, or if he was being hit hard in a game that was still in question. A first line pitcher being used in relief could be expected to pitch several innings, anywhere from two to five. By the time the ninth inning rolled around, if the original starter was still in the game, it would be left to him to close the door, either winning or losing his own game. Starting pitchers of the period, in view of their double-duty responsibilities, carried heavy workloads, often pitching more than 300 innings a year. Many of them started 38 to 41 games a year and relieved in another 5 to 10. Lefty Grove, for example, appeared in 50 games in 1930, starting 32 and relieving in 18, pitching 291 innings. He led the American League in both victories with 28 and saves with 9. Guy Bush pitched in 50 games for the Chicago Cubs in 1929, starting 30 and relieving in another 20, pitching 271 innings. He won 18 games and led the National League in saves with 8. But first and foremost among the double-duty giants of the period was Walter Johnson who, although he was 32 years old when the lively-ball era kicked in, continued to pitch 260 to 280 innings a year for the next seven years.

Although Johnson was only a shadow of his former self during the 1920s, he still enjoyed considerable success during his final years, particularly in 1924 and 1925. His team, the lowly Washington Senators, "First in War, First in Peace, and Last in the American League," a perennial second division club, finally broke the mold and captured the pennant both years. And the Big Train was still their ace. He went 23–7 in 1924, leading the league in victories, winning percentage (.767), shutouts (6), and strikeouts (158). And, in the World Series against the New York Giants, the old warrior, after losing games one and five, came on in relief in the eighth inning of the finale, and blanked John McGraw's troops for four innings, finally gaining the victory when his team pushed over the World Championship–winning run in the bottom of the twelfth inning. Walter Johnson exited the major leagues as he had entered, with grace and humility. Although his ERA increased significantly between 1920 and 1927, his 3.30 earned run average compared favorably with the league average of 4.08. And he still completed 61 percent of the games he started from 1921 to 1927.

Grover Cleveland Alexander, who toed the rubber until 1930, produced three 20-win seasons during the first decade of the lively-ball era, including a 27–14 mark in 1920. His complete game percentage decreased from 79 percent to 67 percent during the 1920s, but he still won 165 games during that decade, while pitching out of the bullpen occasionally. His overall career record included 96 relief appearances with 32 saves. And, like Walter Johnson, his most famous victory came in relief, in the seventh game of the 1926 World Series.

Lefty Grove was the first of the legendary pitchers to begin his career after the introduction of the lively ball. The hard throwing southpaw began his major league career with the Philadelphia Athletics in 1925, and he retired in 1941, completing an epic journey of 17 years. The tall, lanky Maryland native stood 6' 3" tall and weighed 204 pounds. He was blessed with a blazing fastball, and was effectively wild, but he didn't hit many batters, averaging only one hit batter every ten games. Still, he didn't like batters to dig in against him, and he brushed them back frequently to keep them off the plate. It was reported that he even threw brushback pitches at his teammates in batting practice. And Lefty Grove's temper was legendary. "On the day he was pitching," said Jim Kaplan, "it was suicide for a photographer to take his picture. He'd throw the ball right through the lens." And if he lost a game, according to one of his teammates, it was best to stay clear of the clubhouse. As noted in Shatzkin's *Ballplayers*, he "shredded uniforms, kicked buckets, ripped-apart lockers, and alienated teammates."

Grove, who was one of the top five or ten pitchers in baseball history, won 20 or more games 11 times, topping out with a spectacular 31–4 season in 1931. That year, his 2.06 ERA was a full 2.32 runs less than the league average, one of the largest differentials in the annals of the sport. His lifetime 3.06 ERA, compared to those of the era in which he pitched, may be the best ever. The terrible tempered lefty retired with a career record of 300–141. And Lefty Grove's achievements were not limited to starting a game. He was also a fearful presence in the bullpen on his days off, appearing in relief 159 times, and averaging 2.4 innings per relief appearance. The big southpaw went 33–22 out of the pen, with 55 saves and a 2.84 earned run average. He is the all-time saves leader for a starting pitcher.

Van Lingle Mungo was a big, high-kicking flamethrowing pitcher who starred for the Brooklyn Dodgers during the 1930s. He became a favorite of manager Casey Stengel when Stengel asked for someone to hit a batter and Mungo volunteered. He went into the game and hit the first batter. From then on, he could do no wrong in Stengel's eyes. Mungo, who was considered to be one of the best pitchers of his era, won just 120 games against 115 defeats in 14 years, pitching mostly for a sixth place team. He led the National League in strikeouts in 1936 with 238. The 6' 2" right-hander started 259 games during his career, completing 47 percent of them. He also pitched in relief 105 times, recording 16 saves.

Guy Bush was another noted fastball pitcher of the period, his career spanning the years 1923 to 1945. He was also noted as a mean pitcher who would send batters sprawling in the dirt if the situation called for it. Although his hit-batter frequency was low, batters seldom tested his intent. The man known as the Mississippi Mudcat was one of his era's most productive two-way pitchers, coming out of the bullpen almost as often as he started a game. In 17 years, Bush started 308 games and completed 49 percent of them. He also relieved in 234 games, winning 43, losing 20, and saving 34. He led the league in saves in 1925 and 1929. And in 1933, he was a 20-game winner, going 20–12 for the Chicago Cubs.

Eppa Rixey, a 6' 5", 210-pound southpaw, threw baseballs at National League batters for 21 years, from 1912 to 1933. In compiling a 266–251 record, the future Hall-of-Famer averaged about 125 pitches per nine innings, according to F.C. Lane. He started 290 games and relieved in 138 games during his career, and his bullpen stats included 20 wins, 17 losses, and 14 saves.

In addition to the above mentioned power pitchers, there were also a number of curveball artists who excelled in the major leagues during the 1920–1946 period. Foremost among them was Vic Aldridge, who pitched in the National League for nine years between 1917 to 1928, primarily with the Chicago Cubs. As Aldridge noted in Neyer and James' book, "In the Cubs' relatively small field with encroaching bleacher seats, the pitcher has to guard particularly against a fluky home run. A curve is less likely to be changed into a homer than a fast-ball." Rogers Hornsby said Aldridge had one of the best sharp-breaking curveballs in baseball, as James and Neyer noted. The slightly built right-hander, who started 204 games during his major league career with 102 route-going efforts, was in the minority during the decade of the '20s, a pitcher who could control the slippery ball well enough to curve it. He also worked out of the bullpen in 44 games, with six saves. In addition to his career record of 97–80, he pitched two complete game victories in the 1925 World Series against the Washington Senators.

Bob Shawkey was one of the top pitchers in the American League for 15 years, from 1913 to 1927, all but 2 and one-half of them with the New York Yankees. His 195–150 win-loss record included four 20-victory seasons, and he averaged 18 wins a season for Miller Huggins' club between 1916 and 1924. According to J.E. Wray in his 1931 book, *How to Pitch,*

> Shawkey has the hardest arm motion of any major league pitcher. He puts all his body from his waist up into his pitching motion and twists himself on his pivot foot long before he lets the ball get away. The result is a very wide curve that is hard to bat, especially when Shawkey has a good day and his speed is at its highest development. His delivery is not advised for a young pitcher to copy, although his finger positions are all right.

His exaggerated motion might have been necessitated by the slipperiness of the baseball during the 1920s. The 5' 11", 168-pound right-hander was another of the hard working pitchers of the pre–World War II period; he routinely pitched more than 250 innings a year and was available for relief duty on his days off. Shawkey started 333 games in 15 years, and completed 197, or 59 percent of them. He also went 30–21 in 155 relief appearances with 28 saves, leading the league in saves in both 1916 and 1919.

Herb Pennock was a tall, lanky southpaw who pitched in the major leagues for 22 years, from 1912 to 1934, most of that time with the New York Yankees. His career totals showed 241 victories against 162 losses, with a 3.61 earned run average. His ERA jumped up one full run after the lively ball came into existence in 1920, but it was still better than the league average of 3.88. He was primarily a curveball pitcher, who mixed speeds, arm angles, and location to keep the batter off balance. According to teammate Ed Wells, as reported by Neyer and James, "Pennock snapped his wrist so hard when he threw the curve ball you could hear his wrist snap if you were sitting on the bench." Pennock had a skinny arm like Satchel Paige, proving that muscles don't lead to longevity for pitchers. Pennock pitched in the major leagues for more than two decades. Paige pitched all over the Western Hemisphere, 365 days a year, for more than three decades.

Earl Whitehill was a durable pitcher, primarily for the Detroit Tigers and the Washington Senators, between 1923 and 1939. As reported in Shatzkin's *Ballplayers,*

The handsome, temperamental Whitehill, called The Earl for his flashy wardrobe and temperamental air, was a bear-down left-hander who told off teammates, umpires, and Ty Cobb, if he
thought they impeded his progress toward victory. Teammates were scorched for less than 100
percent effort, umpires for bad calls, and Manager Cobb for coming in from center field to
demand curveballs when Earl wanted to throw the fast one.

Whitehill, whose career record was 218–185, pitched over 200 innings in 12 of his 17
years in the Big Time. And he started more than 30 games a year, 11 times, with a high of
37 in 1933. He also pitched 68 games in relief, with 11 saves.

Carl Hubbell, the ace of the New York Giant pitching staff for 16 years between 1928
and 1943, won 253 games against 154 losses with a devastating screwball, plus a fastball, a
curveball, and excellent control. King Carl threw his screwball anywhere from 6 to 25 times
a game depending on the score, but he preferred to keep the batters off balance with his
other offerings. Hubbell is best know for his spectacular 1933 All-Star Game performance
when he fanned Ruth, Gehrig, Foxx, Simmons, and Cronin in succession. The tall, skinny
southpaw pitched in three World Series, going 4–2 with a 1.79 ERA. He also worked out of
the bullpen on occasion, relieving in 103 games during his career, with a 20–8 win-loss
record and 33 saves.

According to William Curran, in the early 1930s George Uhle perfected a nasty little
pitch that had been around since the nineteenth century but had not become popular
because of the difficulty controlling it. The sharp-breaking pitch, which looked like a fastball, was called the nickel-curve originally, but was christened the slider by Uhle. George
Blaeholder of the St. Louis Browns also began using the pitch, and before long it became
part of the normal repertoire of many pitchers. It is one of the pitcher's favorite weapons,
even today. Uhle used the pitch to good advantage during his 17-year career, winning 200
games against 166 losses. He was called the Bull for good reason. He routinely handled
heavy workloads early in his career, leading the league in victories twice, games started three
times, complete games twice, and innings pitched twice. In 1919, the Bull tossed a 20-inning
shutout. Uhle was not only a superb pitcher; he could also hit, as evidenced by his career
.289 batting average and nine home runs. He averaged 76 RBIs for every 550 at-bats.

Wes Ferrell, one-half of a famous brother act, starred in the American League from
1927 to 1941, compiling a career win-loss record of 193–128 along the way. Wes' brother
Rick, a major league catcher for 18 years, was inducted into the Baseball Hall of Fame in
1984. Wes, who also deserves to be a member of that exalted community, has thus far been
ignored. In his youth, Ferrell had a blinding fastball that compared favorably with the heat
of the more famous flamethrowers like Grove and Johnson. But Ferrell's ball lost its zip
after three or four years, and he had to rely on his curveball to get the big outs. Still, whether
with a curve or a fast one, Ferrell put together six 20-victory seasons between 1929 and
1936. His best season was 1926 when he led the league in victories with 25, games started
with 38, complete games with 31, and innings pitched with 322. And, in addition to his
pitching prowess, the 6' 2", 195-pound right-handed batter was the most powerful hitting
pitcher the game has yet produced. In 1934, the big slugger hit two home runs in a 3–2,
12-inning win over the Chicago White Sox. He tied the game with a homer in the bottom
of the eighth, and then hit a walk-off, game-winning homer in the bottom of the twelfth.
Wes Ferrell compiled a .280 batting average during his 15-year career. His 38 career home
runs are the major league record for pitchers, as is his 18 home run average for every 550
at-bats.

One of the legendary fastball pitchers of the twentieth century made his major league debut in 1936. Bob Feller, a 17-year-old farm boy from the plains of Iowa, burst upon the baseball scene in the summer of that year when, pitching for the Cleveland Indians, he fanned eight of the nine St. Louis Cardinal batters he faced in an exhibition game. One month later, the high-kicking right-hander dazzled the American League St. Louis Browns 4–1, tossing a six-hitter and fanning 15 men in his major league debut. He finished his rookie season with a record of 5–3, 76 strikeouts in just 62 innings, and a fine 3.34 ERA. Not bad for a youngster who had just finished his junior year in high school. The next year, he rejoined the Indians after completing high school, and put together a 9–7 record. Following a transitional 17–11 season in 1938, the 20-year-old phenom hit his stride. Over the next three seasons, he led the American League in victories with 24, 27, and 25; in innings pitched with 297, 320, and 343; and in strikeouts with 246, 261, and 260. He had also led the league in strikeouts in 1938 with 240, in games pitched and games started in both 1940 and '41, in complete games in 1939 and '40, and in earned run average in 1940. And he tossed a 1–0 opening day no-hitter at the Chicago White Sox, the first of three no-hitters he would pitch in his career. He was not yet 23 years old, and he had already won 107 major league games. His fastball, which was clocked at 98.6 miles per hour, terrorized American League batters. His potential was unlimited.

Unfortunately, World War II exploded in December 1941, and Bob Feller was one of the first major league players to enlist for active duty in military service. Over the next four years, the 6', 180-pound farm boy, as a member of the United States Navy, won eight battle stars for action in the Pacific theatre of the war. On his return to major league action in 1946, Rapid Robert, as he was called, once again dominated the league pitching statistics, leading the league in victories with 26, games pitched with 48, games started with 42, complete games with 36, shutouts with 10, innings pitched with 371, and strikeouts with a major league record 348. Feller pitched another ten years in the American League, with two more 20-victory seasons, before retiring at the age of 38. He left behind a record of 266 wins against 162 losses, with 2,581 strikeouts and a 3.25 ERA. And he added a major league record 12 one-hitters to his three no-hitters. If World War II had not intervened, Bob Feller might well have joined Walter Johnson and Cy Young as the only major league pitchers to win 400 or more games in a career. And he would almost assuredly have added to his no-hit and one-hit totals. Although he was exceptionally wild early in his career, his over-the-top delivery resulted in few hit batters, just one for every seven games pitched. In the final analysis, the man from Iowa has to be recognized as one of the five greatest pitchers in the history of the game. And, in all probability, the greatest pitcher of the last 70 years.

The outstanding double-duty pitchers of the era, in addition to those mentioned above, included Dizzy Trout (170 career victories and 35 saves), Virgil Trucks (177 victories and 30 saves), Al Benton (98 wins and 66 saves), Clint Brown (89 wins and 64 saves), Charlie Root (201 victories and 40 saves), and Jack Quinn (247 victories and 57 saves). Quinn was an interesting case, a true double-duty pitcher until the age of 46, after which time he became strictly a relief pitcher until his retirement at the age of 50. But the time of the double-duty pitcher was nearing an end. Over the next 60 years, the game of baseball would become more specialized, with nonstarters handling almost all the bullpen duties. The following table shows the steady decline in complete games, and the slow emergence of bullpen saves, since the National League began operations in 1876.

Dazzy Vance of the Brooklyn Dodgers led the National League in strikeouts his first seven years in the league (AUTHOR'S COLLECTION).

Year	Percent CG	Percent Saves
1876	91	2.5
1885	87	0.7
1895	81	2.9
1905	80	2.3
1915	53	5.7
1925	49	7.2
1935	45	8.5
1940	44	9.6

By 1925, the number of complete games thrown in the major leagues had dropped from 80 percent in 1905 to 49 percent, while saves had increased from 2.9 percent to 7.2 percent during the same period. The single-season saves leaders were still starting pitchers, but their days were numbered. Mordecai "Three-Finger" Brown's 13 saves in 1911 remained the major league record until Firpo Marberry racked up 15 saves in 1924. Brown's National League record was not broken until 1931 when Jack Quinn of Brooklyn saved 15 games. The American League record holder, prior to Marberry, was Chief Bender, who saved 12 games in 1913.

One of the first bullpen specialists of the lively ball era was Allan Russell of the New York Yankees. The slim, right-handed pitcher toiled for the Yankees, Red Sox, and Senators for 11 years, starting 112 games and relieving in 233. He was the first major league pitcher to relieve in 200 games. His career record is a mediocre 70–76, but out of the bullpen, he was sensational. As a starting pitcher, he posted a 35–55 record but, in relief, he went 35–21 with 42 saves. Russell led the American League in saves twice; in 1919 with five and in 1923 with nine.

Two other early relievers of note were Claude Jonnard and Rosy Ryan, who teamed to give the New York Giants a potent one-two punch out of the bullpen between 1922 and 1924. Over the three-year period, the two men helped John McGraw's club capture three consecutive National League pennants. Jonnard went 13–9 on the mound, pitching in 112 games, 108 of them in relief. In 1922 he appeared in 33 games, all of them in relief, making him one of the first, if not the first, full-time relief pitcher. He led the league with five saves in both '22 and '23, and added another five saves in '24. Ryan, who was the long man out of the pen during that time, relieved in 82 games in support of Jonnard's closing relief efforts, and he led the league in relief victories in both '22 and '23. The 6', 185-pound right-hander was also an occasional starting pitcher for McGraw, in addition to his relief efforts. He started 53 games over the three-year period, completing 24 of them, with a 41–23 win-loss record and a fine 3.50 ERA. His best years were 1922 and '23, when he pitched in 46 and 45 games respectively. In 1922, he went 17–12 with 22 starts and 24 relief appearances, with seven of his wins coming in relief. The following year, he was 16–5 with 15 starts and 30 relief appearances, with nine of his wins coming in relief. The two relief specialists also made significant contributions to the Giants' World Series successes. Rosy Ryan chalked up a fine 3–0 record in relief in six World Series games, a major league record, while pitching a total of 17 innings, with a sensational 1.59 earned run average. Jonnard pitched a total of two innings over three games, with no record. Claude Jonnard's six-year career essentially ended after 1924. He pitched briefly in two other years, for a total of 24 innings. Rosy Ryan relied primarily on a spitball when he first entered the major leagues, but when the spitball was outlawed in 1920, manager John McGraw intentionally left him off the list of protected pitchers, forcing him to develop a curveball, which became a formidable weapon in subsequent years. Ryan pitched in 248 games during his career, with 173 of them coming in relief. He compiled a record of 52–47, along with 19 saves.

Jonnard and Ryan set the table for the next step in the evolution of relief pitching, the emergence of the full-time relief pitcher. That occurred in 1923 when a young, 24-year-old fireballer named Frederick "Firpo" Marberry arrived on the scene in Washington and hastened Allan Russell's retirement. The big, 6' 1", 190-pound right-hander broke in with a 4–0 record in 11 games. The next year he blossomed, appearing in a league-leading 50 games, and setting a new major league record with 15 saves, breaking Three-Finger Brown's old

Firpo Marberry was baseball's best relief pitcher dring the 1920s (JAY SANFORD).

record of 13 saves. But Firpo was just getting started. He saved another 15 games in 1925, and then upped that figure to 22 the following year. That record would stand for 24 years until Joe Page saved 27 games in 1949. Over the three-year period from 1924 through 1926, Marberry appeared in 169 games, 150 of them in relief, while compiling a record of 32 and 24, with 52 saves. Utilizing a rising fastball almost exclusively early in his career, he could blow batters away for two or three innings. The Senators reached the World Series in both '24 and '25, with Marberry pitching in four games in '24 with two saves and a 1.13 earned run average, and pitching in two games the next year with one save and a 0.00 ERA. Manager Bucky Harris' reluctance to take the aging and tiring Walter Johnson out of the seventh game of the 1925 World Series and replace him with his top reliever, Firpo Marberry, probably cost the Senators the world championship, as the Pittsburgh Pirates jumped on Johnson for three runs in the bottom of the eighth inning, to win the game and the title by a 9–7 score. Later in his career, Marberry was used frequently as a starting pitcher, but he wasn't as successful in that capacity as he was when coming out of the bullpen, as he explained to F.C. Lane:

> I am a relief pitcher and have good luck. But when I go the distance I am not so lucky. Evidently I can fool the batters for a few innings, but they get wise to me before the end of a regulation game. It's the same old Abe Lincoln statement. "You can fool some of the batters all the time and all the batters some of the time." But I for one can't fool all the batters all the time.

Obviously, Firpo Marberry managed to fool many batters coming out of the bullpen. He was the first major league relief pitcher to register 50 career saves and the first to register 100 career saves.

Wilcy Moore was an outstanding relief pitcher for one year, 1927. He arrived in New York that year as a 30-year-old rookie after kicking around the minor leagues for six years. Moore's big break came after a broken arm forced him to pitch sidearm. The new delivery gave him a devastating sinker that brought him 17 consecutive victories in the South Atlantic League and earned him a promotion to the Big Show. Pitching in support of the Yankees' Murderer's Row of Ruth, Gehrig and company, Moore pitched in 50 games, starting 12 and relieving in 38 others. Overall, he went 19–7 on the mound while leading the league with 13 saves and a 2.28 ERA. Moore pitched in the majors five more years, but he was never able to duplicate his 1927 season, although he did lead the league in saves in 1931, registering ten saves as a member of the Boston Red Sox. His career win-loss record was 51–44, with 49 saves and a 3.70 ERA.

The Yankees were the first team to fully recognize the value of a full-time relief pitcher. Their dynasty, which is still alive and well after 78 years, has relied heavily on relief specialists, beginning with Wilcy Moore, and continuing down through the decades with the likes of Johnny Murphy, Joe Page, Ryne Duren, Sparky Lyle, Goose Gossage, and Mariano Rivera. No other major league team has yet been able to match the bullpen brigade produced by the Yankees down through the years.

Johnny Murphy was the first of the modern bullpen specialists, and one of the first relief pitchers to be designated as a "fireman." He was also known as Grandma to his teammates because of his fastidious manner. Murphy, a 6' 2", 190-pound right-handed pitcher out of New York City, signed with the New York Yankees following his graduation from Fordham University in 1929. After spending three years in the Yankees' minor league system, where he got knocked around as a starting pitcher, the slick curveball artist was converted to a relief pitcher in Newark in 1933. And, as they say, the rest is history. Grandma Murphy found his niche, making 20 consecutive relief appearances for the Bears without allowing a run. The 25-year-old New Yorker joined the big club as a relief pitcher in 1934, making 20 appearances out of the bullpen, but he was also forced to start 20 games because of injuries to the pitching staff. He completed 10 of his starts, recorded four saves, and compiled a 14–10 record with an excellent 3.12 ERA. From that point on, Johnny Murphy was primarily a relief specialist, starting only 20 more games over a period of 11 years. In 1935, using his curveball to perfection, he relieved in 32 games with five saves, while posting a 10–5 record. Over the next nine years he became the top relief pitcher in the major leagues, earning the title of fireman for his proficiency in extinguishing enemy fires. He led the American League in saves four times between 1938 and 1942. With Murphy protecting the team in the late innings, Joe McCarthy's Bronx Bombers of Gehrig, Dickey, and DiMaggio rolled to seven American League pennants in eight years between 1936 and 1943, missing the title only in 1940; and they converted six of those titles into world championships. Murphy's contribution consisted of two wins without a loss, and four saves, in six games. Over 16⅓ innings, he allowed just two earned runs for a brilliant 1.10 earned run average. When he retired in 1947, Johnny Murphy had proven the value of having a fireman in the bullpen, if a team was serious about winning a pennant. In 13 years, Grandma posted a 93–53 record, with a major league record of 107 saves and a fine 3.50 ERA. Seventy-two of his victories came in relief.

Mace Brown was a contemporary of Johnny Murphy, handling bullpen duties for the Pittsburgh Pirates for six years, the Brooklyn Dodgers for one year, and the Boston Red Sox for three years, between 1935 and 1946. A University of Iowa graduate, Brown entered the major leagues at the age of 26. He was used primarily as a relief pitcher during his career, but was also a spot starter, starting 55 games during his ten-year career. Brown's best pitch was an overhand curveball that had batters pounding the ball into the dirt for easy ground-ball outs. But he also had a decent fastball and a slider. The strong, 6' 1" 190-pound right-hander led his league in games pitched twice, with 51 games in 1938 and 49 games in 1943. He also led the league in saves twice, with seven saves in both 1937 and 1940. His career record was 76 wins against 57 losses, with 48 saves, with a 3.46 ERA.

Another Brown, named Clint, was the first relief pitcher to be called a fireman. Les Biederman, a Pittsburgh sportswriter, gave him that title in 1938, and Clint was the first reliever to have his photograph taken wearing a fireman's helmet, according to *The Cultural Encyclopedia of Baseball*. The 6' 1", 190-pound right-handed pitcher toiled in the major leagues for 15 years between 1928 and 1942, pitching in 434 games with 304 of them out of the bullpen. In 1937, he led the league in games pitched with 53 and saves with 18. Two years later, he led the league with 61 games pitched. His career numbers show an 89–93 win-loss record with 64 saves.

STARTING PITCHER RELIEF RECORD

	Games	W	L	Saves
Lefty Grove	160	33	22	55
Guy Bush	234	43	20	34
Eppa Rixey	140	20	17	14

Johnny Murphy, a relief pitcher for the New York Yankees from 1932 to 1947, was considered to be baseball's first fireman (AUTHOR'S COLLECTION).

	Games	W	L	Saves
Herb Pennock	196	24	17	32
Bob Shawkey	155	30	21	28
Johnny Morrison	132	28	12	23
George Uhle	147	24	19	25
Dizzy Trout	199	25	17	35
Virgil Trucks	189	31	18	30
Charlie Root	291	42	26	40
Carl Hubbell	103	20	8	33

Relief Pitchers Relief Record

	Games	W	L	Saves
Allan Russell	233	35	21	39
Firpo Marberry	364	53	37	101
Claude Jonnard	128	13	7	17
Rosy Ryan	175	26	17	19

Johnny Van Der Meer

Johnny Vander Meer pitched two consecutive no-hitters in 1938 (AUTHOR'S COLLECTION).

	Games	W	L	Saves
Wilcy Moore	229	39	26	49
Johnny Murphy	375	73	42	107
Clint Brown	314	41	35	64
Al Benton	283	33	28	66
Mace Brown	332	57	30	48

The above lists show that there were still more starting pitchers than full time relief pitchers being called on in the late innings of close games, but the gap was narrowing. In the previous era, Doc Crandall of the New York Giants was the only relief pitcher to gain the confidence of his manager and become a prominent member of his team. But in the 1920–46 era, there were a dozen or more top relief pitchers that made a name for themselves. Some of them, like Jonnard, Ryan, and Moore, had short careers, but when they were active they were dominant, and they made significant contributions to their team's world championship successes. And Firpo Marberry and Johnny Murphy were the first relief pitchers to be credited with 100 career saves.

The beginning of the lively-ball era should not be dismissed without recognizing two of the greatest pitching performances in baseball history. They belong to Charlie Robertson and Johnny Vander Meer. Robertson, a journeyman right-hander for the Chicago White Sox between 1919 and 1928, achieved immortality when he threw a perfect game at the Detroit Tigers in just his third major league start on April 30, 1922, winning 2–0. Outfielder Johnny Mostil preserved the gem with a diving catch at the foul line. That game, only the third perfect game thrown since the modern game began in 1893, was the pinnacle of Robertson's career. He pitched in the major leagues for another six years, but a sore arm limited his career record to a mediocre 49–80. It would be 34 years before anyone would pitch another perfect game in the major leagues. Johnny Vander Meer, a 22-year-old southpaw for the Cincinnati Reds, achieved something that will probably never be surpassed. He threw consecutive no-hitters at the Boston Braves and Brooklyn Dodgers in his first full season in the major leagues. On June 11, 1938, the 6', 190-pound flamethrower shut down the Braves' bats in a 3–0 victory. Four days later, in Ebbets Field, he no-hit Burleigh Grimes' Dodgers by a 6–0 count. He added another three no-hit innings to his string in his next start, giving him 21 consecutive no-hit innings.

6

The Golden Age of Baseball:
1947 to 1960

The period from the integration of major league baseball in 1947 through 1960, the last year before the beginning of the expansion era, has been called the Golden Age of baseball, and with good reason. The same 16 teams that began the century were still operating in 1960, although a few of them had relocated to other cities. Major league attendance had increased five-fold from 3.6 million fans in 1901 to 19.9 million fans in 1960. And the skill level of the leagues had increased significantly as well, thanks to two factors: the total population of the U.S. had doubled from 75 million people in 1901 to 150 million people in 1960, and Jackie Robinson's successful debut in organized baseball had provided opportunities to another 10 percent of the population. Over the 12-year period from 1947 to 1960, more than 100 black players entered the major leagues. At first the recruitment was slow, with Robinson, Larry Doby, Dan Bankhead, Roy Campanella, and Luke Easter among the early arrivals. They were followed by an increasing number of Negro league veterans, including Don Newcombe, "Toothpick Sam" Jones, Ernie Banks, Willie Mays, and Hank Aaron. Most of the new major leaguers were position players; this put additional pressure on the pitching fraternity, already besieged by the introduction of the lively ball and the Babe Ruth syndrome, which produced a new generation of baseball players who gripped the bat at the end and swung for the fences. In fact, three of the major leagues' top career home run hitters, Aaron, Mays, and Banks, began their careers in the Negro leagues.

In addition to the Negro league players who took advantage of the elimination of the color barrier, dozens of other black and Latino players made their way north from Mexico, Puerto Rico, the Dominican Republic, Cuba, and areas further south during the 1950s. These included Roberto Clemente, Orlando Cepeda, Felipe Alou, Luis Aparicio, Juan Marichal, Mike Fornieles, and Luis Arroyo. As good as the pitching talent from the black leagues was, however, it was still the booming bats of the big hitters that dominated the baseball landscape. A total of 15 black and Latino players who entered the major leagues between 1947 and 1960 are presently enshrined in the Baseball Hall of Fame in Cooperstown, New York. They are Robinson, Campanella, Doby, Banks, Aaron, Mays, Aparicio,

Cepeda, Clemente, Marichal, Frank Robinson, Billy Williams, Willie McCovey, Satchel Paige, and Monte Irvin. All but two of them were position players.

After the arrival of Ralph Kiner, another generation of heavy hitters, along with the arrival of the former Negro league sluggers, increased the average home run production from 82 home runs per team per 154 games, between 1920 and 1946, to 121 home runs per team, between 1947 and 1960. Kiner, who led the National League in home runs his first seven years in the league, created what has come to be called the Kiner Syndrome, which has contributed to the continual search for home runs by position players. The Pittsburgh slugger once remarked, "Home run hitters drive Cadillacs. Singles hitters drive Chevys," and that bit of advice caused another generation of young hitters to swing from the heels in hopes of one day cruising around town in a Cadillac. Mickey Mantle was one of Kiner's first disciples, and his career average of 36 home runs a year also produced 116 strikeouts. But the Mick was ahead of his time. Although Harmon Killebrew posted career marks of 39 homers and 115 strikeouts beginning in 1959, most of the free swingers began arriving in the late '60s and early '70s. They included Bobby Bonds, Reggie Jackson, Dave Kingman, and Rob Deer. Statistics, however, have shown this flailing to be a complete waste of time. Free swinging doesn't contribute to increased home runs; it only results in a lower batting average. Ted Williams is a perfect example of controlled slugging. His 19-year career produced a .344 batting average with 37 homers and 51 strikeouts for every 550 at-bats. Joe DiMaggio, a .325 career hitter, averaged 29 home runs against just 30 strikeouts for every 550 at-bats. And even the great Babe Ruth, who was called a free swinger in his day, put together a .342 career batting average, with 47 homers and 87 strikeouts. In today's game, Ruth would be considered a contact hitter.

Starting pitchers were still the first line of defense for besieged major league teams. And teams still used a four-man pitching rotation, with another four or five men in the bullpen. Complete games continued to decline during the Golden Age, falling from 42 percent in 1947 to just 27 percent in 1960. The reason for the steady decline is unknown, although it may have been the result of the influx of black sluggers combined with the increase in world-class relief pitchers like Joe Page, Hugh Casey, and Elroy Face. There were still many pitchers, however, who took pride in finishing what they started. Warren Spahn, for instance, completed an exceptional 60 percent of his 507 starts over the 14-year period. Whitey Ford completed 43 percent of his starts, Robin Roberts completed 59 percent, Bob Lemon completed 54 percent, and Early Wynn completed 45 percent. Great pitchers always responded to the challenge in the old days.

Warren Spahn was the ultimate warrior. The 6', 175-pound southpaw started his delivery swinging both arms back low to the ground, then swinging them forward and up to head-height, and finally delivering the ball with a high leg kick. His stylish overhand delivery was smooth, and he always finished it in perfect position to field the ball. He possessed a good fastball as a youngster, but after suffering knee problems, he became a pitcher who prided himself in out-thinking the opposing hitter rather than trying to overpower him. His total repertoire included a fastball, curve, changeup, sinker, and screwball, aided by pinpoint control. Spahn pitched four games for the Boston Braves in 1941 before being called into the army in World War II. After three years of military service, he returned to the Braves to begin his major league career in earnest. After an 8–5 record in 1946, Spahn went 21–10 the next year, the first of 13 20-win seasons the venerable southpaw would realize over the next 17 years. He pitched 200 or more innings 17 times, winning 14, 15, 17, and

Warren Spahn won 363 games for the Braves between 1942 and 1965 (AUTHOR'S COLLECTION).

18 games in those seasons in which he failed to win 20. His career 363–245 record included 63 shutouts and a 3.09 ERA. His 363 victories is the fifth highest total in major league history, the highest total for a southpaw, and the highest total for any pitcher whose career began after 1911. The ageless one pitched two no-hitters in his career, the first one when he was 39 years old, the second one a year later. Warren Spahn also relieved in 85 games in 21 years, recording 29 saves.

Whitey Ford, known as the Chairman of the Board in New York, was Casey Stengel's pitching ace from 1950 to 1967. The smooth throwing southpaw started 438 games over his 16-year career, compiling a win-loss record of 236–106 for an outstanding .690 winning percentage, the third highest winning percentage in major league history. He relied on a slider and a changeup to compile a 2.75 career ERA, the second-best ERA for pitchers in the lively-ball era, trailing only Hoyt Wilhelm. Ford also pitched in 11 World Series, with a 10–8 record in 22 games and a 2.71 ERA. And he was used occasionally in relief, with 60 relief appearances and ten saves, in 498 games pitched.

Robin Roberts, whose career covered the period from 1948 to1966, was one of the National League's workhorses, pitching more than 300 innings in a season six times, and leading the league five times. He was a one-pitch pitcher, relying on his fastball and excellent control to retire batters, although he did spot his curveball from time to time. His 19-year career included 676 games pitched, with 609 starts and 305 complete games, a 50 percent success rate. He won 286 games during his career, against 245 losses, with 45 shutouts and a 3.41 earned run average. And, like his contemporaries, he was available for relief in critical situations, trudging in from the bullpen 67 times, with an 11–5 record and 25 saves.

Bob Lemon was a Cleveland Indian mainstay for 13 years, from 1946 to 1958. He led the Indians to two American League pennants and one world championship. In 1948, he went 2–0 with a 1.65 ERA as Cleveland defeated the Boston Braves in six games. Six years later, he lost two games as his team was swept by the New York Giants. During the regular season, Lemon racked up a 207–128 win-loss record, with 188 complete games in 350 starts, a 54 percent completion percentage. The big, right-handed, curveball pitcher, who had seven 20-victory seasons, also worked out of the bullpen 110 times in his career, with 22 saves. And, on top of all his pitching achievements, he was a dangerous hitter who was used as a pinch hitter frequently. The 6', 185-pound, left-handed hitter had a .232 batting average, with 37 home runs in 1,183 at-bats. His average of 17 home runs for every 550 at-bats is the number-two all-time record for pitchers, behind Wes Ferrell.

Dizzy Trout pitched for the Detroit Tigers from 1939 to 1952, followed by one year with the Red Sox and two games with Baltimore. His career record showed 170 victories against 161 losses, with 158 complete games in 322 starts, and 28 shutouts. He went 1–1 in the 1945 World Series as the Tigers disposed of the Chicago Cubs in seven games. The tall, husky right-hander led the American League in victories in 1943 with 20. The next year he went 27–14, but that was the year Hal Newhouser won 29. However, Trout did lead the league that year in games started (40), complete games (33), shutouts (7), innings pitched (352) and ERA (2.12). In addition to his heavy starting schedule, the 6' 3", 195-pound right-hander also made 199 relief appearances, with 35 saves.

Dizzy Trout's compatriot, Virgil "Fire" Trucks, was just as valuable to his team, compiling a 177–135 record over 17 years, from 1941 to 1958. He pitched in 517 games, with 328 starts, 124 complete games, 33 shutouts, and a 3.39 ERA. He went 1–0 in the 1945 World Series to help the Tigers win the world championship. Trucks' best year was 1953, when he went 20–10 with five shutouts and a 2.93 ERA. The right-handed fireball pitcher was a true double-duty pitcher for Detroit, supplementing his 328 starts with 189 relief appearances. His record out of the bullpen showed 31 victories against 18 losses, with 30 saves.

In spite of the heavy relief pitching load assigned to starting pitchers, the years between 1947 and 1960 were ones of transition from a reliance on starting pitchers to provide late-inning relief in close games, to relief specialists, who were as talented as the starting pitchers, and whose job it was to be ready to step in to rescue a harried or tired starting pitcher on a moment's notice. The above six pitchers were the last of their kind. Over the last 40 years of the century, the starting pitcher who would step in and save a game for his teammate would become a dying breed, as the following table shows.

STARTING PITCHERS:
CAREER RELIEF APPEARANCES, WINS, AND SAVES

Pitcher	Years	Career Relief Games	Career Wins	Career Losses	Career Saves
Kid Nichols	1890–1906	59	15	9	17
Cy Young	1890–1911	91	28	18	17
Joe McGinnity	1899–1908	84	19	13	24
Three-Finger Brown	1903–1916	149	30	20	49
Ed Walsh	1904–1917	115	16	15	35
Walter Johnson	1907–1927	136	42	25	34
Grover Cleveland Alexander	1911–1930	96	23	17	32
Lefty Grove	1925–1941	159	35	22	55
Dizzy Trout	1939–1957	199	25	17	35
Virgil Trucks	1941–1958	189	31	18	30
Warren Spahn	1942–1965	85	5	18	29
Bob Lemon	1948–1958	110	12	10	22
Robin Roberts	1948–1966	67	11	5	25
Lew Burdette	1950–1967	253	36	19	31
Whitey Ford	1950–1967	60	9	7	10
Camilo Pascual	1954–1971	125	7	15	10
Sandy Koufax	1955–1966	83	6	2	9
Bob Gibson	1959–1975	46	6	4	6
Juan Marichal	1960–1975	14	5	2	2

Lou Burdette made 253 relief appearances, in addition to 373 starts, in 18 years, between 1950 and 1967. His relief appearances are the most ever recorded by a starting pitcher, as is his winning percentage of .655. Walter Johnson posted the most victories in relief with 42, and the most losses with 25. Lefty Grove had the most saves with 55. It is interesting to note that, of the pitchers listed above, two of them fared badly in relief assignments. Camilo "Hot Potato" Pascual, in 125 relief appearances, could do no better than a 7–15 win-loss record. And Warren Spahn, one of baseball's greatest southpaw pitchers, posted a mediocre 5–18 record in 85 relief assignments.

Relief pitchers began to gain stature in the major leagues during this era but, unlike today's relief specialists, divided into long relief, short relief, setup men, and closers, the bullpen brigade in the late 1940s and the 1950s had only one fireman who was asked to pitch as many as six or seven innings at a time. Firpo Marberry and Johnny Murphy were the leaders in the bullpen evolution in the 1920s and '30s, and they were followed by a bevy of top notch relief specialists in the '40s and '50s, beginning with Hugh Casey and followed by the likes of Joe Page, Ted Wilks, Jim Konstanty (in 1950), Joe Black (in 1952), Ellis

Kinder, Hoyt Wilhelm, Al Brazle, Clem Labine, Elroy Face, Ryne Duren, Lindy McDaniel, and Don McMahon.

Yogi Berra, in his book *When You Come to a Fork in the Road, Take It*, had this to say about the value of a strong bullpen: "Bullpens and the people in them are real important. They're lifesavers. They get you out of trouble and make it possible for you to win." He didn't, however, agree with the specialization that has taken place, with relief pitchers entering a game to pitch to just one man. "I said you're nothing without a bullpen thirty years ago. That was before starting pitchers considered five or six innings 'a quality start.' And before relief pitching became so specialized — one pitcher coming in to face one batter, another coming in to face another, the closer only pitching the ninth. Call me old-fashioned, but I don't agree with that philosophy. I say, keep a guy in there if he keeps getting outs. Why remove someone if he's doing the job?"

The number of saves per team, based on a 154-game schedule, from 1876 through 1965, is shown below. As can be seen in the table, saves began to increase rapidly between 1945 and 1955 as the relief chores were handed over to bullpen specialists. There was also a change in the philosophy of the managers during this period. Previously, a starting pitcher was used in relief only in close games. In games that were not in question, a mop-up man was used. And if a starting pitcher was still on the mound in the eighth or ninth inning, he was allowed to finish the game, win or lose. By the mid 1950s, however, fewer and fewer pitchers were permitted to finish a game. Most teams had firemen who were ready to step in and pitch the last two or three innings to finish the game and save it for the starting pitcher. This trend continued over the next 50 years, and the number of saves per team continued to increase right up to the year 2004.

Year	Number of Teams	Game Schedule	Total Saves	Saves/Team/ 154 Games	CG/Team/ 154 Games
1876	8	65	13	4	140
1885	8	112	7	1	148
1895	12	133	45	4	124
1905	16	154	56	4	123
1915	16	154	139	9	84
1925	16	154	175	11	76
1935	16	154	207	13	68
1945	16	154	218	14	74
1955	16	154	359	22	47
1965	20	162	678	32	37

As might be expected, there is a strong correlation between complete games by a starting pitcher and the number of saves. There was a sharp drop in the number of complete games after World War II, from 74 complete games per team per 154 games in 1945, to 47 complete games in 1955, with a corresponding increase in saves from 14 per team to 22. Although the table shows the number of saves per team, going back to 1876, saves were not actually counted until 1960, and they didn't become an official statistic until 1969. And there were no closers. The relief specialists were called firemen until the late 1980s.

Joe Page was one of the best of the early firemen, and he often pitched three or more innings in a game. The Yankees were without a full-fledged fireman between the loss of

Johnny Murphy to military service in 1944 and the emergence of Joe Page in 1947. New York's new fireman went 14–8 in 57 games that year, with a league-leading 17 saves. The hard throwing southpaw followed that up with two more sensational seasons. In 1948, he went 7–8, pitching in a league-leading 55 games, with 16 saves. And the following year, he compiled a 13–8 mark, while leading the league with 60 games pitched and 27 saves, a new major league record. No American League fireman would challenge that mark until Luis Arroyo saved 29 games in 1961. In the National League, Page's record was solid until Elroy Face saved 28 games for the Pittsburgh Pirates in 1962. Page, who had a devastating rising fastball, was also a godsend in the 1947 World Series, appearing in four games in seven days, and pitching a total of 13 innings, with a win and a save. In game one he pitched four innings. Three days later, he pitched three innings. And in game seven, he tossed five innings of one-hit ball to beat the Dodgers 5–2. Two years later, the New York fireman hurled the final 5⅔ innings in game three of the World Series, a 4–3 Yankee victory. In all, he pitched nine innings in three games, with a win and a save. As Yogi Berra noted, "Funny, bullpens weren't a real big thing when I broke in. Relievers used to be washed-out starters. They weren't seen as so vital. They didn't get credit for 'saves' the way they do now. They didn't get great respect. But we had Joe Page in the late 1940s, and he helped change that. Joe was probably the first relief pitcher who became a star rather than just a guy who couldn't start."

Hugh Casey, who pitched in the major leagues from 1935 through 1949, was Page's counterpart and World Series opponent. In 1941, Casey was involved in one of the most bizarre incidents in World Series history. In the ninth inning of the fourth game, with the Brooklyn Dodgers leading the New York Yankees by the score of 4–3, and on the verge of tying the series at two games apiece, Hugh Casey, in his fifth inning of relief, threw Tommy Henrich a two-strike, sharp-breaking curveball that Tommy swung at and missed, apparently ending the game. But the ball eluded catcher Mickey Owen and rolled to the backstop, allowing Henrich to reach first base. And before Casey could regain his composure, the opportunistic Bronx Bombers had punched out three base hits sandwiched around two bases on balls to score four runs and snatch the game away from the beleaguered Brooks. Joe McCarthy's cohorts wrapped up the world championship the next day with a 3–1 victory. The following year, the Georgia native pitched in 50 games for Brooklyn, 48 in relief, with six victories against three losses and a league-leading 13 saves. After spending three years in the United States Navy during World War II, he returned to spark the Dodgers to two National League pennants in 1947 and 1949. Casey matched swords with Joe Page of the Yankees in the 1947 series, and came away the winner, although his team lost the series in seven games. Page pitched 13 innings in four games with one win, one loss, and one save, while Casey pitched 10⅓ innings in six games, with two wins, no losses, and one save. Page and Casey were both photographed climbing over the bullpen fence wearing a fireman's helmet at various times during their careers.

Jim Konstanty, who toiled in the National League for 11 years, from 1944 to 1956, spent most of his career with the Philadelphia Phillies. He was a finesse pitcher with outstanding control. He threw a palm ball, a screwball, a slider, a curve, and a fastball. But his fastball was only for the batter to look at, not hit. The palm ball was his out-pitch. Over his career, Konstanty won 66 games against 48 defeats, with 74 saves and a 3.46 ERA. He is best remembered as one of the key members of the famed pennant-winning 1950 Whiz Kids. The 6' 2", 200-pound right-hander had a career year that year, coming out of the bullpen

Joe Page, the Yankee fireman in the late 1940s, was the first bullpen celebrity (AUTHOR'S COLLECTION).

a league-leading 74 times, recording a 16–7 win-loss record, and saving a league leading 22 games, with a 2.66 ERA. His superb season was rewarded with the National League's Most Valuable Player award, and he was the first relief pitcher to be so honored.

Hoyt Wilhelm was one of the most amazing pitchers ever to play the game. His career, which spanned the years from 1952 to 1972, encompassed 1,070 games, including 52 starts and 1,018 relief appearances. His career totals showed 143 victories against 122 losses, with

Hoyt Wilhelm pitched in 1,070 games, 1,018 in relief, during his memorable 21-year career. He retired at the age of 49 (AUTHOR'S COLLECTION).

227 saves. The lanky knuckleball artist joined the New York Giants in 1952 as a 30-year-old rookie, and stayed around for 21 years, finally hanging up his glove at the age of 49. He was able to pitch that long because he threw the ball with almost no effort, like one of the primitive "feeders" of the 1850s. But in Wilhelm's case, no one, not even Wilhelm, knew where the ball would end up. Sometimes it sailed up near the shoulders before falling off the table. Other times, it would dart to the right or to the left. He has been called the greatest knuckleball pitcher in major league history, and his record certainly validates that claim.

The six-foot-tall right-hander led the National League in games pitched, his first two years in the league. In 1952 he went 15–3 with 11 saves in 71 games, all in relief, and he led the league with a .833 winning percentage and a 2.43 earned run average, in addition to leading in games pitched. Two years later, he helped the Giants capture the National League pennant, going 12–4 in 57 games, with seven saves and a miniscule 2.10 ERA. He added a save in the Giants' World Series sweep of the Cleveland Indians. Unlike today's closers, he pitched an average of two innings per relief appearance, and could go four or five, or more, innings if required. Hoyt Wilhelm's 2.52 career ERA is the lowest ERA for any pitcher in the modern lively-ball era, covering the last 85 years, and his 1,070 games pitched are number three on the all-time list.

Lindy McDaniel pitched in the major leagues for 21 years, from 1955 to 1975. His repertoire included a forkball, a curve, and a sinking fastball, which he threw both sidearm and overhand. The Oklahoma native pitched out of the bullpen his first two years with the St. Louis Cardinals, and then joined the starting rotation for two years. After an excellent 15–9 record with ten complete games in 26 starts in 1957, he slumped to 5–7 with two complete games in 17 starts the next year, and was on his way back to the bullpen. There he found a home. He quickly became the top fireman in the National League, leading the National League in saves three times. In 1959, his first year out of the bullpen, he went 14–12 on the mound, with 15 saves in 62 games pitched. The following year, he pitched in 65 games with an outstanding 12–4 record and 26 saves, the most saves ever recorded in the National League up to that time. He started only 22 games during his last 17 years in the major leagues, while coming out of the bullpen on 866 occasions. When he retired, he left behind a 141–119 win-loss record with 172 saves. His 987 games pitched are ninth on the all-time list.

Ted Wilks was another flamethrower who began his career as a starting pitcher but took his heat to the bullpen after a couple of years. Wilks had a spectacular major league debut with the St. Louis Cardinals, going 17–4 as a rookie in 1944 and leading the league with an .810 winning percentage. He completed 16 of his 21 starts, with a 2.64 ERA. His sophomore year, however, was forgettable, a 4–7 record with four complete games in 19 starts. That essentially ended Wilks' career as a starting pitcher. Over the next eight years, he pitched in 331 games, all but eight of them out of the bullpen. His sinking fastball was particularly effective for a few innings, and Wilks threw it from a variety of angles, overhand, sidearm, and occasionally with a submarine delivery. The 178-pound right-hander led the league in saves twice. He also led the league in games pitched twice, with 59 in 1949 and with 65 two years later. When his ten-year career ended in 1953, he had compiled a record of 59–30 with 46 saves.

Ellis "Old Folks" Kinder, a native of Atkins, Arkansas, joined the St. Louis Browns in 1946 as a 31-year-old rookie. The 6', 195-pound right-hander was a starting pitcher until 1951, at which time he joined the bullpen brigade. His best pitch was his slider, but he also had a good curveball, a change of pace, and a fastball. Kinder was traded to the Boston Red Sox prior to the 1948 season and enjoyed his greatest successes there over the next eight years. He had his finest year in 1949, going 23–6 with 19 complete games in 30 starts. He led the league in winning percentage at .793 and in shutouts with six. The year ended on a sad note for Kinder, whose Red Sox visited Yankee Stadium for the final two games of the season, needing only one victory to clinch the pennant. They didn't get it. After the Sox lost the opener of the series, Kinder took the mound in the season finale, after telling his teammates that he would guarantee them a victory if they could score just three runs. The courageous pitcher departed after seven innings, on the short end of a 1–0 score, and the Bronx Bombers pummeled the Sox bullpen for four big runs, to win the game and the pennant by a 5–3 score. After one more year as a starter, Old Folks, now pushing 36, volunteered for bullpen duty, where he developed into one of the league's top fireman. When he retired in 1957, he left behind a 102–71 win-loss record and 102 saves. He had started 122 games during his career and relieved in another 362 games.

Elroy Face, like many of his peers, entered the major leagues as a two-way pitcher. The diminutive, 5' 8", 155-pound right-hander was a spot starter and a relief pitcher for the Pittsburgh Pirates in 1953 and 1955, with 23 starts and 60 relief appearances. By the time the 1956 season got underway, however, Face was essentially a relief specialist. He pitched in a league-leading 68 games that year, with just three starts, going 12–13 with a 3.52 earned run average, and six saves. At one point during the season, he pitched in nine consecutive games, setting a major league record that was subsequently broken by Mike Marshall. The tough little fireman had developed a forkball during his minor league assignment in 1954, and he used it to befuddle National League batters over the next 14 years. He also had a fastball, a curve and a slider, but it was the forkball that saved his career. As the National League's top relief pitcher over the next decade, Face pitched in 50 or more games a season, for nine consecutive years and 11 out of 12. In only one of his 16 major league seasons did he pitch in less than 41 games. His 28 saves in 1962 made a new National League mark. The Stephentown, New York, native had a career year in 1959 when he went 18–1, with a major league record .947 winning percentage and a 2.70 ERA. His 18 wins are the most wins ever recorded in relief. The following year, he was 10–8 during the season and saved three games in the Pirates' dramatic seven-game World Series triumph over the New York Yankees. When he retired in 1969 at the age of 41, he had amassed 104 victories, 96 of them in relief, against 95 losses, with 193 saves. He pitched in 848 games, all but 27 of them out of the bullpen.

Al Brazle was the prototypical relief pitcher of the early days, the starting pitcher who was demoted to the bullpen when he could no longer handle a starting role effectively. The 29-year-old Brazle joined the St. Louis Cardinals in 1943 and had an excellent rookie season, going 8–2 with a 1.53 ERA. After spending three years in military service, the lanky southpaw averaged between 10 and 14 victories a season, from 1946 to '49, with ERAs from 2.84 to 3.80. Beginning in 1950, with his effectiveness declining, the aging hurler concentrated on relief pitching, and he did a fine job for three years, leading the National League in saves in both 1952 and 1953, with 16 and 18 saves respectively. He put his glove away for the last time after the 1954 season, at the age of 41.

Clem Labine may have been one of the most underrated firemen of the post–World War II era. The crew-cut right-hander from Lincoln, Rhode Island, enjoyed a notable 13-year major league career with the Dodgers, both in Brooklyn and Los Angeles. In his rookie season of 1951, the sinkerball specialist put together a 5–1 record with a 2.20 earned run average and, in the famous 1951 playoff against the New York Giants, after Leo Durocher's boys had taken the first game in the best-two-out-of-three series by the score of 3–1, Labine was handed the ball and asked to stem the tide. And stem it he did, blanking the hard-hitting New Yorkers 10–0. But it was not enough to stop the Giants from snatching the pennant away from the stunned Dodgers on Bobby Thomson's dramatic home run in the bottom of the ninth inning of game three. In 1955, during the Dodgers' world championship victory over the New York Yankees, Labine appeared in four games, with one save and a 2.89 ERA. The following year, he was once again asked to keep his team from elimination in game six of the series with the Yankees holding a 3–2 lead in games. And once again the Rhode Island native rose to the occasion, and shut down the vaunted Yankee attack for ten innings, retiring the last eight men he faced, as the Dodgers eked out a 1–0 victory. When Labine retired after the 1962 season, he had pitched in 513 games including 38 starts, and had compiled a 77–56 record with 96 saves.

Ryne Duren was another of the New York Yankees' outstanding relief aces. The bespectacled, flame-throwing right-handed pitcher came to the Yankees from the Kansas City Royals in 1958 and gave the Bronx Bombers an excellent relief effort that year and the following year. He intimidated opponents when he entered a game, squinting through thick glasses and then firing his 95-mile-per-hour fastball over the catcher's head and all the way to the screen. It was an effective performance. Very few batters dug in against the 6' 1", 195-pound fireman. It was reported that, one time in the minors, the wild-throwing Duren hit the on-deck batter. In 1958, the New York relief ace went 6–4 with a league-leading 20 saves in 44 games, with a 2.02 ERA; and, in the World Series against the Milwaukee Braves, he pitched in three games with one win, one loss, and one save, as the Yankees won the series, four games to three. The next year, the native of Cazenovia, Wisconsin, had only a 3–6 record, but he saved 14 games in 41 appearances, and compiled an excellent 1.88 ERA. Unfortunately for Duren, his career hit the skids in 1960 because of a drinking problem, and he faded from the major league scene in 1965. His ten-year career showed a 27–44 record, 57 saves, and a 3.83 ERA.

The aforementioned relief pitchers were just a few of the many bullpen specialists who emerged after 1946. Other notable firemen included Harry Gumbert, Stu Miller, Don McMahon, Jim Hughes, Jack Meyer, Ed Kleiman, Russ Christopher, Mickey Harris, Harry Dorish, Johnny Sain, Ray Narleski, George Zuverink, Bob Grim, Turk Lown, and Mike Fornieles. All these men led their league in saves at least once. Don Elston of the Chicago Cubs led the league twice in games pitched. Marv Grissom, who pitched in more than 50 games in a season four times, went 10–7 with 19 saves in the New York Giants' world championship year of 1954, and he also won one of the Giants' four victories in the World Series.

Lefty Grove in 1930 was the last starting pitcher to lead the American League in saves. Ken Raffensberger of the Cincinnati Reds was the last National League starting pitcher to lead the league in saves when he recorded six saves in 1946. From that point on, the bullpen became the domain of the relief specialist, although a few starters, like Warren Spahn, continued to be a factor in late-game emergencies.

When World War II ended and the boys came marching home, exchanging their khaki or blue uniforms for baseball white, major league teams—noting the success the New York Yankees had enjoyed by employing bullpen specialists over the previous 26 years (14 American League pennants and 11 World Championships)—began to scour the bushes for relief pitchers, and even converted some of their starting pitchers to firemen, in an effort to become competitive. In 1947, in addition to the Yankees' Joe Page and the Dodgers' Hugh Casey, Ken Trinkle of the Giants led the National League with 62 games pitched while saving ten. Hank Behrman pitched in 50 games for Brooklyn and Pittsburgh, and Ed Kleiman pitched in 58 games for the Cleveland Indians. In 1948, the Indians rescued the ancient Satchel Paige from the Negro leagues in their successful pursuit of the American League pennant, and he went 6–1 down the stretch, relieving in 14 games with one save. In the senior circuit, 38-year-old Harry Gumbert, after 12 years as a starting pitcher, led the league in relief appearances with 61, posting a 10–8 record and a league-leading 17 saves. Ted Wilks pitched in 57 games and Kirby Higbe pitched in 56. The next year Wilks led the league in games pitched with 59, in relief wins with ten, and in saves with nine. Jim Konstanty pitched in 53 games for the Philadelphia Phillies.

In 1950 the strike zone was redefined as the area from the batter's armpits to the top of his knees. Previously it had been defined as the area between the batter's shoulders and his knees. The new strike zone shrunk the pitcher's target significantly, adding to his woes. That didn't stop Jim Konstanty from achieving his career season, however. And in the World Series that year, he made a surprise start in the opening game, scattering four hits over eight innings, in a brilliant but losing effort, as Vic Raschi of the Yankees tossed a two-hitter, to win 1–0. Konstanty came back to relieve in two other games, throwing a total of 15 innings in four days, but he couldn't prevent a New York sweep. Two years later, a former Negro league pitcher dazzled the baseball world. Joe Black of the Brooklyn Dodgers trudged in from the bullpen 54 times, winning 15 games against just four losses, with 15 saves and a 2.15 ERA. Then, like Konstanty, he started game one of the World Series against the New York Yankees. But he was more fortunate than the Philadelphia fireman as he bested Allie Reynolds 4–2. He also started game four and game seven, but lost both games as New York prevailed, four games to three.

The mentality of major league managers was still focused on starting pitching in the early 1950s. Even though Joe Page and Hugh Casey demonstrated the value of a fireman to a pennant contending team, and Jim Konstanty and Joe Black confirmed that fact during regular season play, managers Eddie Sawyer of the Phillies and Chuck Dressen of the Dodgers retreated to the 1930s strategy during the World Series, putting relief pitching on the back burner and using their firemen in starting roles. That strategy proved fatal, as Casey Stengel's New York Yankees swept the overmatched Phils and the Yankee bullpen brought the New York team back from the brink of disaster against Brooklyn, to take the last two games of the seven-game series. Major league teams began to rely more and more on their bullpens in the World Series after that. Hoyt Wilhelm pitched in two games in the 1954 series, with one save in the Giants' sweep, and Clem Labine went 1 and 0 with one save in four games in Brooklyn's historic victory over the Yankees the following year. In 1956, George Zuverink, pitching for the sixth place Baltimore Orioles, went 7 and 6, while leading the league in both games pitched (62) and saves (16). His National League counterpart, Elroy Face, with the seventh-place Pittsburgh Pirates, recorded a 12–13 record in 68 games, with six saves, an outstanding effort pitching for a team that won only 66 games. The 1956 World Series witnessed the greatest pitching exhibition ever seen in the 101 years of series competition. In game five between the New York Yankees and the Brooklyn Dodgers, Yankee pitcher Don Larsen achieved the impossible. Pitching without a windup, the big right-hander, who had compiled an 11–5 record during the regular season, set down 27 Dodgers in a row, the first and only perfect game in World Series history.

Three years before Larsen's gem, major league owners initiated a new personnel policy that would have significant ramifications on ballplayer injuries over later decades. The owners replaced the existing inactive list with a disabled list, which was intended to protect an injured player from further injury. Before a player could be placed on the disabled list, his injury or illness had to be certified "unable to play" by a doctor. Once a player was placed on the disabled list, he could not play in a game for at least 15 days. If a player was placed on the 60-day disabled list, the team could replace him on the roster with another player, but the injured player could not play for at least 60 days.

The year of 1959 belonged to two pitchers, Harvey Haddix and Larry Sherry. Haddix, a diminutive, right-handed pitcher who would complete a 14-year major league career with a record of 136–113 in 1965, carved out his niche in the record books on the evening of May 26, pitching for the Pittsburgh Pirates against the Milwaukee Braves in Milwaukee. The Kitten, as he was called, relying on his fastball and slider, retired the hard-hitting Braves in order for 12 consecutive innings, but his team couldn't dent the plate against Lew Burdette, so the game moved into the thirteenth inning still scoreless. Felix Mantilla, leading off the inning, broke the string when he reached first base on an

Harvey Haddix, known as the Kitten, pitched 12 perfect innings against the Milwaukee Braves in 1959 before losing the game 1–0 in the thirteenth (AUTHOR'S COLLECTION).

error. Then, following an intentional walk to Hank Aaron, Haddix was clipped for a home run by Joe Adcock, ending his no-hitter at 12⅔ innings. The final score was only 1–0 because Adcock was called out for passing Aaron on the basepaths.

Larry Sherry's adventure was much more satisfying. After finishing seventh the previous year, Walter Alston's Los Angeles Dodgers came together in '59, led by two of the aging Boys of Summer, Gil Hodges and Duke Snider, who combined for 48 homers and 162 RBIs between them. Don Drysdale (17–13) and Johnny Podres (14–9) led the pitching staff, but it was Sherry, who was called up to the Dodgers in midseason, who put the team over the top, posting a 7–2 record with three saves in 23 games. And in the postseason, he was sensational. In the first game of a three-game playoff against the Milwaukee Braves to determine the National League pennant winner, the hard-throwing right-hander came on in relief in the second inning of game one and proceeded to blank the Braves over the last 7⅔ innings, as the Dodgers went on to win by a count of 3–2. Los Angeles met the Go-Go Chicago White Sox in the World Series, an event that turned out to be the Larry Sherry Show. The 6' 2", 205-pound pitcher, mixing his fastball and his slider for maximum effect, pitched in all four Dodgers victories, winning two and saving two others. Fittingly, he was on the mound during the final 5⅔ innings of game six, as L.A. brought the city its first world championship. The next year, it was Elroy Face's turn. Pitching in a league-leading 68 games out of the bullpen, the little right-hander won ten games against eight losses, and saved another 24 games. In the Fall Classic against the mighty Yankees of Maris and Mantle, the forkball artist appeared in four games, saving three of them to pace a seven-game Bucs victory and bring the coveted world championship trophy home to Pittsburgh.

In the ensuing years, the role of the bullpen brigade would become more and more important. From a single fireman in the 1930s, '40s, and '50s, the relief corps would evolve into a small band of experts, each one dominant in his role. There would be a long reliever, a short reliever, a setup man, a closer, and right- and left-handed situational specialists who would be called on to get just one critical out.

The Golden Age of Baseball ended in exciting style on October 13, 1960, with the Pittsburgh Pirates' dramatic World Series victory over the New York Yankees, fashioned by Bill Mazeroski's ninth-inning home run in game seven that broke a 9-all tie. Curiously, Casey Stengel's Bronx Bombers outscored their Steel City foes by a count of 55–27 in the series, by winning their three games by scores of 16–3, 10–0, and 12–0, while the Bucs captured the close contests by scores of 6–4, 3–2, 5–2, and 10–9.

7

The Modern Era: 1961 to 2004

The period from 1961 to the present has been one of constant change and chaos in major league baseball. It has been a period of expansion, free agency, player-management confrontations, free swingers, juiced-up baseballs, and smaller ballparks; and it has seen a steroid scandal, a disappearing strike zone, the invention of the designated hitter, the disappearance of complete games by starting pitchers, the introduction of pitch-count limits for starting pitchers, and the emergence of the closer with a corresponding increase in saves.

The era began with unbridled optimism based on the success of integration in the previous era, the continued growth of the minor leagues, and healthy attendance figures that approached 20 million per year. Major league owners responded to that success by initiating a period of uncontrolled expansion that has resulted in a dilution in the talent in the major leagues over the past 44 years. The 60 percent population increase has not been able to keep up with the demand for players to fill the rosters of 30 teams, 88 percent more teams than the 16 teams that made up major league in 1960. The expansion began in 1961 with the addition of the Los Angeles Angels, and a new team in Washington replacing the original Senators team, which relocated to Minnesota. The National League followed suit the next year with the birth of the New York Mets and the Houston Colt 45s. Over the next 37 years, ten more teams were added to the major league mix, six teams in the National League and four teams in the American League. Not only did the number of teams increase, the number of pitchers required on each team increased, from four starting pitchers to five, and from four relief pitchers to six, a total increase of three pitchers per team. Whereas the total number of pitchers required for all major league teams before expansion was 128, the number rose to 330 pitchers by 2004, an increase of a whopping 158 percent.

The decrease in the number of major league baseball prospects also resulted from a continuously shrinking minor league baseball system. Over the past 50 years, the minor leagues have declined from about 58 leagues to approximately 18 leagues. Fifty years ago, the Brooklyn Dodgers had in the neighborhood of 700 minor and major league players at their spring training facility in Vero Beach, Florida. Today the average team has fewer than 150 players under contract. Many high school and college players who would have entered the major league farm system in the past are now opting for professional basketball and professional football, where they can go directly from school to the NBA and NFL without having to struggle through a minor league system to prove themselves. And other major league prospects who are leaving college with professional degrees are choosing careers in industry that command decent salaries and provide the security for themselves and their families that organized baseball cannot offer.

Free agency, which was not anticipated when the era began, has played havoc with major league baseball over the past three decades. In 1975, pitchers Andy Messersmith of the Los Angeles Dodgers and Dave McNally of the Montreal Expos refused to sign contracts for the 1975 season. After playing the season without a contract, the two pitchers filed arbitration grievances against major league baseball's reserve clause that tied a player to a particular team for his entire career, unless he was traded. The arbitration panel ruled in favor of the players, essentially ending the owner's monopoly that had governed baseball for 100 years. A subsequent labor agreement gave the players the right to go to arbitration after two years, request a trade after five years, and become a free agent after six years. Free agency resulted in skyrocketing player salaries and long-term contracts, which removed much of the players' incentive from the game. Many players today coast through the middle years of their contract, only bearing down in the year their contract expires. The loyalty that existed between a team and its players disappeared, and players moved from team to team frequently, some annually. And labor relations between the players' union and management became hostile, producing some confrontations that still haunt the game today.

In 1981, a two-year disagreement over compensation to a team for losing a free agent to another team came to a head. The collective bargaining agreement had expired on December 31, 1979, and, after months of haggling over the free agency issue, the players went on strike on June 12, 1981. The strike lasted 50 days, which resulted in a split playing schedule, with the winners of the first half being matched against the winners of the second half to determine each division champion. There was a two-day strike in 1985 over a salary cap and arbitration, a spring training lockout by the owners over contract issues in 1990, a threatened strike in 1993, and finally a bitter strike that began on August 11, 1994, that forced the cancellation of the rest of the season as well as all postseason series including the World Series. The strike continued into the spring, and the owners began spring training with replacement players, but an arbitration ruling that reinstated the previous collective bargaining agreement (pending further negotiations) ended the strike and saved the season. But the atmosphere remains charged as of 2006, and future strikes that may jeopardize the future of major league baseball are likely.

The integrity of the game has been further damaged by the admissions of some players, such as Jose Canseco, Ken Caminiti, Jason Giambi, and Barry Bonds, that they used steroids during their careers. Canseco averaged 36 home runs for every 550 at-bats during his 17-year career. Caminiti said he was using steroids during his MVP season, when he batted .325 with 40 homers and 130 RBIs, while pacing the San Diego Padres to the National League Western Division title. Giambi hit 163 homers with 486 RBIs and a .310 batting average between 2000 and 2003. Bonds admitted taking steroids in 2003 and, although he has yet to admit taking them during his record-breaking season of 2001 when he broke the single-season home run record by hammering 73 home runs, his former mistress has testified that he began taking steroids as early as 1999. The steroid problem came to a head in 2004 when the U.S. Congress threatened to take action against steroid use in the major leagues unless the league owners and the players' union did something about it. The owners and the players' union, under duress, finally agreed to increase the testing program, both in season and out, with stronger penalties for violating the substance abuse policy. At the present time, the use of illegal drugs is probably the most serous threat to the continued success of major league baseball. Fans are fickle, and they demand dedication and integrity from their heroes. If the major league owners and the players' union are not successful in eradicating the use of illegal substances from the game, attendance will plummet, team profits will disappear, and the game may suffer financial losses from which it may never recover.

The above problems affect major league baseball in general, although since all the admitted steroid users to date are position players, that problem does have a direct effect on pitchers. Several other changes over the past 45 years also have a direct effect on pitchers. One of the first changes in the game that affected the pitcher was the introduction of the designated hitter in the American League. On January 11, 1973, American League owners voted 8–4 to institute the rule using a designated hitter to bat for the pitcher, to put more offense in the game. The National League has never used the DH because the use of a designated hitter removes much of the strategy from the game. An American League manager doesn't have to worry about pinch-hitting for a pitcher in a close game. He can now leave a pitcher in the game as long as the pitcher is doing an effective job. The designated hitter also prevents pitchers from making an offensive contribution to the outcome of the game with a timely base hit or sacrifice bunt. Some of baseball's most outstanding pitchers were dangerous hitters as well, and took pride in their skills with a bat. Probably the most famous hitting pitcher of all time was Babe Ruth, who batted .300 and led the American League in home runs in 1918, while going 13–7 on the mound. Other good hitting pitchers were Wes Ferrell, Bob Lemon, and Don Newcombe. Ferrell hit .280 over an 18-year career, and holds the record for the highest home run rate for pitchers, with 18 homers for every 550 at-bats. He also holds the record for the most home runs hit in a season, excluding Ruth; he batted .319 with nine home runs in 116 at-bats for the Cleveland Indians in 1931. Bob Lemon, another Cleveland Indian hurler, averaged 17 home runs for every 550 at-bats during his 15-year major league career. Between 1948 and 1950, Lemon smashed 18 home runs in 363 at-bats, with 66 RBIs. Don Newcombe had one of the most devastating offensive seasons for a pitcher, when he slugged the ball at a .359 clip, with seven homers in 117 at-bats, in 1955. He also did his bit on the mound that year, compiling a 20–5 record. Jack Bentley, who pitched for the New York Giants between 1913 and 1927, was a career .291 hitter. Don Drysdale of the Los Angeles Dodgers, who twice hit seven home runs in a season, averaged 14 homers for every 550 at-bats. George Uhle had a career batting average of .289 with seasons of .361 and.343. Win Murcer batted .285 over nine years, Red Lucas hit .281, Red Ruffing hit .269, Schoolboy Rowe hit .263, and Ken Brett hit .262.

Pitching in the modern era has suffered in total, but there was a period from 1963 to 1969 when it was revitalized. The strike zone had been redefined in 1950 as the area over the plate, between the batter's armpits and the top of his knees. That rule was changed again in 1963, this time returning it to the strike zone that existed between 1887 and 1950, identifying the top limit as the top of the batter's shoulders. Some of baseball's greatest pitchers took advantage of the expanded zone. Sandy Koufax, in particular, dominated the baseball scene during the 1960s, leading the league in victories three times, winning percentage twice, complete games twice, shutouts twice, innings pitched twice, strikeouts three times, and earned run average four times. Some baseball historians have minimized Koufax's achievements by categorizing them as the result of an expanded strike zone, but the fact is that the strike zone that existed when Koufax was terrorizing batters was the same strike zone that had existed for 69 of the previous 82 years. Also, during Koufax's period of dominance, when he fanned more than 300 men in a season three times, only one other major league pitcher topped the 300 mark. Sam McDowell registered 325 strikeouts in 1965, but no other pitcher had more than 275 strikeouts during that period. That six-year period from 1961 through 1966 compares favorably with the six-year period from 1998 through 2003, when seven pitchers exceeded 300 strikeouts in a season. And, except for Koufax's three years with ERAs less than 2.00, only three American League pitchers and no National League pitchers were able to produce sub-2.00 years. Bob Gibson, who would shock the world with a 1.12 ERA in 1969, could do no better than a combined 2.98 ERA between 1963 and 1966. In 1969, as a result of the pitching dominance of the 1960s, capped off by Gibson's career year, the strike zone was returned to the 1950 definition: the area between the batter's armpits and the top of his knees. At the same time, the pitcher's mound was reduced from a maximum of 15" to 10", further punishing the pitchers. Sometime in the 1970s, according to Curran, the upper limit of the strike zone mysteriously shrank from the armpits to somewhere between the armpits and the waist, causing former American League umpire Ed Runge to state, "Today's strike zone is the smallest it has ever been." Another change was made to the strike zone in 1995, to further punish the pitchers. The new rule placed the strike zone in that area over home plate, the upper limit of which is a horizontal line halfway between the top of the shoulders and the top of the uniform pants, and the lower limit of which is a line at the hollow beneath the kneecap.

The strike zone obviously was an important factor in the pitching success of the 1960s, but the evolution of the free swinger was also a factor. Strikeout records fell like rain over the last half of the twentieth century, helped by the new free-swinging mentality of the modern hitter. Home runs were paramount in the minds of most hitters. Strikeouts no longer had a stigma associated to them. This mentality also led to higher pitch counts, as batters swung and missed at more pitches than their predecessors. As noted earlier, Mickey Mantle and Harmon Killebrew were among the pioneers of the free-swinging group. But they were pikers in the strikeout race. Bobby Bonds averaged 137 strikeouts for every 550 at-bats, Reggie Jackson struck out 145 times a year, and Dave Kingman, who never saw a pitch he didn't like, dragged his bat back to the dugout no less than 150 times a season. But Rob Deer is the king of whiffs, striking out an average of 200 times for every 550 at-bats. And the beat goes on. In 2004, Mark Bellhorn of the Boston Red Sox set a new Red Sox team record by fanning 177 times in 523 at-bats. Adam Dunn of Cincinnati set a new major league single season record by striking out 195 times in 568 at-bats. Two other players struck out more than 160 times in 2004, and numerous players went down on strikes more than 120 times. It is an age of all or nothing at all.

In spite of the continually shrinking strike zone, pitchers recorded ever increasing strikeout totals as batters closed their eyes and swung for the fences, hoping to make contact with the ball. Roger Clemens, for instance, struck out 20 batters in a game twice in his career. On April 29, 1986, the Rocket established a new major league record by fanning 20

Seattle Mariners in a 3–1 victory. Ten years later, on September 16, 1996, he duplicated that feat. Kerry Wood of the Chicago Cubs on May 6, 1998, and Randy Johnson of the Arizona Diamondbacks on May 8, 2001, also struck out 20 men in a nine-inning game. The record for most strikeouts in an extra-inning game belongs to Tom Cheney of the Washington Senators, who struck out 21 Baltimore Orioles in a 16-inning game on September 12, 1962. Cheney's career was forgettable except for that game. He suffered a severe elbow injury the following year, and was out of the majors by 1966, leaving with a career record of 19–29.

The concern over juiced-up baseballs continued into the new millennium, with strong arguments pointing to increased rabbit in the ball. In 1975 the major leagues approved the use of white cowhide in place of horsehide, for baseball covers. The following year, the A.G. Spalding Co. was dropped by the major leagues as the manufacturer of their baseballs because of price considerations. The Rawlings Sporting Goods Company became the official supplier of major league baseballs. In 1980, Rawlings Sporting Goods Company began manufacturing baseballs in Haiti using American materials, machinery, supervision, and quality control. The balls contained 108 stitches, sewn by hand. The quality control specifications included a measurement of the resiliency of the ball. The quality control test measured the coefficient of restitution of the ball with an initial velocity of 85 feet per second. The rebound velocity specification was 54.6 percent of the initial velocity, which is the velocity required to propel the ball a distance of 400 feet. In 1994, baseballs began being manufactured in Costa Rica, and since that change was made, baseballs have been leaving major league parks in record numbers. The period from 1941 to 1960 averaged 109 homers per team per 154 games, while the period from 1961 to 1993 averaged 123 homers per team. But the record from 1994 to 2004 is even worse. Since baseballs began being manufactured in Costa Rica, there have been 166 home runs hit per team over a 154-game schedule. That's an increase of 52 percent since 1941–1960, and 35 percent over the period from 1961 to 1993.

On top of everything else, major league stadiums are getting smaller and smaller. The average ballpark today is approximately 20 percent smaller than the parks Babe Ruth took aim in. This problem will be discussed in detail in chapter 9. Suffice it to say, the size of the modern baseball stadium, combined with the new generation rabbit-ball, makes the feat of hitting a home run commonplace, even for lightweight hitters who previously went to bat hundreds of times without hitting a home run. Singles hitters are now able to hit balls out of the park to the opposite field without even taking a full swing. For the game's top sluggers, hitting a ball out of today's ballparks is nothing more than a chip shot.

A complete game by a pitcher is a rare occurrence in the modern major league baseball game. Pitchers completed 59 percent of their starts in 1919. That number had dropped to 46 percent by 1945, but the emergence of firemen cut that percentage to 23 percent by 1965. And, with the era of the closer, beginning in the middle to late 1980s, the percentage continued its downward spiral, finally reaching a low of just 5 percent in 2004. This trend, which does not reflect on the skills of the pitcher but rather on the modern-day philosophy as practiced by the team owners and managers, will be discussed in more detail in chapter 10. The following table of some of the game's greatest pitchers shows the dramatic decrease in the number of complete games pitched in the major leagues over the decades.

STARTING PITCHERS: GAMES PITCHED,
INNINGS PITCHED, AND COMPLETE GAMES
AVERAGE STATISTICS PER YEAR

Pitcher	G	GS	CG	W	L	IP	SO	BB	ERA
Grover C. Alexander	39	33	24	21	12	288	122	53	2.56
Walter Johnson	40	33	27	21	13	296	175	68	2.17
Lefty Grove	39	29	19	19	9	246	142	74	3.06
Bob Feller	38	32	19	18	11	255	172	118	3.25
Warren Spahn	38	33	19	18	12	262	129	70	3.09
Bob Gibson	33	30	16	16	11	243	195	84	2.91
Tom Seaver	34	33	12	16	11	245	187	71	2.86
Roger Clemens	32	32	6	16	8	225	216	73	3.19
Randy Johnson	35	34	7	18	9	240	298	97	3.10
Pedro Martinez	39	32	5	18	7	218	255	61	2.58
Greg Maddux	34	34	6	17	10	233	163	49	2.89

The period from 1961 to 2004 saw the gradual change from a four-man starting pitching rotation to a five-man pitching rotation, as noted above. At the same time, additional pitchers were assigned to the bullpen to relieve the starting pitchers of the responsibility of having to relieve on their days off. And major league teams also began to maintain records of pitch counts for their pitchers, and to limit starting pitchers to approximately 100 pitches an outing. As soon as a starting pitcher reached the magic 100-pitch mark, he was given the rest of the day off. These changes combined to increase the average major league team's pitching complement from approximately eight pitchers to about 11 pitchers, after the beginning of free agency. They also significantly reduced the workload of starting pitchers from 280 or more innings a year to about 200 innings a year, a move that most major league representatives believed would extend the careers of the starting pitchers. But that belief may have been incorrect, as will be seen presently.

The most significant change in the game over the last 45 years may be the separation of relief pitching responsibilities, with the designation of a long reliever, a short reliever, a setup man, and a closer.

Year	Teams	Scheduled Games	Total Saves	Saves/Team/ 154 Games	CG/Team/ 154 Games
1955	16	154	359	22	47
1965	20	162	678	32	37
1975	24	162	669	26	44
1985	26	162	977	36	24
1995	28	144	1,006	34	10
2004	30	162	1,130	39	5

Closers came into their own in the 1980s with the emergence of Dennis Eckersley, Jeff Reardon, and John Franco. Actually, as late as 1989, late-inning relief specialists were still being called firemen, although they were occasionally being referred to as short relievers, stoppers, and closers. By the early '90s, the team's key late-inning relief pitcher was called the closer. The other relief specialists in the bullpen were designated as long relievers, middle relievers, and setup men. While Eckersley began his major league career as a starting pitcher, being converted to a closer when his stamina began to decline as he approached his mid–30s, Reardon and Franco were relief specialists their entire major league careers, although both men were starting pitchers in the minor leagues.

The era of the starting pitcher who comes out of the bullpen on his second day off was drawing to a close, as shown in the following table.

STARTING PITCHERS: CAREER RELIEF APPEARANCES, WINS, AND SAVES

		Games	*Wins*	*Losses*	*Saves*
Bob Gibson	1959–1975	46	6	4	6
Juan Marichal	1960–1975	14	5	2	2
Nolan Ryan	1966–1993	34	5	0	3
Tom Seaver	1967–1986	9	0	2	1
Roger Clemens	1984–2004	1	0	0	0
Greg Maddux	1986–2004	4	0	0	0
Pedro Martinez	1994–2004	3	0	0	0

Bob Gibson saved six games during his career in 46 relief appearances. Juan Marichal relieved 14 times, but after him, relief appearances by a starting pitcher have been few and far between. Nolan Ryan did have 34 relief appearances, but they were all early in his career when he was still trying to find his niche in the game. He didn't make any relief appearances over his last 19 years. Roger Clemens, who is one of baseball's greatest modern-day pitchers, has made just one relief appearance in 21 years, and that was in his rookie season. He has not relieved in 20 years. Greg Maddux has made four relief appearances in 19 years, one in his rookie season and three the following year. He has made no relief appearances in 17 years.

The new era got underway in 1961 with one of the more exciting races in baseball history. It was a race between two individuals, Roger Maris and Mickey Mantle, for Babe Ruth's single season home run record. The two New York Yankee outfielders battled neck-and-neck through the summer months, first one and then the other taking the lead in the home run race. Finally, an injury to Mantle took him out of the race, leaving it up to Maris to challenge Babe Ruth's legendary record. The native of Hibbing, Minnesota, was up to the challenge. On the last day of the season, he took a pitch from Tracy Stallard of the Boston Red Sox and deposited it ten rows up in the right field stands at Yankee Stadium for home run number 61.

The season also produced a hint of things to come. The American League introduced two new teams, the California Angels and the (new) Washington Senators. The next year, the National League welcomed the New York Mets and the Houston Colt .45s with open arms. The Mets were worse than the typical expansion franchise, losing 120 of their 162 games. Manager Casey Stengel expressed his frustrations with the talent that was made available for the new franchise when he said, as quoted in Frommer, "I've got a catcher who can hit, but can't catch. I've got another catcher who can catch but can't hit. And I've got another catcher who can't do either."

In the 1960s and '70s a new breed of relief specialists marched out of the bullpen to save the game. They usually only pitched an inning or two, but they occasionally pitched as many as six innings in a game, as Ron Perranoski did during the heat of the 1965 pennant race. A full time fireman in the bullpen was considered a necessity if a team was serious about winning the pennant. In New York, Luis Arroyo was the man the Yankees depended on, and he had a career year in 1961. He recorded 15 of his 40 career victories that year, as well as 29 of his 44 career saves. He led the American League in games pitched with 65, and in saves. And he recorded a sensational earned run average of 2.19 against a league ERA of 4.02. His performance sparked the Yankees to the pennant by an eight-game margin over the Detroit Tigers. He was particularly valuable to Whitey Ford, who once remarked, "I think I'll have a great season if Arroyo's arm holds out." And there was more truth than jest to that remark. The Yankee southpaw went on to record a 25–4 season mark in 283 innings, but he only completed 11 of 39 starts, with little Luis picking him up time after time.

Dick "the Monster" Radatz, a 6' 5", 235-pound, right-handed flamethrower was the Boston Red Sox' bullpen ace from 1962 through 1965, leading the league in saves twice and relief wins twice. He went 15–6 with 25 saves in 1963 and 16–9 with 29 saves the following year. His career statistics included a 52–43 win-loss record, 122 saves, and 1.82 innings pitched per game. And the Monster struck out 9.7 batters for every nine innings pitched. Don McMahon was another of the early firemen, pitching for several teams from 1957 to 1974. He went 90–68 on the mound, while appearing in 874 games, with 153 saves. He led the National League with 15 saves in 1959, to go along with a 5–3 record and a fine 2.57 ERA. His career ERA of 2.96 is one of the lowest in modern baseball history, although his 1,310 innings pitched is not enough to qualify him for official recognition.

In 1963, with the return of the strike zone to the pre–1950 specifications, pitchers assumed control of the game, particularly Sandy Koufax. The tall, slender southpaw for Walter Alston's Los Angeles Dodgers came of age that year after six preliminary years of being a thrower, followed by two years of fine-tuning his pitching game. Koufax went 25–5 in '63 with 11 shutouts, 306 strikeouts, and a brilliant 1.88 ERA. Over the next three years, until his retirement, the Dodger's flamethrower put together seasons of 19–5, 26–8, and 27–9. His earned run average between 1963 and 1966 was a combined 1.85, with a high of 2.04 in 1965. Three times he struck out more than 300 batters in a season, and he still holds the National League single season strikeout record of 382 batters. He also tossed four no-hitters including a perfect game. And his excellence continued into the World Series as the Dodgers embarrassed the New York Yankees with a four-game sweep. The 6' 2", 210-pound lefty struck out a series-record 15 batters in a 5–2 opening game triumph. Then, following victories by Drysdale and Podres, Koufax nailed down the title with a tense 2–1 win over Yankee ace Whitey Ford. As one player put it at the time, "Koufax belongs in a higher league."

Sandy Koufax was not the only outstanding pitcher to show his stuff during the 1960s. His teammate Don Drysdale, a 6' 6", side-wheeling right-hander, terrified opposing batters with his buggy-whip delivery that approached the batter by way of third base. "Big D" was mean, and he was always one of the league leaders in hit batters. But he was also a winning pitcher, compiling a career record of 209 victories against 166 losses, including a 25–9 mark in 1962 and a 23–12 record in 1965. At one point in the 1968 season, he set two major league records, throwing six straight shutouts and pitching 58⅔ consecutive scoreless innings. The Dodgers also had other excellent starting pitchers at that time, including Johnny Podres, a career 148–116 pitcher, and Claude Osteen, a career 196–195 pitcher with two 20-victory seasons to his credit.

Los Angeles had the league's top fireman in Ron Perranoski. The 6', 192-pound New Jersey native was a starting pitcher in the minor leagues, but had only one start in the major leagues in 737 games pitched. His 13-year career included seven years in Los Angeles where he sparked the pitching-rich Dodgers to three National League flags and two world championships. His greatest year was 1963, when he led the league with 69 games pitched and a .842 winning percentage based on his 16–3 win-loss record. He also saved 21 games for the National League champs. His biggest game of the season was on September 22, 1965, when, in the heat of a pennant race, Perranoski relieved a battered Sandy Koufax in the sixth inning against the Milwaukee Braves, with the Dodgers down by a score of 6–2. He pitched six shutout innings, with the Dodgers finally pushing over the winning run in the eleventh inning. Los Angeles, who trailed the San Francisco Giants by three games entering the fray, went on a six-game winning streak after Perranoski's clutch performance and clinched the pennant along the way. The husky southpaw had a good fastball, but relied mostly on breaking pitches to get outs. He had an outstanding curveball that was aided by a slight hesitation in his delivery. And, like other firemen of his time, he was not a one-inning pitcher. He often pitched three or more innings in a game, in pursuit of a victory or trying to save a game for a starter.

Out in St. Louis during the 1960s, Bob Gibson held court. According to Shatzkin's *Ballplayers*, "There have been few pitchers more intimidating or more dominating than Bob Gibson. His great physical stamina and tremendous concentration gave him an enormous edge enhanced by his willingness to pitch inside and sometimes hit batters." Like Drysdale, Gibson insisted on owning the inside of the plate, and was not averse to sticking a pitch in the batter's ribs if he dug in too much. The rugged, 6' 2" fireballer had five quality pitches: a rising fastball, a sinking fastball, a slider, a curve, and a change. He had an attitude that made it all work, and he was one of the game's best money pitchers. During his 17-year career, he won 251 games against 174 losses. His greatest year was 1968, when he went 22–9 while leading the league with 13 shutouts, 268 strikeouts, and a 1.12 ERA, the third-lowest ERA in the lively-ball era. And, like all great money pitchers, Gibson was at his best in the World Series. He appeared in three Series, starting nine games, completing eight of them, and compiling a 7–2 record. In game one of the 1968 Fall Classic, he broke the single game strikeout record by fanning 17 Detroit Tigers en route to a 4–0 victory. He also had a 13-strikeout game and two 10-strikeout games in Series play. Overall, he registered 92 strikeouts in 81 innings in his nine starts.

The year 1968 has come to be known as the Year of the Pitcher, after National League and American League batting averages fell to just .243 and .230 respectively. The major league owners took immediate action to add more offense to the game, feeling that that was what the fans paid to see. In 1969 the strike zone was returned to its 1950 specification: that area over home plate between the batter's armpits and the top of his knees. At the same time, the pitcher's mound was reduced from a height of 15" to 10". Coincidentally, the leagues also expanded that year, with the National League adding the Montreal Expos and San Diego Padres, and American League adding the Kansas City Royals and the Seattle Pilots. The Pilots moved to Milwaukee as the Brewers the following year. All these changes did increase the offense in the game; runs scored increased by 19 percent, while home runs

Tom Seaver, who won 311 games between 1967 and 1986, was one of the most outstanding pitchers in the annals of the game (NEW YORK METS).

shot up by 30 percent and batting averages increased from .237 to .248. They went up again the next year, with home runs increasing another 10 percent in 1970, runs scored advancing another 6 percent, and batting averages going up another six points. But that was just a blip on the screen. After 1970, the offense settled back down to the 1967 level, where it would remain until the Costa Rican ball hit the marketplace in 1994.

The 1970s were a chaotic period in major league baseball, with the introduction of the designated hitter, bitter player-management confrontations, free-swinging batters, the proliferation of firemen in the game, and free agency. The American League voted to use a designated hitter to bat in place of the pitcher, again to stimulate the offense. The concept of a designated hitter was not new to the game. It had been proposed as early as the 1890s, and again during the first decade of the twentieth century. But it had never found enough advocates to make it a reality until 1973. The reserve clause was declared to be unconstitutional in 1975, and free agency became law of the land.

Some of baseball's greatest starting pitchers were at their peaks during the 1970s, including Nolan Ryan, Tom Seaver, and Steve Carlton. Ryan entered the major leagues with a 100-mile-per-hour overhand fastball and little control. It took him six years to begin to realize his potential, but when he did, he became the most overpowering pitcher the game has ever seen. He gradually improved his control, and added a sharp-breaking curveball that was thrown at almost the same speed as his fastball, causing batters to freeze in their tracks. The man who became known as the Ryan Express won 19 games in 1972 with nine shutouts and a league-leading 329 strikeouts in 284 innings, with a 2.28 ERA. And from there he just got better. Over the next 22 years, the 6' 2", 195-pound Texan led the league in strikeouts ten more times, and pitched a mind-boggling seven no-hitters, three more than the next man, Sandy Koufax. By the time he had retired, he had accumulated 5,714 strikeouts, almost 1,400 more than Roger Clemens, who is presently in second place. Nash and Zullo reported in *Baseball Confidential*, "Nolan Ryan — even though he's over 40 — still scares the hell out of batters. At the peak of Ryan's career, a strange phenomenon occurred in the opposing clubhouse — hitters suddenly complained of injuries and took themselves out of the lineup." Ryan's career totals include 324 victories against 292 losses, and eight all-star selections.

Tom Seaver was a finished pitcher when he arrived at the New York Mets' spring training camp in 1967. He had a complete repertoire of pitches, including a rising fastball, a sinker, a slider, a curveball, and a change of pace, all thrown with a three-quarter overhand delivery. Plus, he had control of all of them. The handsome, 205-pound fireballer was the club's ace from day one. He sparked the amazing Mets to the National League pennant in 1969, leading the league with 25 victories and a .781 winning percentage. And he pitched the Mets to a 2–1, ten-inning victory in game five of the World Series, as Gil Hodges' underdogs whipped the favored Baltimore Orioles in six games. On April 22, 1970, "Tom Terrific" fanned 19 San Diego Padres, including a major league record ten in a row. His 20-year career produced 311 victories against 205 losses.

Steve "Lefty" Carlton came out of Miami, Florida, in 1965 and mesmerized National League batters for two decades. Initially, scouts questioned his fastball, but a dedicated conditioning program added bulk to his 6' 4" frame, making him one of the most feared pitchers in baseball. The high kicking southpaw had three devastating pitches, a rising fastball, a curveball, and a slider, all thrown with either a straight overhand or a three-quarter delivery, giving him a decided edge over the man at the plate. Carlton quickly developed into one of the league's top left-handed pitchers, recording six 20-victory seasons during his 24-year major league career. On September 15, 1969, he fanned 19 New York Mets in a 4–3 loss. He pitched the Phillies to the world championship in 1980, compiling a brilliant 24–9 win-loss record, with 286 strikeouts and a 2.34 ERA, and he beat the Kansas City Royals twice in the World Series, including the deciding seventh game. By the time he retired in 1988, Steve Carlton had become the game's second-winningest southpaw, behind Warren Spahn, with a 329–244 win-loss record.

The 1970s were not only the abode of great starting pitchers; they were also the spawning ground for some of the most effective relief pitchers the game had yet seen. The first fireman of note was Dave Giusti, who paced National League relievers from 1970 to 1975.

The 5' 10", 195-pound, right-handed reliever pitched in the major leagues for 16 years, compiling a 100–93 record, with 145 saves in 668 games pitched, 535 of them out of the bullpen. Another top fireman was a 6' 1", 192-pound southpaw out of DuBois, Pennsylvania: Albert "Sparky" Lyle. The zany Lyle was one of the top firemen of the decade, pitching as many as 72 games in a season and averaging 1.55 innings per game. One of the lefty's greatest attributes was his coolness under pressure, and he thoroughly enjoyed watching batters trudge back to the dugout grumbling about his devastating slider. Sparky Lyle began his major league career with Boston and was a relief specialist from his first day in the majors. He was traded to the New York Yankees in 1972, where he blossomed into the league's top fireman. He led the American League in saves in both 1972 and 1976, and completed his 16-year career with 99 wins against 76 losses, with 238 saves in 899 games pitched, all in relief.

The next fireman to come along was Rollie Fingers, considered by many baseball experts to be the best fireman in baseball history. The 6' 4" right-hander joined the Oakland Athletics in 1968, beginning a memorable nine-year career there. Armed with a pitching repertoire that consisted of a fastball and a slider, he led the major leagues in total saves between 1972 and 1984. In Oakland, he played for one of the most dysfunctional major league teams in years but, even though they fought like cats and dogs in the clubhouse, they came together on the field to win three consecutive world championships. Decked out in their gaudy gold and green uniforms, the flamboyant A's won 277 games over the three-year period, and Fingers played a major role in their success. The big, 195-pound bullpen specialist, sporting a Gay Nineties handlebar mustache, pitched in 16 of the 19 World Series games between 1972 and 1974, winning two, losing two, and saving six. Rollie Fingers enjoyed a 17-year major league career, during which he went 114–116 in 944 games, 907 of them in relief, with 341 saves in 450 opportunities, a 76 percent success rate.

The Oakland A's' seven-game triumph over the Cincinnati Reds in the 1972 World Series had several interesting facets. In the eighth inning of game three, Fingers relieved Vida Blue with runners on first and third, only one out, and the dangerous Johnny Bench at the plate. After the count reached two and two, catcher Gene Tenace stepped outside and signaled for an intentional walk. As Bench stood relaxed at the plate, Fingers slipped a slider over the outside corner for strike three, sending the embarrassed Reds catcher back to the dugout. Surprisingly, Gene Tenace, who had caught only 49 games all year and hit a feeble .225 with five home runs, was the series' Most Valuable Player. He was behind the plate in six of the games, hit a solid .348, and clubbed four home runs with nine RBIs, to lead both teams in offense.

Mike Marshall, a stocky, right-handed fireman for the Los Angeles Dodgers, set major league records for relief pitchers that may never be broken. The 5' 10", 180-pound student of kinesiology, the study of the proper use of muscles, was a combative individual whose conflicts with managers kept him on a major league merry-go-round, playing for nine teams during his 14-year career. He came of age while pitching for the Montreal Expos in 1972, using three pitches with equal success— a fastball, a screwball, and a slider — to lead the National League with 65 games played, while registering a 14–8 record and 18 saves. The next year, he once again led the league in games played with a record-setting 92, and in saves with 31. Traded to the Los Angeles Dodgers over the winter, he embarked on a season for the ages in 1974. As the Dodgers' fireman, he sparked the team to the National League pennant by relieving in an amazing 106 games, with 21 saves and a 15–12 win-loss

Sparky Lyle was another of the New York Yankees' sensational firemen (BOSTON RED SOX).

record. At one point during the season, he pitched in 13 consecutive games, winning five games in six days in one stretch. Although the Dodgers fell to the Oakland A's in five games in the World Series, Marshall did his best to stem the tide, pitching in every game and recording one save and a 1.00 ERA. His career totals were 723 games pitched, 97 victories, 112 losses, 188 saves, and a 3.14 ERA.

Richard "Goose" Gossage was a fireballing right-handed pitcher who terrified opposing hitters with his all-out, back-to-the-plate, three-quarter overhand delivery. He was just wild enough, and hit just enough batters, that players were afraid to dig in against his 96-mph heat. The 6' 3", 217-pound Gossage was a tireless pitcher who worked 142 innings in 62 games in 1975, an average of 2.28 innings per game. After a failed attempt to make him a starting pitcher, the White Sox traded him to Pittsburgh, where he became a permanent bullpen fixture. In 1977, he went 11–9 on the mound, pitching 133 innings in 72 games, with 26 saves and a 1.62 ERA. That brought him to the attention of the New York Yankees, who quickly acquired him in a trade, hastening the departure of 33-year-old Sparky Lyle. Gossage handled the Yankees' fireman chores for six years, leading the league in saves twice and posting ERAs between 0.77 and 2.62. In 1978, he led the league with 27 saves, won another ten games himself, recorded a save in the American League playoff game, and picked up two wins and a save in postseason play.

Goose Gossage saved 310 games over a 22-year career (NEW YORK YANKEES).

Three years later, he saved all three games in the League Championship Series (LCS) and both Yankees victories against the Dodgers in the World Series. The Goose went on to realize a memorable 22-year career in the Big Time. He won 124 games against 107 losses, while pitching in 1,002 games, 965 of them in relief. He saved 310 games for a 73 percent success rate, and compiled a 3.01 ERA.

Bruce Sutter, who pitched from 1976 to 1988, may have been the best fireman in the annals of the sport. The tall, bearded right-hander was successful primarily because of one pitch, the split-finger fastball he introduced into the major leagues in 1976 after perfecting it in the minors for three years. During his 12-year major league career, the splitter was his out-pitch, set up by his fastball and his slider. According to Tim McCarver, as James and Neyer report, Sutter almost never threw the splitter for a strike, always leaving it in the dirt with a harried batter flailing away at thin air. Sutter, who joined the Chicago Cubs in 1976, became the team's fireman the following year. He led the National League in saves five times in six years between 1979 and 1984, with a high of 45 saves in '84 to go along with a 1.54 ERA. After ten years of spectacular performances, Sutter, like many firemen, developed shoulder problems that effectively ended his career. Over his 12-year career, the father of the split-finger compiled a 68–71 win-loss record in 661 relief appearances, with an excellent 2.83 ERA, and 300 saves at a 75 percent success rate. His ERA would be the fifth-best ERA in baseball history after 1920, if he had enough innings to qualify.

Dan Quisenberry, who pitched from 1979 to 1990, was a submarine-style pitcher who threw a sinker, a curve, and a changeup with control that is unmatched in the game today. The tall lanky right-hander's 80-mile-per-hour delivery yielded a hit an inning, but his low walk rate, which averaged just 1.4 walks per nine innings, coupled with his superb location, resulted in a career ERA of just 2.76. Quis starred for the Kansas City Royals from the first day he put on a uniform. He dominated the American League statistically between 1982 and 1985, leading the league in saves all four years with totals of 35, 45, 44, and 37. When he retired in 1990, he left behind a 56–46 win-loss record, and 244 saves in 674 games. The five-time Rolaids Relief Man of the Year was quoted by Paul Votano after his 1982 selection as saying, "I want to thank all the pitchers who couldn't go nine innings, and manager Dick Howser who wouldn't let them."

Another relief specialist of note is Jesse Orosco, a seemingly ageless southpaw who evolved from a closer to a situational lefty, developing different pitches over the years to retire batters, in compensation for his advancing age. He used a fastball when he was young, switched to a slider several years later, and relied on a split-finger fastball in his sunset years. The tall, lanky Orosco holds the record for most career games pitched, with 1,252, all but four of them in relief. In 1986, he appeared in 58 games with 21 saves and a 2.33 earned run average. He recorded two saves against the Boston Red Sox in the World Series that year, including the game seven clincher. In his declining years, he was frequently used as a situational lefty, called on to get one out in a tight situation. He finally hung up his glove for good in 2003 at the age of 46, finishing a notable 24-year major league career with 87 wins against 80 losses, and 144 saves.

The pitchers noted above, as well as many other major league players, would benefit over the rest of their careers from the actions of Andy Messersmith and Dave McNally. Free agency became the law of the baseball land in 1976 after an arbitration panel ruled against the practice of major league teams' retaining the rights to a player throughout his career unless he were traded or released. A subsequent agreement negotiated between major league owners and the Player's Association granted players the right to free agency after six years. In 1976, more than two dozen free agents hit the jackpot, with salaries averaging $200,000, more than five times their previous contracts. Bobby Grich of the Baltimore Orioles, who had been paid $68,000 in 1976, received a five-year contract for $1,500,000.

Free agency and the new astronomical salaries demanded by the players also affected the disability list. The DL, which was initiated in 1953, was not used very much during the first 20 years of its existence; but after the introduction of free agency, the percentage of pitchers on the disabled list during a season doubled from 24 percent to 50 percent, indicating that perhaps pitchers were using the DL for reasons other than for treating actual injuries, perhaps for being overprotective of their pitching arm, or for avoiding having to pitch if they were having an off year, or just coasting a bit between contracts.

Expansion continued unabated during the '70s. The American League added two more teams in 1977, the Toronto Blue Jays and the Seattle Seahawks. Not surprisingly, the Blue Jays held down the cellar spot in the Eastern Division, with a record of 54 wins and 107 losses, finishing a full 45½ games behind the pennant-winning New York Yankees. The Seattle Seahawks did slightly better, finishing sixth in the Western Division, 38 games off the pace of the Kansas City Royals. The new teams gave the American League a total of 14 teams; the National League had 12. The Senior Circuit would not add any new teams for another 16 years.

As the 1970s were drawing to a close, a new generation of relief pitchers appeared on the horizon. Kent Tekulve, a 27-year-old sidearm pitcher, entered the major leagues in 1974 with the Pittsburgh Pirates and stayed around for 16 years. By 1976 Tekulve was a valuable reliever, pitching in 64 games with a 2.45 earned run average and nine saves. The following year, as the team's fireman, he led the National League in games pitched with 91, while pitching 135 innings with 31 saves and a 2.33 ERA. The lanky right-hander, who stood 6' 4" tall and weighed 180 pounds, was one of the most durable pitchers ever to toe the rubber. He used a hard sinker and a slider to keep opposing batters at bay, and occasionally threw the ball with a submarine delivery. Three times in his career, he pitched in more than 90 games in a season, with a high of 94 in 1979, second only to Mike Marshall's 104. There have been only seven occasions in the history of major league baseball when a pitcher has pitched in 90 or more games. Tekulve did it three times, Marshall also did it three times, and Wayne Granger did it once. The Cincinnati native's career numbers included a 94–90 win-loss record in 1,050 games, all in relief, 184 saves and a 69 percent success rate.

Jeff Reardon, a 6', 200-pound right-hander from Pittsfield, Massachusetts, also enjoyed a 16-year major league career, appearing in 880 games with 73 wins, 77 losses, and 367 saves, fifth on the all-time list. He started his major league career with the New York Mets in 1979, but realized his greatest successes with the Montreal Expos between 1982 and 1986, and the Minnesota Twins between 1987 and 1989. He also pitched for the Boston Red Sox and the Atlanta Braves. Reardon's most satisfying year was 1987, when he saved 31 games for the Minnesota Twins en route to their world championship. He added four more saves in the postseason, including two in the Series, which the Twins won over the St. Louis Cardinals four games to three. The Twins closer set the Cardinals down in order in the bottom of the ninth inning of game seven, preserving a 4–2 victory for Frank Viola. Reardon used a fastball to advantage early in his career, but relied on a slider in later years.

The year 1981 was a traumatic year for major league baseball. The simmering feud between the owners and the Players' Association came to a head. After months of haggling over free agency issues, the players called a strike on June 12. It lasted 50 days causing a shakeup in the playing schedule. The season was reduced to 107 games, and the season was split into two halves, with the first half winner meeting the second half winner to determine a league champion. The Los Angeles Dodgers, thanks to a poised 20-year-old southpaw named Fernando Valenzuela, captured the first-half crown in the Western Division. "Fernandomania" gripped the country during the summer as the chubby Mexican youngster quickly ran up a perfect 8–0 record with four shutouts and a sizzling 0.50 ERA. The Dodgers eventually defeated the Houston Astros in the division playoff, the Montreal Expos in the LCS, and the New York Yankees in the Fall Classic, and they had to come from behind in each series to win. Down two games to one against the Yankees, they came from behind three times in game four, took Yankees ace Ron Guidry downtown twice in the seventh inning of game five to win 2–1, and routed the Bronx Bombers 9–2 in the finale.

Seven years later the Dodgers struck again. Led by all-world pitcher Orel Hershiser, they accomplished the impossible to win the 1988 world championship. The man called Bulldog broke Don Drysdale's consecutive scoreless inning streak in late September by throwing ten scoreless innings of no-decision baseball against the San Diego Padres, giving Hershiser 59 consecutive scoreless innings, one more than the Big D. His September ERA of 0.00 can never be broken. The Dodgers won the Western Division title by seven games over Cincinnati and faced the New York Mets in the NLCS. Somehow, after losing 10 of 11 games to the Mets during the regular season, Tommy Lasorda's cohorts had enough momentum to derail the powerful New Yorkers, with Hershiser throwing a shutout in game seven. Then facing the Oakland A's with the "Bash Brothers," Jose Canseco and Mark McGwire, in the World Series, they shocked the world by winning the world championship easily in five games. The turning point in the series came in the opening game when, with the American League's top closer, Dennis Eckersley, on the mound, the impossible happened. A crippled Kirk Gibson, sidelined with two bad legs, hobbled to the plate in the bottom of the ninth inning, with two men out, one runner on base, and the A's in front, 4–3. The determined Gibson, with two strikes on him, hit a backdoor slider into the right field stands for the most dramatic home run in World Series history. It was Gibson's only at-bat in the series, but it was all the Dodgers needed.

Dennis Eckersley was a unique case in the annals of pitching specialization. An outstanding starting pitcher for Cleveland and Boston in the late '70s, the flamethrowing right-hander tossed a no-hitter at the California Angels in 1977, and won 20 games the next year. But during the early '80s he became a journeyman starter, whose fastball had lost some of its zip. Then, he had a rebirth. The Oakland Athletics converted the 32-year-old pitcher into a fireman, and after one year as a relief specialist who pitched two or three innings if needed, he became the closer in 1988, specializing in stints of one inning or less. He led the American League with 45 saves that year, and again with 51 saves in 54 save opportunities in 1992. Eckersley's 24-year major league career included 12 years as a starter and 12 years as a closer. During that time he won 197 games against 171 losses, and amassed a total of 390 career saves, the number-four all-time record, with an excellent 85 percent save rate. The cocky right-hander, who delivered his pitches almost sidearm, survived with his fastball plus a curve and a slider.

Lee Smith, who pitched in the major leagues from 1980 to 1997, is still baseball's all-timer saves leader, with 478 saves. Nash and Zullo in *Baseball Confidential* say Smith

> was named by many hitters as "the most fearsome figure on the mound." Combining his awesome size — 6 feet, 6 inches and 220 pounds — with a fastball that has been clocked at 99 miles per hour, Smith is at his most terrifying at Wrigley Field. "You can't help but be a little scared when he takes the mound in the ninth inning of a game that started at three P.M. in Wrigley Field and he throws pure gas from out of the shadows," says an Astro. "He looks like he's throwing about 150 miles per hour and, as big as he is, you don't pick up the ball at all."

Smith was one of the most durable and consistent firemen around, as he recorded 20 or more saves for 13 straight years. During his 18-year career, Lee Smith won 71 games against 92 losses, pitched in 1,022 games — all but 6 of them in relief — and recorded 478 saves with an 82 percent success rate, and a 3.03 ERA. His 1.26 IPG makes him one of the game's first closers, along with Jeff Reardon and John Franco.

Lee Smith, at 6' 6" and 225 pounds, was an imposing figure from the pitching mound from 1980 to 1997 (BOSTON RED SOX).

John Franco was still going strong in 2004, 20 years after his debut. The 5' 10", 170-pound southpaw had pitched 1,088 games through the 2004 season, the number-two all-time total, all of them in relief. He holds the major league record for most games pitched without ever having made a start. He began his major league in 1984 with the Cincinnati Reds, but was traded to the New York Mets in 1990, where he still pitches. Using a sinking fastball, a slider, a screwball, and a crafty approach to the game, Franco has led the National League in saves three times, with a high of 39 saves in 1988. He has recorded 28 or more saves 11 times in his career. He has averaged 1.21 innings per appearance over his career, the mark of a genuine closer. Over the course of his career, John Franco has compiled a 90–86 win-loss record, with 424 saves and an 81 percent success rate.

Major league pitchers received another serious blow to their pitching strategy when the strike zone rule was changed again in 1988 to read, "the area over home plate the upper limit of which is a horizontal line from the midpoint between the top of the shoulders and the top of the uniform pants, and the lower level is a line at the top of the knees." Now, according to a former umpire, the strike zone was no bigger than a postage stamp. Curiously, the change didn't seem to have any effect on the batting averages or the number of home runs hit in the major leagues after 1987.

But there were a couple of changes that did have a profound effect on both the batting averages and the home run rate. In 1993, the National League added two teams to bring itself into balance with the American League. The new teams were the Florida Marlins and the Colorado Rockies. Both teams managed to stay out of the cellar, each coming in sixth in its respective seven-team division. The average home run rate increased dramatically in the National League, the 32 percent increase partially the result of having put a team in Colorado, at an altitude of one mile. Balls flew out of Coors Field as though they had wings, at a rate 70 percent higher than at the other National League stadiums. American League home runs increased by 17 percent for unknown reasons.

Beginning in 1994, the major league baseball manufacturing operation was located in Costa Rica, and from that point through the 2004 season, home runs increased from 123 home runs per team per 154 games to 166 home runs per team, an increase of 35 percent.

Two years later, the lower end of the strike zone was moved to the bottom of the knees, with perhaps a 4 percent increase in the home run production around the major leagues.

And in 1998, the National League added two more teams, bringing the major league total up to 30 teams. The Arizona Diamondbacks and the Tampa Bay Buccaneers joined the Big Show, with Tampa Bay going to the American League and Arizona going to the National League. At the same time, the Milwaukee Brewers shifted leagues, joining the Senior Circuit. That gave the National League 16 teams to the American League's 14.

The decade of the 1990s belonged to the Atlanta Braves, who formed a dynasty, winning eight division titles, including five in a row. They won five National League pennants and one world championship. And they continued their domination of the Eastern Division by winning the first five division titles in the first decade of the new century. The key to the Braves' domination was their highly skilled pitching staff that, during the '90s, was led by Greg Maddux, Tom Glavine, and John Smoltz. Between the three of them they won seven Cy Young awards over that period, led the league in games won eight times, in ERA four times, and even in saves once.

Greg Maddux is arguably one of the greatest pitchers in baseball history. His ERA differential from the league average is number-four all-time. The Atlanta ace is still active in 2005, as he begins his twentieth year in the major leagues. During his 11 years in Atlanta, Maddux, a disciple of pitching coach Leo Mazzone, was constantly testing the umpire. In every game he would throw pitches farther and father outside to see how much latitude the umpire would give him, and then he would zero in on that spot for his key pitches. In most cases, he was able to con the umpire into giving him strike calls on pitches that were as much as six inches off the plate. The native of San Angelo, Texas, was almost invincible during the regular season, with a .639 winning percentage. He was more human in postseason play. He started 29 games in the postseason, with just two complete games and a mediocre 11–14 record. His career numbers are much different. He has won 305 games with 174 losses through 2004, with a 2.89 ERA. It is a sign of the times that Maddux has relieved in only four of the 608 games he has pitched.

Roger Clemens is another of baseball's world-class pitchers, and he will undoubtedly be elected to the National Baseball Hall of Fame, probably on the first ballot. He is one of the top two or three pitchers active today, a powerful, 6' 4", 220-pound right-hander who throws three-quarter overhand at speeds in the middle to upper 90s. And he is not afraid to throw one under the batter's chin to keep him loose. The Rocket's repertoire includes two devastating fastballs, a slider, and a splitter that has batters lunging at it in the dirt. Twice in his career he has struck out 20 batters in a nine-inning game, and he has also fanned 18 batters once. He has captured seven Cy Young awards, two more than the next highest man, Randy Johnson. His career totals, through 2004, include 328 victories against 164 losses, with a .667 win-loss percentage and 4,317 strikeouts. But like most modern pitchers, he is not available for relief duty, pitching out of the bullpen only once in 640 games pitched. And he has one serious chink in his armor that may prevent him from sharing the pedestal with such legendary pitchers as Walter Johnson, Grover Cleveland Alexander, Sandy Koufax, and Bob Gibson: The Rocket apparently suffers either from a lack of stamina or some other mysterious malady, because in 30 postseason starts, he has been able to pitch only one complete game. That weakness cost the 1986 Boston Red Sox the world championship.

Randy Johnson, a 6' 10", 225-pound southpaw, slings the ball plateward from a three-quarter overhand to a sidearm delivery, at speeds approaching 100 miles per hour. He insists on owning the inside of the plate, and will not hesitate to throw at the batter's head to keep him from digging in. In fact, during an All-Star Game, he threw a heater over the head of John Kruk of the Philadelphia Phillies, the ball eluding the catcher and going all the way to the backstop. A visibly shaken Kruk took feeble swings at Johnson's next three pitches and headed for the safety of the dugout. The man known as the Big Unit completed his seventeenth year in the major leagues in 2004, with a career record of 246–128. And he shows no signs of slowing down, as he led the league in strikeouts for the ninth time. His career total of 4,161 strikeouts places him third on the all-time list, behind Clemens and Nolan Ryan, but it is likely that he will pass Clemens before he retires. He has struck out 20 men in a game once, 19 men twice, and 18 men once. Although his blazing fastball is unequaled in today's game, his hard slider is his strikeout pitch. And his intimidation makes that possible. He has hit 17 batters for every 40 complete games, the third-highest total of the pitchers studied. Without a doubt, Randy Johnson is the most feared and the most overpowering pitcher in the game today. He pitched a no-hitter in 1990, and in 2004 he realized the dream of every pitcher, a perfect game. Over his career he has relieved in ten games, finishing five games and recording two saves. But his most important relief appearance came in the 2001 World Series when, after having pitched seven innings the previous day in a 15–2 rout of the Bronx Bombers, he came on in relief of Curt Schilling in the game seven finale and shut down the New York Yankees over the final 1⅓ innings to gain the victory.

There is one other starting pitcher who deserves to be recognized for his achievements on the mound during the 1990s and into the new century, and he may be the best of the modern pitchers. Pedro Martinez, who was traded away by the Los Angeles Dodgers, eventually ended up in Boston, where he became almost unbeatable. A two-time Cy Young Award winner, Martinez has won 182 games through 2004 against just 76 losses, for a .705 winning percentage, the second-highest winning percentage in the major leagues since 1920. His best season was 1999, when he went 23–4, an .852 winning percentage. In addition to leading the league in victories, he also led the league with 313 strikeouts and a 2.07 ERA. The slightly built, 5' 11", 170-pound, right-handed pitcher throws a mid–90s fastball and the best changeup in the majors, both with the same arm motion and from a variety of arm angles. The native of the Dominican Republic, who relieved in 64 games early in his career, has relieved in only three games over the past 11 years.

As the twenty-first century got underway, four world-class closers dominated the major league baseball scene. They were Trevor Hoffman of the San Diego Padres, Mariano Rivera of the New York Yankees, John Smoltz of the Atlanta Braves, and Eric Gagne of the Los Angeles Dodgers. Hoffman began his professional baseball career in 1991 in the Cincinnati Reds organization, joining the San Diego Padres two years later. He has been the Padres closer for 11 years, although he lost most of the 2003 season after undergoing shoulder surgery. He came back fully recovered in 2004, appearing in 55 games, while saving 41 games in 45 opportunities. In his career to date, he has pitched in 696 games, all in relief, posting a 48–47 win-loss record, with 393 saves against 48 blown saves and a 2.74 ERA. His 89 percent success rate is the number-three all-time since blown saves were first recorded in 1969.

Mariano Rivera began in the Yankee organization as a starting pitcher, compiling a brilliant 0.17 ERA in 22 games for the Yankees in the Rookie League in 1990. After undergoing elbow surgery in 1992, he worked his way up to New York three years later. In his rookie season he started ten games but failed to complete any of them. Yankee management decided he was too frail to withstand the rigors of starting, and assigned him to the bullpen in 1996. The rest, as they say, is history. He pitched in 61 games that year, mostly as a middle reliever, won eight against three losses, and posted an excellent 2.09 earned run average. Beginning in 1997, Mariano Rivera became Joe Torre's closer, and over the next eight years he pitched in 506 games, winning 34, losing 25, and saving 331 games with just 44 blown saves, and a sparkling 2.14 ERA. His 88 percent success rate is one of the highest in major league history, trailing only Eric Gagne, John Smoltz, and Trevor Hoffman. And Rivera was even better in postseason play. Pitching in 70 postseason games over ten years, he went 8–1 with 32 saves and a brilliant 0.75 ERA.

John Smoltz took another route to bullpen glory. He started out as a starting pitcher in the Braves organization, arriving in Atlanta just three years after his minor league baptism of fire. He quickly became one of the aces of the Braves staff, going 12–11 in 208 innings as a 22-year-old starter in 1989. His best year was 1996, when he led the National League in victories and strikeouts, compiling a 24–8 record with 276 strikeouts in 254 innings, and a 2.94 ERA. In 2000, after suffering from elbow problems for four years, Smoltz underwent Tommy John surgery, and was sidelined for the season. When he returned, he was assigned to the bullpen and quickly rose to the position of closer, becoming one of the top three in the major leagues. Between 2001 and 2004, the 6' 3", 210-pound right-hander appeared in 236 games, with 154 saves in 169 opportunities, a 91 percent save record. John Smoltz is the twenty-first century edition of Dennis Eckersley, a world-class starting pitcher who became a world-class closer. With a 163–121 win-loss record and 154 saves, Smoltz should be an easy HOF member when he finally hangs up his glove.

Eric Gagne of the Los Angeles Dodgers is another starting pitcher who made the switch to the bullpen, but his is a different story. Gagne worked his way up through the Dodgers' minor league system as a starting pitcher, finally arriving in the City of Angels in 1999. For three years he tried to break into the starting rotation, without success. He pitched in 58 games over that period, with 48 starts and no complete games, compiling an 11–14 record and a sorry 4.81 earned run average. Still, when spring training opened in 2002, Gagne was penciled in as the fifth starter. He didn't make it because, as he said, he couldn't pace himself. He threw as hard as he could for as long as he could and eventually ran out of gas, sometimes as early as the third inning. When the regular season began, he found himself in the bullpen, where a "closer by committee" setup awaited him. That arrangement didn't survive the first week of the regular season. As soon as the big Canadian got his chance, he nailed down the closer's job, and quickly established himself as one of the best closers in the major leagues. He finished the year with a 4–1 record in 77 games, with 52 saves in 56 chances and a 1.97 ERA. The next year, he was even more dominant, going 2–3 in 77 games, with 55 saves, no blown saves, and a barely visible 1.20 earned run average. In 2004, he appeared in 70 games, with a 7–3 win-loss record, 45 saves in 47 opportunities, and a 2.19 ERA. And along the way, Gagne set a major league record that may never be broken. Between August 28, 2002, and July 3, 2004, he saved 84 consecutive games, breaking the old record by 30 saves. His career save record, through 2004, shows 152 saves against six blown saves, for an amazing 96 percent success rate.

The year 2004 saw one of the most exciting postseason adventures ever witnessed in major league baseball. The Boston Red Sox, long known as a team of losers, perennial bridesmaids to the New York Yankees, and still cringing under the "Curse of the Bambino" that had prevented them from winning a world championship since Babe Ruth was traded to the Yankees in 1919, thrilled the baseball world with a stirring comeback victory against their hated rivals. After disposing of the Anaheim Angels in the American League Division Series, the Red Sox quickly fell behind New York three games to none in the LCS, including a 19–8 laugher in game three, and were written off by even their most ardent fans. Somehow, they clawed their way back into the series with two thrilling extra-inning victories in games four and five. Then, in game six, a miracle happened. Curt Schilling, who had severely injured his ankle in the Angels series, and couldn't make it through an earlier start against the Yankees, underwent an experimental surgery to sew the tendons to keep them from moving. Amazingly, the strategy worked, and Schilling stopped the Bronx Bombers in game six, even though blood kept oozing through his socks throughout the game. After Derek Lowe put the final nail in the Yankee coffin in game seven, it was off to the World Series. A rejuvenated Red Sox team, with the Curse off their shoulders, swept the shocked St. Louis Cardinals four straight. Curt Schilling once again went through the surgical procedure to tie off his tendon, and once again pitched a win with blood dying his socks crimson. And for the third time in the postseason, Derek Lowe wrapped up a series, this one giving the fans of Beantown their first world championship in 86 years.

As the twenty-first century got underway, it was apparent that the closer was going to be an important fixture on any pennant-contending team for the foreseeable future. Times have changed drastically since Johnny Gorsica came out of the Detroit Tigers bullpen in the 1940s. Gorsica told John Thorn that as a relief pitcher, "you either won or lost the game, and there was no credit except experience in no-decision games." That situation began to change in 1969 when Jerome Holtzman of the Chicago *Sun-Times* first suggested

Mariano Rivera has been the major leagues' premier closer since 1997 (NEW YORK YANKEES).

the recognition of saves to measure the effectiveness of relief pitchers. His newspaper and the *Sporting News* began recording saves at that time, but it was another nine years before major league baseball adopted it as an official statistic. As late as the 1970s, relief pitchers were still considered to be subs. Even in 1989, the top relief pitchers in the major leagues were still being referred to as firemen or stoppers. Bobby Thigpen of the Chicago White Sox was called the "closer" in Street and Smith's baseball annual of that year. That year he averaged 1.30 IPG. One candidate for the title of baseball's first closer was Bruce Sutter,

Curt Schilling changed from an outstanding major league pitcher into a legend during the 2004 League Championship Series against the New York Yankees (JULIE CORDEIRO).

who, beginning in 1976, appeared in 661 games between 1976 and 1988, all in relief, and averaging just 1.58 innings pitched per game. He saved 300 games, and won 68 games against 71 losses. Another candidate was Rollie Fingers who, between 1972 and 1985, pitched 790 games in relief, with no starts, averaging 1.65 innings pitched per game. He saved 310 games over that period with a record of 97–96. Jeff Reardon, who pitched from 1979 to 1994, had statistics that read more like those of a closer, as he averaged only 1.29 innings per game as early as 1984. Sutter was used to pitching more than one inning per appearance, as was Fingers. Dennis Eckersley began his career as a relief pitcher in 1987 after being a starting pitcher for 12 years. Within a year of his introduction into relieving, he became the Oakland Athletics' closer, averaging just 1.15 IPG.

The following list gives the innings pitched per game (IPG) for the most prominent relief pitchers since 1920:

F. Marberry	1.73 IPG	D. Eckersley	1.15 IPG	J. Reardon	1.29 IPG
J. Murphy	2.15 IPG	M. Rivera	1.16 IPG	E. Face	1.48 IPG
J. Page	2.09 IPG	E. Gagne	1.10 IPG	K. Tekulve	1.37 IPG
B. Sutter	1.58 IPG	J. Smoltz	1.08 IPG		

In an effort to identify baseball's first closer, this study first focused on late-inning relief pitchers who averaged less than 1.5 IPG. Elroy Face could have been the first true closer, based on that guideline. He averaged 1.48 innings per game during his 16-year career, but over his last seven years, he averaged just 1.29 IPG. Jeff Reardon averaged slightly over 1.5 IPG his first three years in the major leagues. Then he averaged just 1.29 IPG over his last 13 years, beginning in 1982.

In reviewing the careers of recent known closers like Mariano Rivera, John Smoltz, Eric Gagne, and Trevor Hoffman, it became apparent that closers don't win many games. Generally, relief specialists who win ten or more games in a season are not genuine closers. They are more like the firemen of the '30s, '40s, and '50s, such as Johnny Murphy, who twice won 12 games; Joe Page, who won 13 and 14 games; Ron Perranoski, who won 16 games one year; and Rollie Fingers, who had season victory totals of 11, 10, 13, and 11. John Franco won 12 games in 1985, but that was before he moved into an actual "closer" category. In that year, he averaged 1.48 IPG.

The modern closer averages less than 1.25 IPG and, except on rare occasions, rarely pitches more than two innings in a game. Dennis Eckersley was one of baseball's first true closers, based on that guideline. He averaged 1.15 IPG beginning in 1988, and never had a year higher than 1.20 over an 11-year period. Lee Smith had a career IPG average of 1.26 IPG, but he averaged 1.53 IPG between 1980 and 1986, and then just 1.10 IPG from 1987 through 1997. John Franco averaged less than 1.25 IPG beginning in 1987. Bruce Sutter has been called baseball's first closer by many historians, but his 1.58 IPG indicates that he often pitched three or more innings, and wasn't restricted to just closing a game out over the last inning or two. This area will be examined in greater depth in chapter 10.

The 1920s and 1930s were still the domain of the starting pitcher, and particularly the fastball pitcher, who didn't rely as heavily on the slipperiness of the ball as the curveball pitchers did. The starting pitchers on all teams were the best pitchers available. As John Thorn noted, "The school of thought was still, if you had a lead late in the game, why put your fate into the hands of a second-rater? If the starter was too pooped to pitch any further, bring in another starter." And as noted earlier, John A. Heydler, the president of the National League, welcomed the introduction of a new slower baseball in the 1930s by saying it should result in more complete games.

There are a finite number of outstanding pitchers in the major leagues at any given time, and they are always allocated to starting pitching responsibilities if they have the stamina to pitch a complete game. Some people claim that pitchers such as middle relievers, setup men, and closers are less talented, or have less stamina, than starting pitchers. They say it should be the objective of management, therefore, to condition pitchers to be able to pitch a complete game of nine innings, with a pitch count that averages about 135. A number of former pitchers and managers have been voicing the same concerns about the quality of major league pitching today. They say the best way to condition an arm to throw 135 pitches a game is by throwing a baseball. Satchel Paige said he threw a ball every day of the year, and he never had any arm "miseries" (actually, he did have a sore arm one year because of pitching in Mexico City at a 6,000-foot altitude, but it disappeared with rest). Herb Pennock, like Paige, was a tall, skinny pitcher with not much muscle visible in his arm, just sinew and bone, yet he pitched frequently over a long career without an arm problem.

Years ago, some of the top pitchers in the major leagues were big, strong farm boys, conditioned by the heavy workload required to run a successful farm. Cy Young, Walter Johnson, and Dazzy Vance fell into that category. Many of today's pitchers are pampered athletes who were the stars of their Little League teams, the stars of their high school teams, and often the stars of their college teams. Many of them have never done any physical labor in their entire lives, which may be one reason there are so many arm injuries among pitchers today. Their arms have never been properly conditioned to withstand the rigors of pitching a full nine-inning game of 135 pitches. Nolan Ryan, in a lot of ways, is a throwback to the old days. He didn't work on a farm as a child, but there was a strict work ethic in his family, and he had a paper route when he was in high school. And, like most kids of his generation, he wasn't allowed to play in the house. Children usually played outside until it got dark. As a result, Ryan played baseball up to eight hours a day, strengthening his arm by throwing the ball.

PART II. THE ELEMENTS OF PITCHING, YESTERDAY AND TODAY

8

The Rule Changes That Have Affected the Pitcher

The first seven chapters of this book discussed the growth of baseball and the evolution of pitching, from its murky beginnings in the 1840s when a pitcher (or feeder, as he was called) was expected to do nothing more than lay the ball over the plate for the batter to hit, to the present day where starting pitchers throw darts at batters for six or seven innings, then turn the game over to setup men and closers who overpower or befuddle the batters in the eighth and ninth innings. In the next three chapters, the rule changes, strategic changes, and other factors affecting pitchers will be investigated in detail, beginning with an examination of the rules changes over the past 150 years and the effect those rules changes had on the pitching game down through the years. Next, other factors that have affected the game, such as the introduction of relief specialists, setup men, and closers; the reliance on pitch counts and pitch count limits to determine when a pitcher should be relieved; and the continuing saga of the lively ball, will be reviewed and discussed. Finally, 14 former pitchers, including one of the five greatest pitchers of all time, will give testimony as to the effect that various changes in the game have had on pitchers. These pitchers, whose contact with the game over the past 40, 50, 60, and even 70 years qualifies them as experts, have remained close to the game since their retirement from active play. Many of them have served as major league pitching coaches, instructors, and scouts, as well as minor league coaches and college coaches.

The rule changes over the past 150 years, along with the effects of the changes on the pitcher, are presented below.

The Pitcher's Box, Pitcher's Plate, and the Distance to Home Plate

• In 1845, the distance from the pitcher's position to home plate was set at 45 feet. The pitcher was nothing more than a feeder at this time. His only job was to gently toss the ball under-

119

hand, over the plate, so the batter could hit it, making the distance from the pitcher's position to the plate unimportant.

- In 1857, the pitcher's position was identified as a line four yards in length, drawn at right angles to a line from home plate to second base, having its center upon that line, at a fixed iron plate placed at a point 15 yards distant from the home plate. The distance from the pitcher's position to home plate became more important after 1858, when James Creighton used an illegal wrist snap to obtain more speed on his ball. Creighton was the first pitcher of note to challenge the batter. Pitchers had been challenging the batter for several years prior to the appearance of Creighton, in the New York–Brooklyn National Championship series of 1858, and in the Amherst-Williams college baseball game played in Pittsfield, Massachusetts, in 1859, for instance, but the names of the pitchers in those games are unknown. With Creighton, the pitcher was beginning to evolve from a feeder to an enemy of the batter, whose job it was to make sure the batter didn't get a base hit.
- In 1863, the pitcher's box was defined as lying between two lines, each 12 feet in length, with the front line 45 feet and the back line 48 feet distant from home base. The pitcher's lines were to be marked by flat, circular iron plates.
- In 1866, the back line of the pitcher's box was moved back one foot. The next year, the pitcher's box was defined as being six feet wide and four feet long.
- In 1869, the pitcher's box was defined a six-foot square.
- In 1879 the pitcher's box was defined as being four feet wide and six feet long.
- In 1881, the distance from the pitcher's box to home plate was set at 50 feet. As a result of this change, home runs increased, as did pitchers' earned run averages.
- In 1886, the pitcher's box was made seven feet long by four feet wide. The next year the pitcher's box was changed to 5½ feet long by 4 feet wide.
- In 1890, the pitcher's box was set at 6 feet long by 4 feet wide.
- In 1893, the pitcher's box was replaced by a pitching rubber. The size of the rubber was initially 4" × 12", but it was increased to its present size of 6" × 24" in 1895. The distance from the pitching rubber to home plate was set at 60' 6".

The Pitcher

- When the first rules were written in 1845, the pitcher, called a feeder, was directed to throw the ball in an easy underhand motion to the batter, to give the batter an opportunity to hit the ball. The object of the game at this point was not for the pitcher to try to retire the batter. It was for the fielders to try to retire the batter after he hit the ball.
- After 1858, with the emergence of James Creighton, the pitcher became a competitive force whose job it was to prevent the batter from getting a hit. He was still limited to throwing the ball underhand and was prevented by the rules from putting a wrist snap on the ball. Creighton's illegal wrist snap was virtually undetectable. At that time, starting pitchers were expected to pitch a complete game. Once a game got underway, no substitutes were allowed to enter the game except in the case of illness or injury. If a pitcher was being hit hard, he could only be relieved by changing positions with another player. Often, a hard-throwing outfielder would come in to pitch, and the pitcher would go to the outfield. The relief pitcher was called a change pitcher.
- In 1881, sidearm pitching was legalized, but the expected pitching dominance never mate-

rialized because the pitchers had been cheating for years and were already throwing near-sidearm. But the extra five feet of distance from the pitcher's box to home plate played havoc with their strikeouts, which decreased by an average of 10 percent.

- 1884, overhand pitching was legalized, and the pitchers did dominate the hitters. Strike-outs in the eight-team National League increased from 2,877 to 4,335, an increase of 51 percent. Home runs increased from 124 to 322, but that number has to be taken with a grain of salt because it was caused by a rule change in Chicago's Lake Front Park. The park measured only 180 feet to left field and 186 feet to right field, and in 1883 any ball hit over the short fence was ruled a double, but in 1884 it was a home run.
- A rule change in 1891 permitted teams to substitute players during the game, allowing relief pitchers to be brought in from the sidelines rather than having to use a change pitcher. It was about this time that a special area was reserved on the sidelines for a pitcher to warm up before entering the game. That area was called the bullpen.

The Bat

- In 1857 the rules called for a round bat not exceeding 2½ inches in diameter in the thickest part. The bat had to be of wood and could be any length.
- In 1868, the bat was limited to 40 inches in length.
- In 1869 the rule stated that the bat could not be over 42 inches in length.
- In 1872 a player was allowed to use his own personal bat. The rule was dropped in 1874. At the same time, it was stated that the bat had be made wholly of wood.
- In 1885, it was legal to have one flat side on the bat.
- In 1893, the bat had to be wholly of hard wood. It had to be round, and could not exceed 2½" in diameter or 42" in length. Previously, one side of the bat could be flat.
- In 1895 the maximum diameter of the bat was set at 2¾ inches.
- In 1940, the rule on bats stated that the bat had to be made entirely of hardwood in one piece.
- In 1950, the bat rule restated the limitations as noted above: 42 inches long, 2¾ inches in diameter, and made of hardwood in one piece. The rule added that twine could be wound around it, or a granulated substance applied to it, for a distance of 18 inches from the end of the handle, but not elsewhere.

Height of the Pitcher's Mound

- Until 1903, there was no pitching mound defined in the rule book, although unofficially mounds varied in height from flat to about 20" high.
- In 1903, a pitcher's mound was established in the rules, with a maximum height of 15". A mound with any height less than 15" was legal, at the determination of the home team. This rule definitely favored the pitcher, giving him extra leverage to increase the speed of his pitches. It also favored the home team, who could vary the height of the mound to suit the preference of its pitcher.
- In 1969, the height of the pitcher's mound was changed to an exact height of 10". This rule change was made after the "Year of the Pitcher" in 1968 resulted in batting averages of

.243 in the National League and .230 in the American League. Bob Gibson led all major league pitchers with an earned run average of 1.12.

Location of the Strike Zone

- The original strike zone, defined in 1887, identified the strike zone as the area over the plate, between a batter's knees and his shoulders.
- In 1900, the shape of the plate was changed from a 12" square to its present five-sided shape, 17" wide. This change increased the width of the strike zone by 42 percent.
- In 1901, any foul hit but not caught was a strike, unless two strikes had already been called.
- In 1950, the strike zone rule was changed to read "from the top of the batter's knees to his armpits." This change gave the umpires a more specific definition than the previous vague strike zone that was defined as being between the batter's knees and his shoulders. The new strike zone was advantageous to the batter, but he still had to defend himself against pitches thrown at the top of his shoulders and at the bottom of his knees.
- In 1963, the strike zone was identified as that space over home plate between the top of the batter's shoulders and his knees. This change restored the strike zone to its original position, and once again favored the pitcher. Sandy Koufax, Don Drysdale, and Bob Gibson took advantage of the change to establish several pitching records, including Koufax's National League single-season strikeout record and his four no-hitters, Drysdale's 58 consecutive scoreless inning streak, and Gibson's 1.12 ERA.
- In 1969 the strike zone was returned to its 1950 location, which was the space over home plate between the batter's armpits and the top of his knees.
- The 1988 strike zone was changed to read, "that area over home plate, the upper limit of which is a horizontal line at the midpoint between the top of the shoulders and the top of the uniform pants, and the lower limit is a line at the top of the knees." That change has brought confusion to the game. It reduced the strike zone from its original definition by at least 25 percent, giving the batter a huge advantage. But more important, the vagueness of the location of the strike zone has resulted in each umpire visualizing his own strike zone. There is no longer just one strike zone. There are as many strike zones as there are umpires working behind the plate.
- The 1995 strike zone, which dropped the lower limit to the hollow beneath the kneecap, did nothing to simplify the strike zone. Today the batter still has a huge advantage, but that advantage has been partially offset by the stubborn actions of the umpires, who each have their own special strike zone. In many cases, the strike zone is no higher than the belt. And most umpires totally ignore the rule that the ball must pass over the plate. The typical strike zone covers pitches that are four to six inches off the plate. However, on the inside of the plate, the pitcher is at a distinct disadvantage. If he pitches inside, he is in danger of being given a warning by the umpire, who may accuse him of intentionally throwing at the batter. And if he repeats the action inside, he could be ejected from the game. This situation has created a dangerous environment in the batter's box. Batters, who feel they are completely protected by the umpire, have become bolder and are crowding the plate trying to get in position to hit an outside pitch with authority. According to former major league umpire Ed Runge, as quoted in Curran, "Today's strike zone is the smallest it has ever been."

Don Drysdale routinely led the National League in hit batters during his 14-year career (AUTHOR'S COLLECTION).

The Major League Baseball

The construction of the baseball used by the major leagues has changed many times since the National League was formed in 1876. The first rule governing the size and weight of the baseball was written in 1854. It established the specifications, as noted in Thorn et al.'s *Total Baseball*, as "from 5½ to 6 ounces in weight and from 2¾ to 3 inches in diameter." Three years later, the specifications were redefined, with the size of the ball being measured by its circumference rather than by its diameter: "The ball must weigh not less than 6 nor more than 6¼ ounces avoirdupois. It must measure not less than 10 nor more than 10¼ inches in circumference. It must be composed of India rubber and yarn, and covered with leather."

- In 1859, the specifications were changed to a weight of 5¾ to 6 ounces and a circumference of 9¾ to 10 inches.
- The specifications were changed again in 1861: "The ball must weigh 5½ to 5¾ ounces and measure 9½ to 9¾ inches in circumference."
- In 1868 the weight of the ball was reduced to 5 to 5¼ ounces, and the size of the ball was reduced to 9¼ to 9½ inches in circumference.
- In 1870 the specifications called for a ball with a hard rubber core, tightly wrapped with wool, covered by a figure-eight horsehide. Previously the leather cover construction had been an orange peel design.
- In 1871, the weight of the ball was changed again, to 5 to 5¼ ounces, and the size of the ball was changed to exactly 9¼ inches in circumference. The next year, the specification for the size of the ball was redefined as from 9 to 9¼ inches. The ball had to contain one ounce of vulcanized rubber in mold form. A new rule stated, "If a ball becomes ripped, out of shape, or, in the umpire's opinion, unfit for play, the umpire shall call for a new ball at the end of a complete inning."
- In 1874, the yarn used in the manufacture of the ball was specified as woolen.
- In 1875, the rule regarding injury to the ball was rewritten as follows: "When the ball becomes out of shape, cut or ripped to expose the yarn, or in any way injured to be unfit for fair use, the umpire, at the close of an even inning at the request of either captain, shall call for a new ball."
- In 1876, one of the manufacturers of baseballs, Kelley Brothers, advertised their ball as follows: "Our professional dead balls are the deadest balls made."
- In 1879, A.G. Spalding Company was designated as the official supplier of National League baseballs.
- In 1882, the Mahn Sporting Company was designated as the official supplier of baseballs to the American Association.
- The following year, the Mahn ball was determined to be unsatisfactory, and A.J. Reach and Co. was designated as the official supplier of American Association baseballs. In the National League, if a ball was found to be unfit for play, the umpire could call for a replacement "at once," and did not have to wait until the end of the inning.
- In 1886, a rule was added stating that if a ball was hit outside of the enclosure or lost during a game, the umpire should call at once for another ball.
- In 1887, the National League and the American Association agreed to be governed by the same rules. Each league would retain its own approved official baseballs.

- In 1890, a rule stated that no ball could be intentionally discolored by rubbing it with soil or otherwise.
- In 1896, the home club was directed to have at least one dozen baseballs on the field ready for use by the umpire.
- In 1897, a rule was added stating that if a new ball was intentionally discolored, the umpire, at the request of the opposing captain, could put a new ball in play and could fine the offending player $5.
- In 1900, A.G. Spalding Company was designated as the official supplier of American League baseballs.
- In 1911, a cork-centered baseball was used in a major league baseball game for the first time.
- In 1955, the rule stated that "the ball shall be a sphere formed by yarn around a small core of cork, rubber or similar material, covered with two strips of white horsehide, tightly stitched together. It shall weigh not less than 5 nor more than 5¼ ounces avoirdupois, and measure not less than 9 nor more than 9¼ inches in circumference."
- In 1975, white cowhide, as well as white horsehide, was allowed as the covering material in the construction of the baseball.
- In 1976, Rawlings Sporting Goods Company replaced Spalding as the official supplier of major league baseballs.

The Specifications for the Construction of Major League Baseballs

- The nucleus of each baseball is called a pill, or cushion cork, which is a small sphere of a cork-rubber mixture, covered by two thin rubber layers, one black and one red. The weight is ⅞ of an ounce.
- The pill must be 1.375 inches in diameter, plus or minus 0.01 inches.
- The cemented surface of the pill is then wound with three layers of wool yarn and one layer of a cotton/polyester yarn.
- The first layer is approximately 121 yards of four-ply blue-gray woolen yarn to make a circumference of 7¾ inches with a weight of 2⅞ ounces.
- The second layer is approximately 45 yards of three-ply white woolen yarn to make a circumference of 8³⁄₁₆ inches with a weight of approximately 3¹¹⁄₁₆ ounces.
- The third layer is approximately 53 yards of three-ply blue-gray woolen yarn to make a circumference of 8¾ inches with a weight of 4¼ ounces.
- The fourth layer is approximately 150 yards of 20/2-ply fine white cotton/polyester yarn to make a circumference of 8⅞ inches with a weight of 4½ to 4⅝ ounces.
- The yarn used, with the exception of the cotton finishing yarn, is to be 99 percent wool, one percent other fibers. Seventy-five percent of the wool must be virgin wool, and 24 percent reprocessed.
- The ball is then coated with a latex adhesive, and a figure-eight cowhide cover is attached and hand stitched with 88 inches of waxed thread.
- The special alum-tanned leather is sewn with a double stitch of 10/5 red thread. The weight of the cover must be ½ to ⁹⁄₁₆ ounces. The thickness must be .045 to .055 inches. The finished ball is machined for about 15 seconds to compress the 108 stitches.

• The ball must measure 9 to 9¼ inches in circumference and weigh between 5 and 5¼ ounces. Random balls are tested on an approved indoor driving machine to determine and measure the resiliency of baseballs through the coefficient of restitution with an initial velocity of 85 feet per second. The rebound velocity must be from 0.514 to 0.578 of the initial velocity, a total range of 12 percent. (Eighty-five feet per second is determined to be approximately equal to the velocity of a baseball that, after being hit by a bat, would carry 400 feet.)

Rules Involving Trick Pitches and the Application of Foreign Substances to the Surface of the Baseball

• In 1920, trick pitches such as spitballs, emery balls, and shine balls were banned from the game. A new rule was also added to prevent discoloring the baseball with soil, rosin, paraffin, licorice, or any other foreign substance, or intentionally damaging the baseball by the use of sandpaper or other substance. The rule also called for a new ball to be put in play whenever a ball became discolored. That rule was particularly harmful to the

pitcher because he could no longer take the sheen off a new ball by rubbing it with dirt or rosin. As a result, pitchers had difficulty making the ball curve, and the batters gleefully attacked the ball. Major league batters love to hit straight balls.

• In 1921, a total of 17 spitball pitchers, nine in the National League and eight in the American League, were exempted from the ban for the remainder of their careers. Burleigh Grimes was the last spitball pitcher, retiring in 1934.

• In 1926, a National League pitcher was allowed to dry his hands with rosin, but still could not rub the ball with rosin.

• In 1931, umpires were directed to rub dirt on new balls before each game, and pitchers were allowed to use the rosin bag on the ball to remove the sheen.

• In 1938, umpires began using a special mud from the Delaware River to rub on new balls before the game.

Burleigh Grimes, the major leagues' last legal spitball pitcher, was also one of the game's leading headhunters (AUTHOR'S COLLECTION).

9

Lively Balls, Deadly Bats, and Shrinking Ballparks

Major League Baseballs: A Chronology

1911: The cork-center baseball was introduced.

1920: The baseball manufacturing process was changed, with new winding machines producing a ball that was wound tighter and was livelier. Some researchers have said that during World War I cheap yarn had to be used to manufacture baseballs because the high quality yarn was being used in the war effort, for uniforms, blankets, etc. The cheap yarn required higher tension settings on the winding machines in order to produce a tight ball, but when the war ended and superior wool, possibly from Australia, became available again, the winding machine tension settings were never returned to their prewar settings.

1920: The Hubbert Company of Perkasie, Pennsylvania, began stitching major league baseballs as a subcontractor for the Spalding Company. Three hundred of the 350 employees of the Hubbert Company stitched the balls at home. The contract expired in 1950.

1920: A new rule was introduced banning trick pitches, such as the spitball, emery ball, and shine ball.

1920: A rule banned the application of any foreign substance to the ball. This rule prohibited, among other things, the use of rosin to rub on a ball to take the sheen off it.

1921: After the tragic death of Cleveland shortstop Ray Chapman in a beaning accident, the umpires were ordered to replace dirty balls as often as possible in order to allow the batter to have a good look at every pitch. Previously, one ball was ordinarily kept in play for the entire game. By the later innings of the game, the ball could be badly misshapen and almost black in color. This move had a further negative effect on the pitcher since new balls were glossier and more difficult to curve than dirty balls.

1925: A cushioned, cork-center baseball was introduced for the first time. Batting averages increased by a modest five points that year but home runs jumped up by 30 percent and ERAs went from 4.05 to 4.33. The cushioned cork nucleus was a mixture of cork and rubber, making it livelier than the ball with a 100 percent cork center. According to

Jonathon F. Light, "Julian Curtis of Spalding said there were no new balls introduced in the 1920's, but that the wool was better after World War I and new winding machines made for a tighter, springier ball. George Reach (Al's son) claimed that the manufacturers occasionally tinkered with the balls."

On February 4, 1931, the *Los Angeles Times* headlined the news, "Major Leagues Act To Curb Home Run Hitters." The subheadlines noted, "New Baseball Aids Hurlers," "Rabbit Ball is Slowed Up by Manufacturers," and "Bulb Has Raised Seams and Heavier Cover." The National League, in an effort to combat the lively ball that was introduced in 1920, began using a number-five ball, having a thicker cover and a heavier stitch. The American League adopted the heavier stitch but did not adopt the heavier cover. *The L.A. Times* noted, "The changes made in both leagues were designed not only to eliminate some of the 'rabbit' tendencies of the ball, but also to give the pitchers a 'break' against the batsmen who have had it all their own way in recent years. It was explained that the new ball in each league would give the pitchers a chance for a better grip and therefore increase their effectiveness." Babe Ruth seemed unconcerned about the changes to the baseball, commenting, "Say, you can make that ball all cover and let the stitches stick out like grapevines and I'll still hit it. I hit that ball when it was said to be dead back in 1918 and 1919, and I sailed a lot of those 'dead' balls a lot of feet. The ball will go if it's hit."

Also in 1931, the umpires were directed to rub the balls with dirt before the game began, to remove the sheen, and pitchers were allowed to use the rosin bag on the ball for the same purpose. Three years later, the National League began using the American League ball, with the heavier stitch but thinner cover.

The headlines in the *Sporting News* of December 16, 1937, noted, "Major Leagues Split on Changing Ball." The subheading said, "N.L. Adopts 'Slower' Ball For Next Year."

The National League began using a new "dead" ball, with a heavier cover, although the number-four ball was not as dead as the number-five ball used by the league between 1931 and 1933. The number-four ball used five strands in the seams instead of four. The American League voted to retain the faster number-three ball. Also in 1938, the umpires began using a special mud to prepare balls before a game. The mud, called Lena Blackburn Rubbing Mud, was obtained from the Delaware River.

In 1939, both leagues adopted the number-four baseball.

In 1945, Dr. Lyman J. Briggs, director emeritus of the National Bureau of Standards, U.S. Department of Commerce, published a technical paper titled "Methods for Measuring the Coefficient of Restitution and the Spin on the Ball." Dr. Briggs continued to do research on COR through the 1950s, issuing a report in 1959 on how far a baseball curves. The Coefficient of Restitution (COR) was not used to measure the quality of major league baseballs until the end of the twentieth century.

1975: The official supplier of major league baseballs was changed from Spalding to Rawlings Sporting Goods Company. Rawlings, which became an independent company in 1968, had originally been part of Spalding and had manufactured major league baseballs since 1955. As Light noted, "Both the American and National League balls were manufactured by the same company even though the American League balls were stamped with the Rawlings name and the National League balls were stamped with the Spalding name (consistent with earlier practice)." The baseballs manufactured by Rawlings Sporting Goods Company in the United States between 1976 and 1979 behaved like the balls manufactured by Spalding Sporting Goods Company prior to that time. The balls manufactured by Rawlings Sporting Goods Company in Haiti between 1980 and 1993 also behaved in a similar manner. But the balls manufactured by Rawlings in Costa Rica between 1994 and 2004 have been a disaster. There have been 35 percent more home runs hit off Costa Rican baseballs than baseballs manufactured between 1961 and 1993. The finished baseballs are tested on an indoor driving machine that shoots a ball from a cannon against a wall made of northern white ash, the same wood used to make bats. Each ball has to rebound at between 0.514 and 0.578 of the initial velocity. At the lower end of the specification, a COR of 0.514, a typical batter would be able to hit a ball 400 feet, while at the high end of the spec, 0.578, that same man could hit the ball 449 feet. It should be no surprise that baseballs can vary by more than 10 percent from one to another.

The National Labor Committee called the Turrealba, Cost Rica, plant where the major league baseballs are manufactured, a sweat shop. Workers in the plant have to hand-sew one baseball every 15 minutes to meet the minimum requirements. They work 10⅔ hours a day, five days a week, and mandatory overtime can occasionally extend the workday to 15 hours. A worker is paid 0.28 cents for every ball stitched, or $44.28 for the weekly minimum of 158 baseballs. A representative for the Labor Committee asked, "How can you expect a worker, who is paid almost minimum wage, and who works ten hours a day, to stitch a ball just as tight at the end of the day when he is tired as he did at the beginning of the day when he was fresh?"

THE EFFECT OF BASEBALL MANUFACTURING ON HOME RUNS

	Home Runs per 154 Games
Balls manufactured by Spalding, 1961–1975	123
Balls manufactured by Rawlings in the U.S., 1976–1979	122
Balls manufactured by Rawlings in Haiti, 1980–1993	123
Balls manufactured by Rawlings in Costa Rica, 1994–2004	166 (+35 percent)

AMERICAN AND NATIONAL LEAGUE
HOME RUN STATISTICS, 1980 TO 2004
(STATISTICS BASED ON A 154-GAME SEASON)

Year	*Teams*	*Games*	*AL HRs*	*NL HRs*	*AVG*
1980	26	162	125	98	110
1981	26	107	109	86	97
1982	26	162	141	103	122
1983	26	162	129	111	120
1984	26	162	134	110	122
1985	26	162	148	112	130
1986	26	162	155	120	138
1987	26	162	179	144	162
1988	26	162	129	101	115
1989	26	162	117	108	113
1990	26	162	122	120	121
1991	26	162	133	113	122
1992	26	162	122	100	111

Year	Teams	Games	AL HRs	NL HRs	AVG
1993	28	162	141	133	137
1994	28	114	171	147	159
1995	28	144	165	146	156
1996	28	162	186	151	169
1997	28	162	168	147	158
1998	30	162	170	151	161
1999	30	162	179	171	175
2000	30	162	183	177	180
2001	30	162	170	174	172
2002	30	162	167	153	160
2003	30	162	170	160	165
2004	30	162	177	168	173

The Resiliency of the Ball

In 1993, the National League averaged 133 home runs per team per 154 games. It has not been below 146 since that time. In 1993, the American League averaged 141 home runs. It has not been below 156 since that time.

A research team at the University of Rhode Island conducted a study in 2000 to compare the resiliency of major league baseballs manufactured in 1963, 1970, 1989, 1995, and 2000. It should be noted that the study was not a scientific study, so it cannot be used as the final word on the characteristics of major league baseballs; but the results are so shocking that it should lead to a thorough scientific study by official agencies. The URI team conducted drop tests from a height of 182 inches. These gave dramatically different results for the 20 balls tested. The balls manufactured in 1963, 1970, and 1989 bounced back 62 inches, while the balls manufactured in 1995 and 2000 bounced back 83 inches. The test results were in perfect agreement with the home runs hit in the major leagues during those years. Balls manufactured in 1963, 1970, and 1989 behaved the same in the bounce tests and they also yielded the same number of home runs in actual major league play. Balls manufactured in 1995 and 2000 behaved like each other and decidedly unlike the other three balls. Their 32 percent increase in resiliency matches the increase in home runs experienced in those years. The URI study also determined that the balls from 1989, 1995, and 2000 contained synthetic fibers in the windings, which is contrary to the specifications that require wool. Also, there was more rubber in the core than is specified. One of the conclusions of the URI research team was that "the manufacturer is not meeting Major League Baseball specifications for the balls. The composition of the inner core yarns includes synthetic fibers, probably polyester. Rawlings specifies woolen yarn for the first, second, and third winds. The 1963 and 1970 balls fit the specifications better than the newer balls." They also said, "The large amount of synthetic fiber in the balls from 1989, 1995, and 2000 is bound to affect the performance of the balls. If the synthetic fiber is polyester as we suspect, then it has good elasticity, resiliency, and loft." Major League Baseball once again denied that anything had been done that would increase the liveliness of the ball.

A research study conducted by the Larchmont Corp. in California in 2000, sponsored by the *Cleveland Plain Dealer* newspaper, tested a new major league baseball and a 1942 ball. Their tests showed the official big league baseballs to fly up to 48 feet farther than a 1942 ball, and concluded that the new big league balls are significantly more lively. Alan Nathan, a physicist at the University of Illinois, was quoted in the *Cleveland Plain Dealer* on September 29, 2000, as saying, "What you can say unequivocally is that the balls you tested [Larchmont] are 'hotter' than the ones they had in play so long ago."

Another study, conducted at the Penn State University, and reported in the *Plain Dealer*, noted that starting around 1970 the big league ball had been pumped up on polymers and manufactured by state-of-the-art machinery. Penn State has scanned more than 100 major league balls dating to the 1930s. David G. Zavagno, the president of Universal Systems, Inc., was quoted as stating, "Clearly the core of the baseball changed with each era, indicating that the baseball was made differently. The cores have changed dramatically from cork to a composite material that resembles rubber. I think that's what's giving the balls additional pop or liveliness."

After listening to a continuous stream of complaints about the liveliness of the base-ball, Major League Baseball commissioned the University of Massachusetts at Lowell to con-duct a study to determine if the baseball used in 2000 was livelier than the baseball used previously. Unfortunately, balls from only two years were tested, the 2000 ball and a 1999 ball. Jim Sherwood, the director of the Baseball Research Center at the university, found no significant difference between the two balls. He did make one startling discovery, how-ever. The specifications for major league baseballs are so loose that two balls, both within specifications, one on the light side and harder, and the other on the heavy side and softer, can vary in batted-ball distance by as much as 49 feet. An online article on the study in AASE Prism magazine noted, "Home runs have been increasing steadily for most of the past decade, not just this season [2000]. Moreover, the study showed that the balls, although within specifications, have COR values toward the higher end of the acceptable range — and no one yet knows how long they have been that way. Testing older balls would be an obvious solution." In other words, the University of Massachusetts study indicated that major league baseballs can be manufactured within the present specifications and still be "juiced."

Jim Kaat, a former major league pitcher who won 283 games during his career, wrote an article for *Popular Mechanics* titled "Baseball's New Baseball," in which he examined the lively ball debate. According to Kaat, major league baseball began using a new ball in 2000, with Bud Selig's name on it (the new baseball commissioner). At the time, MLB spokesman Sandy Alderson echoed the party line that there was no difference in any of the balls, at least as far as MLB specifications are concerned. He may have been right, but it is now known that the specifications are much too generous. Alderson also referred to the COR, which would show if a ball was juiced, but COR has only been in use since the late 1990s, and MLB has not contracted any studies to compare the current ball, such as the 2000 ball or the 2001 ball, with baseballs manufactured over the past century. It would be of inter-est to initiate a study using balls from the 1920s, '30s, '40s, and every other decade through the end of the century. Jim Sherwood at the University of Massachusetts said that type of study couldn't be done because earlier balls were not stored under controlled temperature and humidity conditions. That may be true, and the study might not be perfect as Sher-wood suggested, but it might still shed some light on the problem and expose differences in baseballs from different eras. All balls used in the study could be stored in controlled temperature and humidity conditions for a month or more to allow the balls to equilibrate

Bob Gibson was a fearless warrior, who was particularly effective in the World Series. He went 7–2 in three series, with seven complete games in nine starts (JAY SANFORD).

before testing. And the balls could be scanned, as was done by Penn State University, to compare the construction of the balls from one decade to another. Representative balls from different eras could be dissected to compare the interior of the different baseballs, including the type of core, the type of yarn used, and whether or not there are any synthetic materials in the modern balls. Kaat reported, "Juiced or not, and MLB's position notwithstanding, pitchers, umpires, and coaches—folks who handle the ball every day—say there is a difference. Everyone we spoke to says that the cover is slick. Mike Reilly, who has been an umpire for more than 20 years, thinks so. Before every game, umpires rub up five-dozen brand new balls with a specific mud from the Delaware River to take the shine off. He said that the mud doesn't adhere to the new ball the way it did to the old ball."

In October 2000, Jim Kaat wrote for *Popular Mechanics*: "Cal Eldred, veteran pitcher with the Chicago White Sox, says, 'You used to get a baseball, gather a little perspiration off your brow or off your wrist, rub the ball maybe twice in your palms, and you got the feeling you wanted. Now, I go to my wrists and I rub the ball 10 or 12 times and my hands just keep slipping off it.' With the old ball, a pitcher would mix perspiration with rosin to get the tacky feeling he wanted for better control. That doesn't seem to work with the new baseball."

David Cone and Andy Pettite also feel the ball has changed in recent years. Both told Kaat the ball is smoother and the stitches are flatter than they used to be, and Pettite also feels that the National League ball has higher seams than the American League ball. Kaat, Eldred, Cone and Pettite may be correct in their feeling that the ball has changed, and the problem could be the result of something as simple as the recent practice of machine-rolling the ball after manufacture. As Kaat noted, "Baseball can say all it wants about the components of the ball being the same. Every major league clubhouse I go into provides an opportunity to talk to players who handle the ball, and they all tell me the same thing: there's a slickness to the ball that wasn't there before." Scientific tests were carried out at SGS U.S. Testing Company in Fairlawn, New Jersey, using dozens of 1999 balls and 2000 balls. The test results showed a lower Coefficient of Friction for the new ball, indicating that it has a slicker surface. The tests also measured a higher stitch for the 1999 ball. Once again, the liveliness of balls that fell within the MLB specifications for weight and COR were drastically different depending on the balls. Balls at the lightest (low weight) and liveliest (high COR) ends of the specs traveled about 49.1 feet farther than balls at the heaviest (high weight) and deadest (low COR) end of the specs.

A statement made by Rawlings spokesman Ted Sizemore on the company's website just increases the suspicion about the liveliness of the baseball. Sizemore acknowledged that improved manufacturing techniques have eliminated the soft or "dead" spots that were in vintage baseballs. If the material in the core has changed, if polymers are being used for some of the wool in the windings, if cowhide is being used in place of horsehide, and if "improved manufacturing techniques" such as machine-rolling the baseball after manufacture have eliminated the dead spots in the old baseballs and flattened the seams, it would be a miracle if the liveliness of the ball had not changed over the past 40 or 50 years. Rawlings has stated that the baseball has undergone very little change since the early days of the game, at least in the specifications prescribed in the rules. The last part of that statement also gives cause for concern —"at least in the specifications prescribed in the rules." Without knowing how tight the specifications are, that statement could open a Pandora's box of evil deeds. Both the American and National Leagues have admitted they changed the thickness of the cover and the number of stitches in the seams several times between 1931 and 1939. They have allowed cowhide to be substituted for horsehide in the cover. They have changed the official supplier of baseballs to the major leagues. The manufacturer has twice changed the country where the baseballs are being manufactured. And the manufacturer changed the structure of the core and may have added polymer to the windings of the ball.

Since the Costa Rican baseball has been in routine use, major league batting averages have averaged .267, and teams have averaged 166 home runs per team per 154 games, 762 runs scored per team, and a 4.54 ERA. The year 1930 was known as the Year of the Hitter because of changes in the baseball that allowed hitters to tee off on pitchers with abandon. But 1930 would have been a typical year in today's Costa Rican era. In 1930 the major league batting average was .296, home runs averaged 98 per team, runs scored averaged 856 per team, and the league ERA was 4.81. The Costa Rican period, from 1994 to date, is the most embarrassing period in major league baseball history. Major league baseball appears to have prostituted itself to maximize the number of home runs hit in the leagues at the expense of the game's proud traditions.

Bob Gibson, in his biography *Stranger to the Game*, said, "The honchos in the commissioner's and league offices can keep denying that the ball has been juiced up, but I was taking batting practice before an Equitable game at Busch Stadium a few years ago and deposited one just under the Stadium Club in the upper deck. There's no way in hell I could have done that with the 1968 ball."

And Virgil Trucks seconded that opinion, in his autobiography, when he said, "The ball is more lively now — you can't tell me it isn't when a little guy like Rafael Furcal hits the ball to the opposite field for a home run. They're all going for home runs now — even the little guys."

Baseball Bats

In the early days of the game, players made their own bats. Then, in 1884, Pete "the Gladiator" Browning, a slugging outfielder for the Louisville Colonels in the American Association, broke his favorite bat. He asked Bud Hillerich, a local wood-turner, to make him a new bat. Hillerich obliged and, when Browning went three for three the first day he used the bat, a new industry was born. The 17-year-old Hillerich was soon making bats, called Louisville Sluggers after Browning, for many major league players. The company J.F. Hillerich and Son prospered over the years, with such stars as Ty Cobb and Honus Wagner using Hillerich's bats. Wagner began a new practice when he had his signature burned into his bats in 1905, and soon all the players were following suit. Fred Bradsby, the sales manager for the company, was made a partner in 1916, and the name of the company was changed to the Hillerich and Bradsby Company.

Hillerich's early bats were made from northern white ash, which had the characteristics the ballplayers wanted: light weight and high strength. Today, the white ash comes primarily from the Adirondack Mountains of Pennsylvania and New York. Major league baseball rules governing the characteristics of the bat state that the bat has to be made of one piece of hardwood, with a maximum length of 42 inches and a maximum diameter of 2¾ inches. But within those specifications, considerable personal variations exist. For instance, in the early days, players preferred heavy bats with thick barrels and thick handles so they could be more assured of making contact with the ball. The stigma of striking out was of paramount importance to major league players during the first 90 to 100 years of play. Edd Roush, a career .323 hitter during the 1920s, used one of the heaviest bats on record, a mammoth 48-ounce bludgeon. Babe Ruth used a 44-ounce bat, 36 inches long. He did try a 52-ounce bat one time, but found it too unwieldy. Al Simmons, a .334 hitter and one of the all-time greats, used one of the longest bats on record, a 38-inch weapon weighing 46 ounces. Wee Willie Keeler, a tiny 5' 4" hitting master of the 1890s, had the shortest bat ever used in the major leagues, measuring just 30½ inches. One of the most unusual bats was the famous "bottle" bat of Heinie Groh, a singles-hitting third baseman from 1912 to 1927. Groh's bat had a thick barrel with no taper; it was reduced to a thin handle within just a few inches.

Once the fear of striking out fell by the wayside in the 1970s, the design of baseball bats changed dramatically. A typical major league bat of the 1920s and '30s had a thick handle and weighed as much as 46 ounces, with the average weight about 36–38 ounces. Today's batters prefer lightweight bats weighing 30–32 ounces, about 35" long, with a thin handle that can be whipped rapidly through the strike zone. It has long been believed that a thin-handled, lightweight bat will produce more home runs because of the faster swing-speed at time of contact, but that is not necessarily true. A thin-handled bat will produce more home runs than a thick-handled bat because of the faster swing-speed if everything else is equal. But everything else is not always equal. If the thin-handled bat is lighter in weight than the thick-handled bat, then the advantage of the faster swing-speed will be lost. Newton's second law of motion states that

$$F = MA$$

where

$$F = \text{force}$$
$$M = \text{mass}$$
$$A = \text{acceleration}$$

The force applied to the baseball by the bat is equal to the mass (or weight) of the bat times the acceleration (or swing-speed) of the bat. The force applied to a baseball as the result of the faster swing-speed of a lighter bat may be neutralized by the lighter weight of the bat.

Another popular misconception about the effect that certain changes to the bat have on home runs is that a corked bat will propel a baseball a greater distance than a legal bat. A corked bat is one where a hole is drilled into the top end of the bat and the cavity, usually about 10" deep, is filled with cork or rubber; this results in a lighter-weight bat with faster swing-speed. Alan Nathan, a professor in the Physics Department of the University of Illinois, and an expert on the dynamics of major league baseballs and baseball bats, conducted a study to determine the practical results of corking a bat. He concluded, "We see that corking the bat leads to higher swing-speed but to less efficient bat-ball collision. These two effects roughly cancel each other out, leaving little or no effect on the hit ball speed or on the distance of a long fly ball." He went on to say, "It is quite unlikely that corking the bat will produce any appreciable effect, either of a beneficial or detrimental nature, on the distance of a long fly ball. It is likely to result in higher batting averages for contact-type hitters."

Jim Sherwood at the University of Massachusetts, Lowell, on the other hand, suspects that the bat might contribute to the rapidly increasing home run distance of major league baseballs. *Prism* magazine stated, "Now he [Sherwood] suspects that bats may play a big part. It seems that hitters have been doing a little engineering design work of their own: "Hitters modify the profile of the bat (by sanding or shaving) to increase their swing speed, which may be causing the ball to travel farther."

Ballparks

Major league baseball parks are the smallest they have been in the history of the game. This fact was detailed in my book *Baseball's Other All-Stars*:

It is a fact that the playing field dimensions of modern baseball stadiums are about 20 percent smaller than the playing field dimensions of sixty or eighty years ago. For example, the left-center field power alley in Yankee Stadium was 460 feet in 1923 and 463 feet in 1967. Today, it is a comfortable 399 feet. The right-center field power alley was 429 feet in 1923. Today it is 385 feet. Center field in Shibe Park in Philadelphia was 468 feet until 1956. Forbes Field in Pittsburgh had a left field foul line of 365 feet, power alleys of 406 and 416 feet, left and right, and 435 feet to center field. Griffith Stadium in Washington, D.C., measured 405'–421'–320', left to right in 1950. And the famous Polo Grounds measured 505 feet to straightaway center field in 1949. Today, most parks have 330 foot foul lines and 400 foot center field walls, a veritable chip shot for sluggers like Babe Ruth and Jimmie Foxx.

Baseball parks today resemble Japanese league parks rather than major league parks. In a few more years, if the trend continues, they will be the size of little league parks. The table below shows the average distances in major league parks when Babe Ruth was chasing the home run title, when Roger Maris was chasing it, and when Barry Bonds was chasing it.

MAJOR LEAGUE BASEBALL STADIUM DISTANCES, FEET

Date	LF	LCF	CF	RCF	RF
1927 AL	338	388	446	386	329
1961 AL	336	379	422	380	325
2001 NL	332	373	406	375	330

The dimensions for San Francisco's Pacific Bell Park are more generous than the average National League park:

2001	335	367	404	361	307

The author's recent ballpark study, reported in my *Single Season Home Run Kings*, noted, "In Barry Bonds' case, 15 of his 16 home runs to center field traveled less than 446 feet, and 5 of his 19 home runs to right-center field traveled less than 386 feet. Additionally, two of his home runs to right field would have stayed in the park in Ruth's time." What that means is that if Barry Bonds had hit today's lively baseball in the same parks that Babe Ruth played in, he would have hit 51 home runs in 2001. If those numbers were converted to a common basepoint, under the conditions described above, Bonds would have hit 59 home runs for every 550 at-bats. The Bambino, on the other hand, would have hit 81 home runs.

10

Pitchers and Pitching Strategy

Illegal Pitches

When the trick pitches were banned, 17 spitball pitchers were grandfathered. Burleigh Grimes was last legal spitball pitcher, but the pitch is still part of some pitcher's illegal repertoire. The most notable violators of the rule were Gaylord Perry and Preacher Roe. Roe, who pitched for the Brooklyn Dodgers for six years, told the author the story of his buddy, Billy Cox, who played third base for the team. "Well, I used to throw a 'wet one' once in awhile, but I think it was really overrated. I usually loaded it up myself. It came out better that way. Ole Hoss [Cox] kept trying to load it up for me, but he did a lousy job. He'd come walking over to the mound and hand me the ball dripping with spit. 'How's that, Preach?' I'd say, 'That's good, Billy.' Then I'd wipe it off and start all over again."

The Disappearance of the Complete Game

In the early days of the game, starting pitchers usually pitched the entire game. Old Hoss Radbourne, for instance, completed 97 percent of all the games he started during his major league career. At that time it was not unusual for a pitcher to complete every game he started during a season. But over the years, the number of complete games gradually decreased as the concept of relief pitching became popular. The last pitchers to complete every game they started during a season were Jack Taylor, who started and completed 39 games, and Mordecai "Three-Finger" Brown, who started and completed 24 games in the National League, both in 1905; and 41-year-old Ted Lyons, who started and completed 20 games in the American League in 1942.

A HISTORICAL PERSPECTIVE OF MAJOR LEAGUE COMPLETE GAMES

Year	Percent CG	Year	Percent CG	Year	Percent CG	Year	Percent CG
1895	81	1925	49	1955	30	1985	15
1905	80	1935	45	1965	23	1995	6
1915	53	1945	46	1975	27	2004	5

Bob Feller pitched 36 complete games in 42 starts in 1946, finishing with a record of 26–15 in 371 innings. Over the course of his illustrious career, he threw 279 complete games in 484 starts, a 58 percent complete game percentage. Bob Gibson, one of the modern-day warriors, pitched the St. Louis Cardinals to three National League pennants and two world championships between 1964 and 1968. In 1968 he completed 28 of 34 starts for an 82 percent completion rate. During his 17-year career, he completed 255 of 482 starts, a 53 percent completion rate. As a measure of the disappearing complete game, it is interesting to note that the last pitcher to throw 40 complete games pitched in 1907. The last pitchers to throw 30 complete games pitched in the 1970s. Steve Carlton pitched 30 complete games in 41 starts in 1972. Three years later, in the American League, Catfish Hunter tossed 30 complete games in 39 starts. The last pitchers to throw 20 complete games pitched in the 1980s: Fernando Valenzuela in the National League threw 20 complete games in 34 starts in 1986, and Bert Blyleven in the American League threw 24 complete games in 37 starts in 1985. The last pitchers to throw ten complete games pitched in the 1990s: Randy Johnson in the National League pitched 12 complete games in 1999, and Scott Erickson in the American League pitched 11 complete games in 1998. Now the question is, who will be the last pitcher to throw a complete game in the major leagues?

PITCHING COMPARISONS

Pitcher	Years Pitched	Won	Lost	Percent CG	IPG
Al Spalding	1871–77	252	65	94	8.8
Charles Radbourne	1881–91	309	194	97	8.9
Cy Young	1890–11	511	316	92	8.7
Christy Mathewson	1900–16	373	188	79	8.2
Walter Johnson	1907–27	417	279	80	8.3
Lefty Grove	1925–41	300	141	65	7.8
Bob Feller	1936–56	266	162	58	7.4
Warren Spahn	1942–65	363	245	57	7.5
Bob Gibson	1959–75	251	174	53	7.8
Phil Niekro	1964–87	318	274	34	6.9
Jim Palmer	1965–84	268	152	40	7.4
Steve Carlton	1965–88	329	244	36	7.2
Don Sutton	1966–88	324	256	24	6.9
Tom Seaver	1967–76	311	205	36	7.4
Nolan Ryan	1966–93	324	292	29	6.8
Roger Clemens	1984–04	329	165	19	7.0
Greg Maddux	1986–04	305	174	17	6.9
Curt Schilling	1988–04	184	123	22	7.2
Randy Johnson	1988–04	246	128	19	7.0
Pedro Martinez	1992–04	182	76	13	6.8
Jason Schmidt	1995–04	104	74	7	6.2

KEY:

Percent CG: Percent complete games

IPG: Average number of innings pitched per game

Do Pitchers Pace Themselves?

The idea of a pitcher pacing himself during a game is as old as professional baseball itself. As soon as overhand pitching was legalized in 1884, it became particularly important for a pitcher to conserve his energy if he was to pitch a complete game every few days. One of the first disciples of conserving his energy was Old Hoss Radbourne, according to Roger Kahn in *The Head Game*, who said, "He [Radburne] later learned, he said, to pitch only as hard as the game situation demanded, saving some strength for another day." And Radbourne knew the value of pacing himself better than anyone; in 1884, he pitched a total 678.2 innings in 75 games, while compiling a fantastic 59–12 record. He pitched 40 of his team's last 43 games, averaging four complete games every week down the stretch. His three-quarter underhand delivery put less strain on his arm than an overhand delivery would have, but he still pitched with such severe pain that he couldn't raise his head above his shoulders after a game.

Christy Mathewson noted in his book *Pitching in a Pinch*,

> I have always been against a pitcher pitching himself out, when there is no necessity for it, as so many youngsters do. They burn them through for eight innings and then, when the pinch comes, something is lacking. A pitcher must remember that there are eight other men in the game, drawing more or less salary to stop balls hit at them, and he must have confidence in them. Some pitchers will put all they have on each ball. This is foolish for two reasons. In the first place, it exhausts the man physically and, when the pinch comes, he has not the strength to last it out. But second, and more important, it shows the batters everything that he has, which is senseless. A man should always hold something in reserve, a surprise to spring when things get tight. If a pitcher had displayed his whole assortment to the batters in the early part of the game and has used all his speed and his fastest breaking curve, then, when the crisis comes, he hasn't anything to fall back on.

In the years before night baseball was in vogue, it was particularly important for a pitcher to pace himself if he expected to pitch a complete game. In those days, when all the games were played during the day, the summer heat could be oppressive, especially in cities such as St. Louis and Cincinnati. Billy Herman, the second baseman for the Chicago Cubs during the 1930s, reminisced with Donald Honig:

> Here's how you went from Chicago to St. Louis to Cincinnati — and I'm talking about July and August when it's always 90 or more degrees. You got on a train at midnight, and maybe that train has been sitting in the yards all day long, under a broiling sun. It feels like 150 degrees in that steel car. You get into St. Louis at six thirty in the morning, grab your own bag, fight to get a cab, and go to the hotel. It's seven thirty and you have an afternoon ball game to play. So you hurry into the dining room — and it's hot in there, no air conditioning — and you eat and run upstairs and try to get a few hours' rest. Then you go to the ballpark, where it's about 110 degrees. You finish the game about five or five thirty and go into the clubhouse. It's around 120 degrees in there. You take your shower, but there's no way you can dry off; the sweat just keeps running off you. You get back to the hotel and go up to your room. You try to sleep but you can't because you're sweating so much. This goes on for four days in St. Louis, and you go on to Cincinnati, and it's the same thing. For eight days you haven't had a decent night's sleep.

To make matters worse, the players wore flannel uniforms that soaked up the sweat and made them feel like they were carrying 100-pound monkeys on their backs. Modern-

Randy Johnson, at 6' 10", may be the game's greatest modern-day pitcher (JAMES R. MADDEN, JR.).

day players have it much easier. The travel is faster and more comfortable. Hotels, clubhouses, taxicabs, and restaurants, are air-conditioned. The uniforms are made from lightweight, comfortable cotton. And most games are played in the cool of the evening.

Major League umpire Tom Gorman once told Jerome Holtzman, as reported by James and Neyer, "Gibson knew how to pace himself. He was one of the very few pitchers whose fastball was as good in the eighth and ninth innings as it was in the first and second."

Bob Feller said he paced himself whenever he had the opportunity. If he had a lead in the middle innings, on a hot day, he would try to get the batter to hit his first or second pitch in order to conserve his energy.

Randy Johnson, in his book *Power Pitching*, said he didn't think he paced himself, but his statements indicate otherwise. At one point Johnson said, "Every pitch I throw, from the first to the last, is at maximum effort. Forget about pacing yourself. Pacing yourself for what?" But then he went on to say, "Your goal is to throw as few pitches as possible. ... I don't like goofing around. The fewer pitches it requires to get the guy out, the stronger I'll be if I'm fortunate enough to be pitching later in the game." It is obvious from Johnson's statements that he concentrated on getting the batter to hit his first or second pitch, to conserve his energy. He did throw with maximum effort on every pitch, as he noted, but he was also unconsciously pacing himself with his pitch selection and location.

A.J. Burnett of the Florida Marlins also paces himself by pitching efficiently and making quality pitches, as reported by Steve DiMeglio in his article "A Whole New Ballgame," in *Sports Weekly*:

> The new approach just comes with experience, Burnett says.
>
> "When I'd get into jams in the past, I'd reach back and try and throw the ball in the mid–100's," says Burnett, who earned his first complete-game victory in more than three years April 12 in an 8–2 win against Philadelphia. In that game, he didn't walk a batter and didn't have a strikeout until the sixth.
>
> "I'd get into situations and it'd be harder, harder, harder. Now I have confidence in my stuff, mixing up off-speed pitches in fastball counts. I'll take ground-ball outs every time."
>
> Josh Beckett seconded that approach. "We're pounding the strike zone, and we're throwing to quality spots. You just can't throw the ball down the middle of the plate. And we have the best defense in baseball behind us." And Dontrelle Willis added, "We have Gold Glovers all around. It makes us more efficient with all our pitches. We can go out there and look for contact early. The way they play behind us, you almost want them to hit the ball early."

John Thorn examined the disappearance of the complete game, the ability of a pitcher to pace himself, and the availability of a bullpen in his book *The Relief Pitcher*. At one point he said,

> If a man has the ability to go nine, these men [former pitchers] imply, he does not need to be relieved. The simplicity of that view is appealing and the logic seems unassailable, but the fault lies in the word ability. If the ability to go nine is found less frequently than it once was, this may be because modern managers have placed less value on it. Today's very best starters know how to coast in spots to make sure they have something left for the last three innings; a Tom Seaver or a Jim Palmer will strive for a complete game as a matter of professional pride. But on a team blessed with a strong bullpen crew, a manager is quite content to get seven good innings from his starter (Gaylord Perry, winner of the 1978 Cy Young Award in the National League, completed only 5 of his 37 starts). Accordingly, most of today's starters scorn pace and go as hard as they can as long as they can."

Pitch Counts and Pitch Count Limits

Johnny Pesky, who has been around baseball as a player and a coach for over 60 years, believes the pitch count limit helps a pitcher. Obviously, modern-day pitchers throw more pitches in a complete game than their predecessors did 50, 60, or 70 years ago. Part of that increase is the result of the lively ball, which causes pitchers to pitch more carefully. But there is another reason for the increase that is not directly connected with the lively ball. Beginning in the early 1950s, hitters began emulating Pittsburgh Pirates home run king Ralph Kiner, as noted earlier. His now-famous "Cadillac" comment spawned a generation of Kiner wannabees, whose main objective was to hit every ball out of the park. The big bombers of the '70s, '80s, '90s, and '00s swing at anything that moves, fouling off numerous pitches and striking out five times as often as they homer. The result is that pitchers' strikeouts have increased dramatically, but have done so at the expense of their pitch count.

The top strikeout pitchers in modern baseball history are Rube Waddell, Walter Johnson, Lefty Grove, Bob Feller, Sandy Koufax, Nolan Ryan, and Randy Johnson. In rating the top strikeout pitchers, it is not possible to rate them on total strikeouts per se, due to the many strategic and philosophical changes, as well as the number of rules changes, that have taken place in the major leagues over the past 130 years. Each pitcher has to be compared to his peers. Then the ratings of the different pitchers can be compared to determine who is the greatest strikeout pitcher in baseball history. Nolan Ryan, of course, holds the major league single-season strikeout record, with 383 strikeouts in 1973, eclipsing Sandy Koufax's National League record by one. Ryan also holds the major league career strikeout record with an incredible 5,714 strikeouts, surpassing Walter Johnson's long-time record by a whopping 2,205 strikeouts. In fact, "the Big Train," who held the major league record for more than 50 years, now finds himself in ninth place on the all-time strikeout list, having been passed by eight pitchers who are members of the free-swinging generation. Randy Johnson, the 6' 10" gunslinger from Walnut Creek, California, holds the record per-game average with 11.2 strikeouts per game. He is followed by Nolan Ryan with 9.5 strikeouts per game and Sandy Koufax with 9.3 strikeouts per game. But, by putting all pitchers on a level field by comparing them with their peers, a different picture emerges. Nolan Ryan, over the course of his career, struck out 89 percent more batters than the league average, while Randy Johnson struck out 87 percent more than the league average. Those numbers were good, but they weren't good enough to put the two flamethrowers at the top of the list. The number-one strikeout pitcher of all time, based on a comparison of his numbers to those of his contemporaries, was Rube Waddell, the eccentric southpaw for Connie Mack's Philadelphia Athletics. Waddell exceeded the league strikeout number by 95 percent. The top strikeout pitchers, with their career average strikeouts per game and their percent strikeout increase over the league average, are as follows:

	SO/G	Percent Increase
Rube Waddell	7.0	95%
Nolan Ryan	9.5	89%
Randy Johnson	11.2	87%
Sandy Koufax	9.3	69%
Lefty Grove	5.2	68%
Pedro Martinez	10.5	67%
Bob Feller	6.1	61%
Walter Johnson	5.3	55%
Roger Clemens	8.6	37%
Curt Schilling	8.8	35%

The following table summarizes the average number of pitches thrown in the major leagues over the years. It also shows the corresponding number of home runs hit by each team over a 154-game season.

Year	P/G	HR/154G
1905	117	21
1915	120	24
1925	—	73
1935	122	83
1945	—	63
1955	128	139

Year	P/G	HR/154G
1965	—	134
1975	130	107
1985	—	131
1996	138	168
2003	135	165

KEY:

P/G: Average Number of Pitches per Game, per Pitcher.

HR/154G: Average Number of Home Runs per Team, per 154-Game Schedule.

The following table shows the estimated number of pitches for a nine-inning game for selected pitchers.

Pitcher	P/G
Roger Clemens	138
Bob Feller	137
Greg Maddux	120
Warren Spahn	118
Pedro Martinez	139
Curt Schilling	132
Randy Johnson	153
1988–1993	161
1994–2003	151
Grover Cleveland Alexander	108
Walter Johnson	117
Lefty Grove	140
Sandy Koufax	142
1955–1960	160
1961–1966	134
Bob Gibson	132
Christy Mathewson	111
Steve Carlton	135
Tom Seaver	128
Cy Young	106
Nolan Ryan	160
Jack Stivetts	127
Kid Nichols	112

Don Newcombe, in an attempt to be a modern Iron Man, started both ends of a September 6, 1950, doubleheader against the Philadelphia Phillies during a pressure-packed pennant race. He pitched a complete game in the opener, winning 2–0. In the nightcap, he pitched seven innings, leaving with a 2–0 deficit. The Dodgers scored three runs in the ninth to win the game 3–2. Overall, Newcombe pitched 16 innings, yielding two runs on 11 base hits, while striking out three men and walking just two. It was estimated that he threw 159 pitches during his gutsy performance, conserving his energy and minimizing his pitch count by not forcing strikeouts.

Daniel R. Levitt compared the pitch counts from the 1919 World Series to the pitch counts from the 1997 World Series. He found that there were approximately 118 pitches thrown per game in 1919 versus 160 pitches thrown per game in 1997. The major reason for the large increase was the higher number of bases-on-balls issued in 1997 and the higher number of strikeouts registered in 1997.

One reason for the conservative pitch count limit of 100 pitches per game per pitcher is the interest of team owners in protecting the arms of their valuable property. Another reason is the concern of agents to protect the arms of their clients, in order to maximize the length of their client's careers. But there is no evidence that these conservative approaches to the game are beneficial to the health of the pitcher. In fact, the oppo-

Don Newcombe was the last pitcher to attempt an Iron-Man feat, starting both ends of a doubleheader against the Philadelphia Phillies during the heat of the 1950 pennant race (AUTHOR'S COLLECTION).

site may be true. Pitchers may not be in the best physical condition to throw 100⁺ pitches a game, and may be more susceptible to injuring their arms when they are forced to bear down in the late innings of a game.

Leo Mazzone believes that pitch counts make sense, but that each pitcher has his own pitch count limit. He has said, "Maddux may be done at 110 pitches. Smoltz will usually still have something left past that point. Glavine can usually go further than 100 pitches. Neagle is borderline at 100 pitches. We have a magic number — about 125 pitches — per start, and that's as far as anyone is going with the Braves. It's usually not a good idea to get into the 140–150 pitch range. But of course, there are exceptions to every rule. Smoltz threw 140 pitches in a 2–0 shutout of the Dodgers."

There is some indication that, as the 2005 season got underway, the era of the low pitch-counts may be coming to an end. Jack McKeon, the manager of the 2003 world champion Florida Marlins, voiced his irritation with the modern pitch-count philosophy, as reported by Steve DiMeglio:

If you've got the time and want to set him off, just ask him about pitch counts. Then buckle up, because one of his pet peeves are the pitch limits many organizations impose on their young pitchers. His disdain for them puts him strongly at odds with today's prevailing wisdom, which holds that young arms are a precious commodity to be protected, not abused.

"My pitchers don't worry about pitch counts. They worry about getting hitters out," McKeon says. "The only people who worry about pitch counts are writers, TV broadcasters, and the guys wearing three-piece suits. ... Too many organizations don't allow the guys in the minor leagues to pitch the innings. They baby them. ... A lot of guys who have never put on a uniform, know all the answers."

DiMeglio went on to say,

McKeon had to go on the defensive when critics questioned his motives, insisting that instead of squeezing an extra 15 or 20 pitches in the ninth inning now, he should save the starter's arm for later.

Hogwash, McKeon says. He believes pitchers are more likely to stay healthy if they throw a lot. That's why, the past two springs, he's had the starters on a four-day rotation the first few weeks of exhibition games.

Four-Man vs. Five-Man Pitching Rotation

Johnny Pesky believes the five-man rotation protects a pitcher's arm. Maybe. Maybe not. Years ago, pitchers pitched in a four-man rotation and were available for relief duty on their second day between starts. Testimony from pitchers who pitched in a four-man rotation, which will be admitted in the next chapter, was almost unanimously in favor of the four-man rotation. Also, the statistics that are available indicate there are proportionately more arm injuries now than there were years ago, as shown in the following table.

Year	No. of Teams	Total No. of Pitchers	No. of Pitchers on D.L.	% Pitchers on D.L.
1933	16	86		
1944	16	127		
1953	16	154	5	3
1959	16	195	14	7
1964	20	221	38	17
1972	24	263	62	24
1981	26	330	165	50
2004	30	342	248	73

The increased number of injuries may be due to the fact that today's pitchers are being babied, and are not in condition to pitch deep into a game, as noted previously. Or it may be due to the fact that, as was also noted previously, both team owners and player's agents are being very conservative in their approach to a pitcher's health, and if he is not 100 percent, placing him on the disabled list. Years ago, pitchers pitched while hurt as a matter of routine. Today, at the slightest twinge, they shut it down.

Another proponent of the four-man pitching rotation is Atlanta Braves pitching coach Leo Mazzone. In his book *Pitch Like a Pro*, Mazzone noted,

A funny thing happened when the five-man rotation came into vogue. The quality of pitching began to slide a little, and you started to hear about a lot of pitchers getting arm injuries. I was a minor league pitcher for many years, and I had experience with both the four and five-man rotation. I always felt that I stayed sharper — and felt better — in a four-man rotation. The idea behind the five-man rotation was to protect pitchers by giving them an extra day of rest between starts. In reality, this coddling of pitchers did just the opposite.

Mazzone could not dictate the rotation to be used in Atlanta. He had to work with a five-man rotation, so he adjusted for the extra day of rest by having his pitchers throw off the mound twice between starts, keeping their arms fresh. Mazzone went on to say, "The pitchers loved it! And the guys whom I worked with went to the post consistently for years— there were no sore arms whatsoever. I can't remember having any sore arms, from 'A' ball all the way through my eight years of coaching at the major league level with the Braves."

The Key to Pitching Winning Baseball: Pitching Inside and Throwing Strikes

If you want to be a winning pitcher, you have to pitch inside. But that is difficult to do today because the umpire will give a pitcher a warning if he pitches inside, and the second time the pitcher does it, he will be ejected from the game. Today, the plate belongs to the batter, and he inches closer and closer to the plate without fear of being hit by a pitch, so he can hit the outside pitch with all the power he can muster.

In the old days, the inside of the plate belonged to the pitcher, and the batter was responsible for protecting himself from errant pitches caused by the wildness of the pitcher. Thousands of times over the past century, batters have been hit by pitched balls, and quite a few of them have been hit in the head, the most notable one in recent memory being Mike Piazza, who was decked by Roger Clemens. But according to baseball historians, no pitcher has ever intentionally thrown a ball at a batter's head. There have been many batters hit intentionally over the years, but the errant balls have been thrown at the batter's body. Branch Rickey, who was part of the major league scene from 1905 until his death in 1965, stated in his book *The American Diamond*,

> The high fast inside pitch is a purpose pitch. It is the strikeout pitch of all ages. After you set up a batter by working around the area of the strike zone, high and inside is the strikeout pitch. But I don't think there is a pitcher in all of baseball who voluntarily and intentionally throws at a batter's head with the full intention of hitting him in the head. And furthermore, no one in the history of baseball has ever been hit on the head by a pitch that was thrown as high as a batter's head when he is set in the batters box. When a batter takes his stride into a pitch, his head moves lower. The Carl Mays pitch that hit Chapman and killed him was chest-high.

F.C. Lane, in *Batting*, examined the dangers associated with inside pitches: "Fear of being hit by a pitched ball is one of the least obvious but still important factors in batting. This fear impels the player to commit both mental and physical faults. In the mental field, it shakes his confidence in himself and disturbs the calm, concentrated mind, which is the proper mental attitude of the batter at the plate. Physically it is a constant urge upon the batter to pull away from the plate and, as the saying is, to hit with 'one foot in the water bucket.'" The testimony of many players in the 1920s indicated that the players considered the act to be accidental, but painful, as noted by Cincinnati Reds first baseman Jake Daubert, a lifetime .303 hitter, who had just recovered from a beaning, in F.C. Lands' *Batting*:

> This is the eighth time I have been beaned since I joined the National League. There are seven pitchers who have the honor or distinction of bouncing a baseball off my cranium. I say seven because Big Jeff Tesreau, when he was with the Giants, did it twice. Either I am getting old or a few rivets have worked loose in my skull, or Sothoron put more steam on that ball than I thought. Anyway, this eighth experience of mine was the worst of the lot. For several hours, I couldn't see. And when my sight did return, it kept coming and going like switching an electric light on and off. Besides, blood oozed out of my ears and I developed a first-class headache, which lasted for three weeks. I tried various remedies, but the thing that seemed to produce the best results was a simple massage.

Later Lane said, "The prime cause of hit batsmen is, of course, pitching wildness. Dazzy Vance said, 'Look up my record. When I was in St. Joe, I gave 110 bases on balls and I hit 25 batters, 10 of them on the head. I had nothing against these batters, you understand. They simply couldn't seem to get out of my way fast enough. It always gave me the cold creeps to hit a batter on the head." Duster Mails, another famous wild man, seconded that opinion: "Anybody who stood up to the plate when I was pitching in Brooklyn was in danger." And no batter is free of the concerns of standing at the plate waiting to hit. Even the great Ty Cobb had anxious moments. "Walter Johnson, for a long time, had me buffaloed. I wouldn't admit it to anyone else, and I don't think I ever showed it. But I had a dread amounting to almost positive fear of his fastball. I have a vivid recollection of how it seemed to me when I faced Walter. That accursed fastball of his used to whistle when it shot past. I found myself unconsciously speculating on just what would happen if that ball hit me on the head. It wasn't a pretty picture."

Van Lingle Mungo was a high-kicking, right-handed flamethrower for the Brooklyn Dodgers from 1932 through 1941, during which time he won 102 games against 99 losses. One day, according to Maury Allen in *You Could Look It Up: The Life of Casey Stengel*, Tony Cuccinello was reminiscing about an incident that took place in 1934:

> We were playing the Cubs one day and they were a real good ball club. They had won in '32 and had most of the same guys in '34. We were getting the hell knocked out of us, 10–1 in the first game and about 12–2 late in the second game. Casey was up and down that bench screaming like it was 1–1 in the ninth inning. The rest of us were pretty quiet. The big, Chicago pitcher, Lon Warneke, the guy with that high kick, had nailed a couple of our guys. Stengel thought we were too timid about it. "Do I have anybody here who will take a crack at them?" All of a sudden, Van Mungo, our best pitcher, says, "I'll take a crack at them, skip." He got up, picked up his glove, and went to the bullpen. He threw a few pitches and Casey called him in. He hit Gabby Hartnett right in the ribs with his first pitch. Mungo was a little smashed when he did that, see, because he had pitched the day before and he was known to take a drink once in a while after a game. I don't think Mungo could ever do anything wrong in Casey's eyes after that.

Another Casey Stengel tale involved legendary southpaw Warren Spahn. During a spring training exhibition game in 1942, Stengel ordered the 20-year-old rookie to hit Dodgers shortstop Pee Wee Reese with a pitch. Spahn refused. Stengel ordered him again to do it. Again Spahn refused. The disgusted Boston Braves manager called Spahn gutless, and said he would never make a major league pitcher. He banished the kid to the minor leagues before the season started, and Spahn responded with a fine 17–12 record for

Hartford in the Eastern League before joining the army. He served three years with distinction during World War II, particularly at the famous battle at the Remagen bridge, where he was slightly wounded, and where he became the only major league player who was given a battlefield commission as a second lieutenant. The stylish left-hander went on to enjoy 13 20-win seasons in the major leagues during a memorable 21-year, Hall-of-Fame career. Stengel went on to have a Hall-of-Fame career of his own, winning five consecutive world championships with the New York Yankees. Later Spahn would say, "I played for Casey before and after he was a genius."

Bob Gibson believes that several recent changes in the game, including lowering the pitcher's mound, reducing the size of the strike zone, and ordering the umpires to crack down on brushback pitches, have been detrimental to the game. In Gibson's mind, the changes have reduced pitchers to being little more than a feeder, a relic of the 1850s. The St. Louis Cardinals legend commented on one issue in particular:

> By looking closely at just one issue — pitching inside — it can be easily perceived how financial considerations have dominated the scene. Owners are against inside pitches because they threaten to nick their million-dollar investments. The whim of the owners of course trickles down to the umpires, whose warnings to pitchers lead the batters to believe that they are well protected at the plate. Nowadays the umpires can eject a pitcher for throwing at a batter even without warning him first. All of this not only gives the batter a false sense of security — accidents happen — but makes them indignant and ready to fight if a pitch merely sounds too close. Some of the pitches that are starting fights these days are only three or four inches off the plate. A few years ago, Kevin Mitchell of the Giants charged the mound after Bruce Hurst of the Padres hit him in the foot with a pitch that first bounced in the dirt. What the hell?
>
> ... Pitchers, on the whole, are so reluctant now to brush hitters back — reluctant even to defend their teammates— that many hitters, on the rare occasions they are knocked down or pitched tight, feel their only recourse is to charge the mound. To avoid this, pitchers keep the ball away from the hitters and the hitters take their whacks and the battle between them becomes less and less compelling as the cycle plays on and the years pass.

Gibson also told a story about Stan Williams, a character who pitched in the "old days"— the 1960s. Williams, as the story goes, kept a list of all the pitchers who hit him, and he kept each name on his list until he gained revenge. One year, after being traded, he was pitching batting practice to his new team when, all of a sudden, he sent one of his fellow pitchers sprawling in the dirt with a well-aimed pitch to the ribs. After the pitcher picked himself up, he asked Williams what the problem was, to which Williams replied, "You were the last one on my list." That couldn't happen today.

Over the years, there have been many so-called headhunters on the mound in the major leagues, but most of them just wanted what belonged to them — the inside corner of the plate. Some of the more notorious headhunters include Don Drysdale, Bob Gibson, Sal "the Barber" Maglie, and Roger Clemens. It's no surprise that Don Drysdale hit more batters per game than most other pitchers in the study. He was fast, he had a nasty side-arm, buggy-whip delivery that sent the ball hurtling plateward from the direction of third base, and he was mean. His teammate Tommy Davis told the author, "The key to hitting Drysdale is to hit him before he hits you." And Davis was serious. Jack Lang, in "These Were Baseball's Eleven Meanest Pitchers" in the January 1989 *Baseball Digest*, told a story about Walter Alston, the Dodgers manager, ordering Drysdale to walk a batter intentionally. Instead of walking him, Drysdale hit him, and then told the manager he saved three pitches by hitting him. One year, National League president Warren Giles said he was going to fine Drysdale $50 every time he hit a batter, to which Drysdale confided to teammates, "It looks like I'm going to be sending Mister Giles a lot of money this year." The list at the end of this section shows the number of batters hit by many of the pitchers in this study, as well as their frequency of hitting batters. And Big D is number two in hit-batter frequency.

Bob Gibson is also no surprise. He, like Drysdale, was fast and mean. He claimed the inside of the plate, and he wouldn't let any hitter get close to it. A reporter, noting his attitude toward opposing batters, once said he thought Gibson would hit his own mother, to which Gibson replied, "I would if she crowded the plate." In his autobiography, Gibson noted, "It was said that I threw, basically, five pitches. I don't believe that assessment did me justice, though. I actually used about nine pitches—two different fastballs, two sliders, a curve, a changeup, knockdown, brushback, and hit-batsman." One day, Gibson watched as a Los Angeles Dodgers batter dug himself a good toehold. After a few minutes, Gibson yelled in to the batter, "You'd better dig it deep because you're going to be in it after the pitch." Gibson fired the ball at the batter with a three-quarter delivery that was thrown with such effort that he hurled himself toward first base in his follow through.

Sal "the Barber" Maglie considered the batter to be his enemy, and he always wanted to keep the upper hand in the battle between them. He was another pitcher who demanded the inside of the plate, and any batter who got too close to it would feel a little "chin music" from the master. He wasn't called the Barber for nothing. Maglie was primarily a curveball pitcher who delivered his pitches from different angles, from straight overhand to sidearm. He had a fastball and a change, but it was his curveballs that won the day for the tall right-hander. And as Branch Rickey noted, the high-inside pitch was one of the most important pitches in his repertoire. In classic fashion, he would set the batter up with a high inside fastball and then finish him with a low outside curveball. Maglie never shaved on the day he was pitching. He always had a five-o'clock shadow, which made him look meaner than usual, and he used it to his advantage. As he said, "When I'm pitching, I own the plate," as quoted in Shatzkin.

Elden Auker, a submarine pitcher who starred for the Detroit Tigers in the 1930s and '40s, also felt he owned the plate. He was never among the leaders in hit batters, but he would send the batter diving for cover if he got too close to the plate. And Charlie Root was another tough pitcher who always challenged the hitter, who took no quarter and asked none. Root was the victim of Babe Ruth's so-called "called shot" in the 1932 World Series, but Root always objected to the validity of the account. Gold and Ahrens quoted Root as saying, "He didn't point. If he had, I'd have knocked him on his fanny. I'd have loosened him up. I took my pitching too seriously to have anybody facing me do that."

Don Drysdale and Randy Johnson are among the leaders in hit-batter frequency, but they have to take a back seat to Pedro Martinez of the Boston Red Sox when it comes to hitting the target. The frail looking pitcher from the Dominican Republic has hit 115 batters through the 2004 season. Pedro is another player who feels the plate belongs to the pitcher, and he is determined to claim what is rightfully his. His fastball rides in on right-handed batters, and the 5' 10", 170-pound pitcher takes full advantage of it. The strategy obviously works for Martinez because his 13-year win-loss record is a brilliant 182–76, with a 2.71 earned run average. His .705 winning percentage is the best ever in baseball history

Sal "The Barber" Maglie claimed the inside of the plate, often giving batters a "close shave" (AUTHOR'S COLLECTION).

and, if he can maintain it throughout his career, he will become the first pitcher with a career .700[+] winning percentage.

The following table shows the number of hit batters and the hit-batter frequency of some of the game's greatest pitchers. It should come as no surprise that many of the pitchers most likely to hit a batter threw sidearm, with their pitches coming at the batter from the batter's backside, in the case of a right-handed pitcher throwing to a right-handed

Pedro Martinez presently owns the game's highest career winning record, a glittering .705 (Julie Cordeiro).

batter, or from the batter's front in the case of a left-handed batter. Some of the more notable sidearm pitchers were Old Hoss Radbourne, Walter Johnson, Don Drysdale, and Ewell "the Whip" Blackwell.

Some of the meanest pitchers in the annals of the game do not appear on the leader's list for hit-batter frequency because they established a reputation for themselves, and once they had done that, batters kept their distance from the plate. One prime example is Pat Malone, who was voted the meanest pitcher ever to play the game by a panel of several dozen former major league players, including Tim McCarver, Leo Durocher, and Billy

Herman, in a *Baseball Digest* poll in 1988. Jack Lang, writing in the magazine, quoted Leo Durocher, a tough street kid from Springfield, Massachusetts, who fought his way through the major leagues as both a player and a manager from 1925 to 1973, describing his first experience with Malone. Durocher said,

> Gabby Hartnett is catching and he warns me not to dig in against Pat. But I do it anyway. The first pitch is right down the middle and I take a good swing at it. Naturally, I miss it. That got Malone mad. 'You're swinging pretty good, kid,' he yells at me. 'Try hitting this one.' He knocks me down on the next three pitches. Then, on the fourth one, he hits me. That was my experience with Pat Malone."

Billy Jurges, a teammate of Malone's, had this to say in the January 1989 *Baseball Digest*: "He wanted to kill you when he got between the lines. He threw at your head. When he was sober, he was the nicest guy in the world. But he drank pretty good and he wasn't often sober. And when he was in that condition on the mound, it was worth your life to face him." Tony Cuccinello, in the January 1989 *Baseball Digest*, explained why Malone wasn't among the leaders in hit-batter frequency. "You didn't give him a chance to hit you. You stayed loose when Pat was pitching because you knew what was coming."

Lefty Grove was one of the meanest pitchers ever to toe a mound, and he talked tough to Donald Honig. "Never bothered me who was up there at bat. I'd hit 'em in the middle of the back, or hit 'em in the foot, it didn't make any difference to me. But I'd never throw at a man's head. In all my years, I've thrown at guys, but never at their heads. Never believed in it." The truth is the flamethrowing Grove intimidated batters, but over the course of 17 years, he actually hit very few of them, as the chart below shows.

Pitcher	G	GS	IP	HB	HB/G
C. Radbourne	527	502	4,527	54(Inc)	0.31
Cy Young	906	815	7,356	163	0.20
W. Johnson	802	666	5,914	205	0.31
C. Mathewson	636	552	4,789	59	0.11
G. C. Alexander	696	600	5,190	70	0.12
L. Grove	616	457	3,941	42	0.10
B. Feller	570	484	3,827	60	0.14
D. Drysdale	518	465	3,084	154	0.45
B. Gibson	528	482	3,884	102	0.24
E. Blackwell	236	169	1,321	44	0.29
S. Koufax	397	314	2,324	18	0.07
T. Seaver	656	647	4,783	76	0.14
N. Ryan	807	773	5,386	158	0.26
R. Clemens	640	639	4,493	147	0.29
R. Johnson	489	479	3,368	156	0.42
P. Martinez	388	321	2,296	115	0.45
G. Maddux	608	604	4,182	118	0.25

KEY:

G: Games pitched   **IP:** Innings pitched   **HB/G:** Hit batters per nine-
GS: Games started   **HB:** Hit batters   inning game

Pitchers, in addition to claiming the inside of the plate as their domain, also have to be able to throw strikes if they expect to win in the major leagues. Many pitchers today are power pitchers who relish blowing batters away with their heat. Unfortunately, their heat doesn't hit the strike zone very often, and they struggle through mediocre careers as journeyman pitchers. Jim Kaplan, in his biography of Lefty Grove, noted,

If you throw a strike on the first pitch, you should retire the batter about eighty percent of the time. Leo Mazzone, pitching coach of the Atlanta Braves, baseball's dominant pitching staff of the 1990's, compiled first-pitch effectiveness. To take a mid-decade sample, in 1994 the Braves' Greg Maddux threw 524 first-pitch strikes and allowed only 31 hits on those at-bats. Tom Glavine was 415 and 35, Steve Avery 360 and 22, John Smoltz 339 and 21, and Kent Mercker 239 and 17. 'People claim Maddux threw inside,' Mazzone says. 'That's nonsense. He put himself in position to pitch inside by getting ahead on the count. Once you're 0–1, you can expand your strike zone and change speeds.' On the other hand, some eighty percent of all walks occur after a ball on the first pitch. Makes you wonder why major leaguers throw strikes on only slightly more than fifty percent of their first pitches.

The careers of three of baseball's legendary southpaw pitchers, Lefty Grove, Sandy Koufax, and Randy Johnson, confirm that theory. All three men had problems throwing strikes early in their careers, and they were just average pitchers until they learned to get the ball over the plate, after which they became three of the greatest pitchers in the annals of the game. During his first five years in the majors, Randy Johnson walked an average of six men a game, while compiling a record of 49–48. Over his last 13 years, the big flamethrower has produced 197 wins against just 80 losses, a .711 winning percentage, while walking only two batters for every nine innings. He has also struck out an average of 11 men a game over that period. Lefty Grove had a similar experience. He walked an average of five men a game during his first two years with the Philadelphia Athletics, with a combined record of 23–25. Once he mastered the art of getting the ball over the plate, he was almost unbeatable, going 277–116, a .705 winning percentage, striking out five men and walking just two. The Dodgers' Sandy Koufax had a similar experience, but it went on much longer than either Grove's or Johnson's. Koufax struggled with his control for six years as he tried to throw every pitch as hard as he could. All he accomplished for his wasted energy was mediocrity. He ran up a record of 36–40, striking out six men a game and walking five. When he finally stopped being a thrower and became a pitcher, in 1961, he became one of the greatest in baseball history. Over the next six years, before his retirement from the game at the age of 31 because of an arthritic elbow, Koufax won 129 games against just 47 losses, for a spectacular .733 winning percentage. And he upped his strikeout average to 10.5 strikeouts a game, with just two bases-on-balls. In fact, in his last four years, Sandy averaged 27 wins, 7 losses, a 1.85 earned run average, and 9.3 strikeouts against 1.9 walks a game.

After Randy Johnson became a pitcher instead of just a thrower, he outlined his pitching philosophy in his book *Randy Johnson's Power Pitching*: "Your job is to throw off the timing of the hitter.... Outsmarting the hitter is one of the most gratifying aspects of pitching.... A pitcher has to be aggressive. He has to be intimidating. To be intimidating, you have to pitch inside.... I'm a firm believer that you have to establish that you own the inside of the plate."

Relief Pitchers and Closers

During the first half of the twentieth century, there weren't many relief specialists in the major leagues, so starting pitchers were recruited to stem the tide of an opponent's late-inning uprising, or to enter a game in the early innings in an emergency. One of the top relief pitchers early in the century was Mordecai "Three-Finger" Brown, the workhorse of the Chicago Cubs pitching staff. He relieved in 149 games over his 14-year major league career, in addition to starting 332 games. The 5' 10", 175-pound right-hander recorded 49 saves during his career, leading the league in saves four consecutive years from 1908 to 1911. In 1909, in addition to leading the league in saves, he also led the league in victories with 27, complete games with 32, and innings pitched with 343.

Two other notable starting pitchers, who also did yeoman's work out of the bullpen, were Lefty Grove and Virgil "Fire" Trucks. Jim Kaplan noted Grove's willingness to relieve, in his biography of the Philadelphia immortal: "Happy to relieve, Grove pitched eight times in ten games over eleven days early in 1933, winning four, saving four." During his 17-year career, the Philadelphia A's southpaw started 457 games and relieved in 159 others. This is his record as a relief pitcher:

G	IP	W	L	SV	ERA
159	377.2	32	22	55	2.84

Virgil "Fire" Trucks started 328 games in 17 years and relieved in 189. This is his relief record:

G	IP	W	L	SV	ERA
189		31	18	30	

Relief pitchers in the '40s and '50s were still primarily starting pitchers doing double-duty if the game was on the line. The regular bullpen pitchers were journeyman pitchers who were used in mop-up situations or games that had gotten out of hand. Bob Feller, for instance, relieved in 83 games over his career, with 21 saves. His teammate Bob Lemon relieved in 110 games between 1946 and 1958, saving 22. And Warren Spahn relieved in 85 games between 1942 and 1965, saving 29. Starting pitchers were usually on a four-day rotation in the 1930s, '40s, and '50s. So, on the day following their scheduled start, they rested. On the second day, they went down to the bullpen. If the game was close in the late innings, they were available to enter the game in relief. If they weren't needed in the game, they would usually throw from 10 to 20 minutes in the bullpen as part of their normal conditioning program. On the third day, they would do wind sprints and engage in some soft tossing, to be ready for their start on the fourth day.

It was during the 1950s that specialized relief pitching first became a widespread phenomenon. Jim Konstanty, whose 22 saves and 74 appearances out of the bullpen sparked the 1950 Philadelphia "Whiz Kids" to the National League pennant, followed in the footsteps of Murphy, Page, and Casey to bring glamour to the position. The tall, husky right-hander relied on a palm ball and excellent control to keep opposing batters at bay. Lindy McDaniel, who recorded 172 saves between 1955 and 1975, and Stu Miller, who saved 154 games from 1952 to 1968, also excelled. Other notable bullpen aces included Clem Labine and Ryne Duren.

As the 1960s got underway, relief specialists, or firemen as they were called, were becoming valuable members of any pennant-contending team. Little Luis Arroyo, of the New York Yankees, was a sensational fireman in 1961, helping Whitey Ford to a 25–4 record by repeatedly coming out of the bullpen to close out one of Whitey's games. Arroyo labored in the major leagues for eight years, but 1961 was his one season in the sun. He recorded 29 of his 44 career saves that year. One of the first long-term career firemen was Elroy Face, a diminutive right-hander from New York State. Face, who was a starting pitcher in the minor leagues and a mediocre starting pitcher for the Pittsburgh Pirates in 1953 and 1955, was converted to a relief pitcher exclusively in '56 with spectacular results. Using a forkball as his out pitch, he compiled a record of 104–95 during a 16-year career, with 193 saves. In 1959, he established the greatest winning percentage in baseball history, .947, based on 18 wins against a single loss. Elroy Face made relief pitching popular.

JEFF REARDON

Jeff Reardon, one of the game's first closers, saved 367 games between 1979 and 1994 (MONTREAL EXPOS).

Other notable firemen followed Face to major league prominence in the '60s and '70s, including Rollie Fingers, Sparky Lyle, and Kent Tekulve. By the late 1980s the relief effort had evolved into specialized niches for long relief, short relief, setup men and closers. The names most familiar to baseball fans include potential Hall-of-Famers Bruce Sutter, Lee Smith, Jeff Reardon, Dennis Eckerlsey, Mariano Rivera, and Eric Gagne.

The following tables show the gradual emergence of the relief specialist over the past 110 years.

MAJOR LEAGUE PERCENT COMPLETE GAMES AND PERCENT SAVES

Year	Percent CG	Percent Saves
1895	81	2.9
1905	80	2.3
1915	53	5.7
1925	49	7.2
1935	45	8.5
1945	46	9.0
1955	30	14.6
1965	23	21.0

Year	Percent CG	Percent Saves
1975	27	17.3
1985	15	23.9
1995	6	25.0
2004	5	25.2

MAJOR LEAGUE CAREER SAVES LEADERS

Career Saves	Pitcher	Year	League
100	Firpo Marberry	1934	AL
	Johnny Murphy	1946	AL
	Elroy Face	1962	NL
	Stu Miller	1964	NL
200	Hoyt Wilhelm	1969	AL & NL
	Sparky Lyle	1977	AL
	Rollie Fingers	1978	AL & NL
300	Rollie Fingers	1982	AL & NL
	Goose Gossage	1988	AL
	Bruce Sutter	1988	NL
	Jeff Reardon	1991	NL & AL
	Dennis Eckersley	1995	AL
400	Lee Smith	1993	AL & NL
	John Franco	1999	NL
500	????		

As can be seen in the tables, complete games have been in decline since major league baseball began, but they went into a free fall for the first time between 1905 and 1915, when relief pitchers were first recognized as valuable members of the team. But at that time, saves were few because starting pitchers were used out of the bullpen in close games, and they normally pitched three or more innings, gaining a victory in many cases. Another free fall in complete games occurred after 1985, when the long reliever began to gain acceptance. The short-term specialists had become popular in the late 1940s thanks to men such as Joe Page and Hugh Casey, significantly increasing the number of saves realized by the bullpen crew. This strategy produced a high number of CG saves for the modern firemen. At first the saves were spread out over several relief pitchers, but with the emergence of the one-inning closer in the late 1980s, the other bullpen specialists were designated to hold a lead, with the closer stepping in in the ninth inning to pick up the save.

Player Size

Players are getting bigger every year and, as a result, can be expected to hit more home runs. Players on the 2004 major league all-star team, for instance, are 35 pounds heavier than the players who made up the nineteenth century all-star team, and 30 pounds heavier than the players who made up the 1900–1925 all-star team. The following table summarizes the change in player size over the years.

ALL-STAR TEAMS—POSITION PLAYERS

Date	Number of Players	Players over 200 Lbs.	Average Weight (lbs.)	Adjusted Home Runs
19th Century	18	3	175	15
1900–1925	18	3	180	15
1926–1950	18	5	188	20
1951–1975	18	7	194	25
1976–2000	18	5	208	26
2001	18	13	204	37
2004	18	13	210	29

Factor = 2.39 lbs per HR.

Adjusted Home Runs = Average number of home runs per 154 games.

In general, a player will be able to add one home run to his total number of home runs per year for every additional 2.39 pounds of body weight he adds. The data for weight and adjusted home runs are from major league all-star teams selected by the author for the periods noted. Today's all-star player is an average of 22 pounds heavier than his 1926 counterpart. That would equate to an additional nine home runs per player in the year 2004. Babe Ruth and Barry Bonds were approximately the same weight, so there was no home run advantage to either player on a weight basis. Unfortunately, the size versus home run relationship has been upset in recent years by the steroid controversy, which has tied some of the game's greatest home run feats, from 1998 to the present, to the use of steroids. This issue will be discussed in greater detail in chapter 13. The use of steroids has a significant impact on the state of pitching in the major leagues, because batters who use steroids have an unfair advantage against pitchers who play fair. As of 2004, no pitcher had been named as a steroid user, only hitters.

The Overall Quality of Pitching Today

Pitchers cannot be directly compared to each other from era to era because of all the rule changes and strategic changes, such as changes in stadium dimensions and changes in batting philosophy. Strikeouts cannot be compared from one era to another because the batting philosophy has changed drastically over the past 40 or 50 years. Prior to World War II, batters cringed at the thought of striking out. It was an embarrassing event to have to walk back to the dugout carrying a bat after failing to make contact with the ball. But all that changed during the '50s, '60s, and '70s, when sluggers such as Reggie Jackson and Bobby Bonds attacked the ball with abandon, and strikeout-be-damned. The era of the free-swinger was underway. These players wanted to hit a home run at any cost. Bonds and Jackson struck out five times for every home run they hit. Jackson, in fact, went the equivalent of five full seasons without ever making contact with the ball.

Today there are probably as many good pitchers as there were 40 or 50 years ago, but expansion has outdistanced the ability of the population to provide enough major league pitchers, so there are many pitchers in the major leagues today who would have been in the minor leagues 50 years ago. Then, there were a total of 16 major league teams in the

American and National leagues, and each team carried approximately eight pitchers on its roster. Teams had a four-man starting rotation and four journeyman pitchers in the bullpen to fill in for a starting pitcher in case of an injury, or to mop up in games that had gotten out of hand. The four men in the regular rotation handled the bulk of the innings pitched, usually 60 percent to 70 percent of the team's total innings pitched. On a starting pitcher's middle day off, he went to the bullpen to relieve if necessary. In a close game, a starting pitcher was sent in to save it or to win it, because there were very few specialized relief pitchers at that time. Today, every team has a five-man rotation, a 25 percent increase over 50 years ago. And they also have a setup man and a closer in the bullpen, which adds two more quality pitchers to their roster. In all, seven quality pitchers are required today to do what four quality pitchers did 50 years ago.

Back then, when each team had four starting pitchers and four relief pitchers, the total number of pitchers in the major leagues was 128, 64 starting pitchers and 64 relief pitchers. Today there are 30 teams, with five starting pitchers per team, for a total of 150 starting pitchers. Each team also has about six relief pitchers, for a total of 180 relief pitchers. The total number of pitchers in the major leagues today, both starting and relieving, is 330, an increase of 158 percent over 50 years ago.

The years from 1947 to 1960 have been called the Golden Age of Baseball, because it was the time when professional baseball finally broke down the color barrier and integrated the sport, bringing in the greatest pool of talent ever witnessed in any professional sport. During that period more than 100 former Negro league players entered the major leagues, including world-class sluggers such as Aaron, Mays, and Banks, and outstanding pitchers like Paige, Newcombe, and Juan Pizzaro.

Beginning in 1961, the talent in professional baseball began to decline, as the American League expanded from eight teams to ten teams. By 1998, the two major leagues had grown to 30 teams, an 88 percent increase that significantly diluted their pitching talent. The total population of the United States, Puerto Rico, the Dominican Republic, and Venezuela couldn't keep up with the expansion, growing by just 60 percent during that time. In addition, the leagues expanded the season from 154 games to 162 games, requiring additional pitching help. And the situation became even more strained when major league teams changed from a four-man pitching rotation to a five-man pitching rotation, which increased the starting pitching requirement by another 25 percent. As late as 1978, the top four pitchers on major league teams accounted for between 55 percent and 65 percent of all the innings pitched by their teams. A few pitching quartets, like Earl Weaver's great Baltimore teams of the 1960s and '70s, handled 70 percent to 75 percent of the team's pitching requirements. But that state of affairs essentially ended when free agency became the law of the land, and agents insisted that their clients be handled with kid gloves to protect their valuable pitching arms. The situation continued to decline into the twenty-first century. In 2004, for instance, the average was down to less than 50 percent, with the better teams topping out at 57–58 percent. And as noted in my book *Backstop*, "The dearth of talent in the major leagues is magnified by the situation in the minor leagues. In 1949, there were 58 minor leagues feeding more than 8000 players up to the major leagues. Today, there are about 18 leagues with less than 4000 players. If the minor leagues had kept pace with the population growth over the past half-century, there should be about 16,000 players in the minor leagues today." Pete Palmer, baseball's foremost statistician, said, in the same book, "from 1901–1960 the population more than doubled and the number of teams stayed the same. I think if you go overall from 1901 to the present, the population has increased more rapidly than expansion (280/75 compared to 30/16). This would state that the best players must have been in the 1950–60 period, after integration and before expansion."

There are many great pitchers who have been active over the past 20 years, including Nolan Ryan, Greg Maddux, and Roger Clemens. However, it might seem almost impossible to compare the performances of modern-day pitchers with pitchers who pitched 40, 50, and even 80 years ago. Pitchers from those earlier eras were conditioned, both mentally and physically, to pitch nine innings or more on every start. As noted earlier, Walter Johnson completed 80 percent of the games he started, Warren Spahn completed 57 percent of the games he started, and Bob Gibson completed 56 percent of the games he started. Compare that with Nolan Ryan's 29 percent completion rate, Greg Maddux's 18 percent completion rate, and Roger Clemens' 19 percent completion rate. But then, everything is not always as it seems. On closer inspection, it's not that the game has changed today. The truth is, the game has been in a constant state of change from the day it was organized.

There is more to pitching a complete game than stamina. There is also a mental aspect to it as discussed in chapter 7. The example used there was Roger Clemens, whose failure to pitch complete games in the postseason has come under severe scrutiny. For instance, in games four and seven of the 2004 LDS, Clemens lasted only six innings on three days' rest, and six innings on four days' rest. His problem is best reflected in the 1986 World Series, when his Boston Red Sox met the New York Mets. After failing to get through the fifth inning in game two, Clemens, pitching in game six on five days' rest, with the world championship in his hand, held a 3–2 lead after seven innings. All he had to do was throw two more scoreless innings and the Boston Red Sox would have their first world championship in 68 years. But, unbelievably, the Rocket asked manager John McNamara to come out of the game because he had a blister on his middle finger. The Sox eventually lost the game, 6–5 in ten innings, and the world championship the next day. By comparison, Sandy Koufax threw a 2–0, three-hitter at the Minnesota Twins in game seven of the 1965 World Series, striking out ten men en route, while pitching on just two days' rest, and suffering from the severe pain of the arthritis in his left elbow. And he had volunteered for that duty by telling his manager, Walter Alston, "If you want to win the Series, you'll pitch me." Then there was Bob Gibson, who was one of baseball's all-time great money pitchers. He appeared in three World Series, starting nine games and completing eight of them, while posting a 7–2 record. Can anyone imagine Gibson asking to come out of a World Series game for any reason short of blindness? And if the manager had insisted on taking him out, there would have been fingernail marks in the ground all the way from the mound to the dugout. Forty years ago, all starting pitchers pitched on three days' rest and, in a World Series, they were mentally and physically prepared to go on two days' rest without any fanfare.

Many people today explain the lack of complete games by saying it is more difficult to pitch today because the ball is so lively that the pitcher has to bear down on every pitch. However, in many ways, it was more difficult to pitch in the old days, as noted previously. Until the 1940s and '50s all the games were played during the day, with summer temperatures often soaring past the 100-degree mark. This took a heavy toll on pitchers, who might sweat off five or more pounds during a nine-inning game. Many pitchers even became dehydrated during the course of a game. Also, the ball carries farther during the day than it does at night.

The effect of rules changes and other changes on the major league batting statistics can be seen in the following chart:

Effect of Rules Changes and Other Changes on Batting and Pitching Statistics
STATISTICS PER A 154-GAME SEASON

Period	BA	HR	ERA
1876–1880	.259	12	2.46 (National League organized)
1881–1883	.258	23	2.93 (Sidearm pitching legalized)
1884–1892	.252	44	3.35 (Overhand pitching legalized)
1893–1900	.275	39	4.32 (60' 6" mound to plate)
1901–1903	.267	26	3.26 (American League begins)
1904–1910	.247	18	2.62 (15" pitching mound)
1911–1919	.256	26	2.96 (Cork-center baseball)
1920–1930	.286	66	4.11 (Lively-ball era begins)
1931–1940	.276	84	4.22 (Baseballs modified)
1941–1960	.259	109	3.95 (WWII + integration)
1961–1993	.256	125	3.76 (Expansion begins)
1994–2004	.267	166	4.54 (Costa Rican baseballs)

In spite of all the changes the game has undergone over the past 100 years, it is still America's national pastime. And Johnny Pesky, the 85-year-old coach for the Boston Red Sox, who played with Ted Williams and company in the 1940s, put it all in perspective when he said, "All of baseball (not only pitching) is a different game today. I wish I could still play."

11

Former Players Speak

Fourteen former major league pitchers participated in this study on the evolution of pitching. They had a combined major league service record of 175 years pitched, with 1,606 victories against 1,374 losses, and they represent the full range of pitching expertise, from journeyman pitchers to Hall-of-Fame legends. Pete Burnside enjoyed an eight-year career, appearing in 196 games for five different teams. Jack Banta was a hard-throwing right-hander with outstanding potential. As a rookie in 1949, he was the winning pitcher in the pennant-clinching game against the Philadelphia Phillies, throwing 4⅓ scoreless innings in relief, as the Dodgers won 9–7 in ten innings on the last day of the season. His promising major league career was cut short by an arm injury in 1950. Arm injuries also cut short the careers of Carl Erskine and Dave Ferris. The periods of active major league service for the 14 pitchers spanned the years from 1933 to 1985. Active pitchers were not included in the survey because they would not be familiar with the situation in the major leagues 30, 40, or 50 years ago. Former pitchers had hands-on experience with the situation as it existed when they were active, and they have kept in touch with the game over the years. Several of them, such as Burt Hooton, Claude Osteen, Sid Hudson, Walt Masterson, Dave Ferris, and Larry Jansen, served as major league pitching coaches or scouts after their retirement, and Jansen, during his service with the San Francisco Giants in the early '70s, helped develop future Hall-of-Fame pitchers Juan Marichal and Gaylord Perry. The following list shows the years of service and the win-loss records of the 14 pitchers.

Pitcher	Years of Service	Win-Loss Record
Bob Feller	1936–56	266–162
Virgil Trucks	1941–58	177–135
Larry Jansen	1947–56	122–89
Carl Erskine	1948–59	122–78
Clem Labine	1950–62	77–56
Dave Ferris	1945–50	65–30
Sid Hudson	1940–54	104–152
Pete Burnside	1955–63	19–36

Pitcher	Years of Service	Win-Loss Record
Elden Auker	1933–42	130–101
Walt Masterson	1939–56	78–100
Claude Osteen	1957–75	196–195
Jack Banta	1947–50	14–12
Hal Brown	1951–64	85–92
Burt Hooton	1971–85	151–136

Sid Hudson and Walt Masterson had the misfortune of pitching for the Washington Senators at a time when the favorite saying around the major leagues was "Washington, first in peace, first in war, and last in the American League." Hudson pitched for the Senators from 1940 to 1952, and the only two years the team finished in the first division were 1943 and 1945, while Hudson was serving his country in the United States Army. Masterson, who pitched for the Senators during the same period, was also in the army in 1943 and 1945. During the tenure of the two pitchers, the senators finished seventh in the eight-team league four times and finished last once.

Additional comments from Dave Campbell, Satchel Paige, Ned Garver, Hal Newhouser, Joe Garagiola, and Harry Danning, gleaned from various books and magazines, are also presented.

Bob Feller, who lost four years to military service in World War II, was one of the five greatest pitchers in the history of the game (AUTHOR'S COLLECTION).

Biographies of Participants

Bob Feller is one of the five greatest pitchers in baseball history, and a longtime student of the game. He burst upon the major league scene in 1936 as a 17-year-old high school kid when he fanned eight St. Louis Cardinals batters in three innings in an exhibition game. That same year, still in high school, he went 5–3 for the Cleveland Indians, fanning 15 St. Louis Browns batters in his major league starting debut, and then fanning 17 Philadelphia Athletics batters as the season drew to a close. During his career, he won 266 games against 162 losses and, if he hadn't lost four years to military service in World War II, he might have had a chance at the magic 400-win mark. During his time in the United States Navy, Feller won eight battle stars for action in the Pacific Theatre of Operations. Among his baseball achievements were three no-hitters and a major league record 12 one-hitters. Using an overpowering fastball that was clocked at 98.6 mph, a nasty curveball and a slider, he went on to lead the American League in victories six times and in strikeouts seven times.

Virgil Trucks, known as Fire Trucks because of his blazing fastball, began his professional baseball career in grand style, going 25–6 for Andalusia in the Alabama-Florida League in 1938, while setting a modern professional baseball record by striking out 418 batters in 273 innings. The 6' 1", 195-pound right-hander joined the Detroit Tigers four years later, and helped them capture the world championship in 1945. He pitched a seven-hitter in game two of the series after the Chicago Cubs had routed the Bengals in the opener, 9–0. Virgil Trucks pitched for 17 years in the major leagues, compiling a record of 177–135, with a fine 3.39 ERA. He won 20 games in 1953, and 15 or more games in four other years. He pitched in a total of 517 games during his career, starting 328 games and completing 124 of them, and appearing in relief 189 times. He pitched 33 shutouts as a starting pitcher and saved 30 games out of the bullpen. In 1952, he became one of just four major league pitchers to throw two no-hitters in the same year. In his fifth start of the season, on May 15, Trucks shut down the Washington Senators without a hit, winning 1–0 on a ninth-inning home run by Vic Wertz. One month later, he almost duplicated the feat, when the Senators visited Briggs Stadium. Washington's lead-off hitter, Eddie Yost, hit the first pitch down the left field line for a single. It turned out to be their only base runner as Trucks retired the next 27 batters. Then, on August 25, the Tigers' flamethrowing right-hander embarrassed the world champion New York Yankees in Yankee Stadium. It was another nail-biter, with Trucks nursing a slim 1–0 lead into the ninth inning, but he sucked up the nerves enough to retire Mickey Mantle, Joe Collins, and Hank Bauer in order, to preserve his masterpiece. But no-hitters were no stranger to the Detroit ace. Counting his minor league service, Virgil Trucks tossed a total of seven no-hitters in his professional career.

Larry Jansen began his professional baseball career with Salt Lake City in the Pioneer League in 1940, going 20–7 and leading the league with a .741 winning percentage and a 2.19 ERA. After spending two seasons with San Francisco in the Pacific Coast League, and sitting out two years, he returned to the game with a vengeance, capturing a league-leading 30 victories against just six losses for San Francisco in 1946, with a barely visible 1.57 earned run average. The next year, the 27-year-old rookie posted a 21–5 mark for the New York Giants, at one time during the season throwing ten consecutive complete-game victories, utilizing an outstanding overhand curveball, an effective fastball, and excellent control. Four years later, as the Giants overtook the Brooklyn Dodgers in the famous "shot heard round the world" pennant race, Jansen went 23–11 on the mound, and was the winning pitcher when Bobby Thomson put one of Ralph Branca's fastballs into the left field seats at the Polo Grounds to win the National League pennant. Over the course of a memorable nine-year career, Jansen won 122 games against 89 losses, completing 107 of the 237 games he started. Following his retirement as an active player, he served as the San Francisco Giants' pitching coach from 1961 to 1971, and helped develop pitchers Juan Marichal and Gaylord Perry. He was the pitching coach for the Chicago Cubs in 1972 and '73.

Carl Erskine pitched for the Brooklyn Dodgers from 1948 through 1960, winning 122

Carl Erskine had a potential Hall-of-Fame career cut short because of arm injuries (AUTHOR'S COLLECTION).

games against 78 losses for an excellent .610 winning percentage. Oisk, as he was called in Brooklyn, pitched some memorable games for the famed "Boys of Summer" in the '50s, using his repertoire of four outstanding pitches: a live fastball, two great curves, and the league's best changeup. In 1953, after going 20–6 during the regular season, he set a single game World Series strikeout record, fanning 14 New York Yankees, including Mickey Mantle four times. He also pitched two no-hitters. The first one against the Chicago Cubs on

June 19, 1952, just missed being a perfect game. With a storm threatening in the third inning, Erskine tried to end the inning quickly and, in his haste, he walked the opposing pitcher. That was the Cubs' only base runner, as "the Little Hoosier" set down the last 19 men to face him, winning 5–0. Four years later, he stopped the New York Giants without a hit, 5–0, walking two.

Clem Labine was a key member of the Brooklyn Dodgers' "Boys of Summer" baseball team during the glory days of the 1950s. He was not only the Dodgers' top relief ace, he was also asked to start some of the most important games in Brooklyn Dodgers history, as related in chapter 6. His 77–56 win-loss record and 96 saves over his 13-year career don't begin to tell the story of his importance to the Brooklyn dynasty.

Dave "Boo" Ferris had a promising major league career cut down by injury. The Mississippi native arrived on the major league scene after being discharged from military service in 1945, and immediately took Boston by storm, running up a record of 21–10 for the seventh-place Red Sox. The next year, he was even better, going 25–6, pacing the Sox to the American League pennant, and defeating the St. Louis Cardinals 4–0 in the third game of the World Series. Then disaster struck. He injured his arm in a night game in Cleveland in 1946, and he was never the same again. His career was essentially over at the age of 25. With the medical technology available today, Dave Ferris' arm injury probably could have been treated, and he could have gone on to a long, productive major league career. But in 1946, there was no solution to his problem.

Sid Hudson was an outstanding pitcher who had the misfortune of spending most of his 12-year career with the lowly Washington Senators, the doormats of the American League. In his rookie year, in 1940, the 6' 4", 180-pound right-hander went 17–16 for the seventh-place Senators, but that was his last winning season in the majors. His 104–152 career win-loss record doesn't do him justice. He had a good sinking fastball, a sharp curve, excellent control, and a world of confidence. His out-pitch was a low outside curveball. Hudson also relieved in 101 games, winning 13, losing 7, and saving 13. He was the pitching coach for the Senators in 1961, and spent the next 26 years with Washington and Texas, before serving as pitching coach for Baylor University for six years.

Pete Burnside was, as he said, a very average pitcher. But remember, only one-tenth of one percent of the young men who play baseball and dream of becoming major leaguers ever make the grade. A "very average" major league pitcher is a very exceptional athlete. Pete Burnside pitched in the major leagues for eight years, appearing in 196 games with five teams, and compiling a record of 19 wins, 36 losses, and seven saves. He also pitched for ten years in the minor leagues and in 1955 had his best season, going 18–11 with Dallas in the Texas League.

Elden Auker made his major league debut with the Detroit Tigers on August 10, 1933, after posting an excellent 16–10 mark with Beaumont of the Texas League. The 22-year-old submarine pitcher went 3–3 in August and September for Detroit with two complete games and one shutout. In 1934, he ran up a record of 15–7 as the Tigers won the American League pennant, and he followed that up with a complete-game victory over the St. Louis Cardinals in the World Series. The following year, he led the American League with a .720 winning percentage based on an 18–7 record. He had one no-decision start in the World Series as Detroit captured the world championship, defeating the Chicago Cubs, four games to two. Over the course of a ten-year career, Elden Auker won 130 games against 101 losses, with 126 complete games. He also relieved in 72 games with an 11–9 record and two saves.

Walt Masterson pitched in the major leagues from 1939 through 1956, with three years out for military service with the U.S. Air Force during World War II. Unfortunately, most of Masterson's career was with the Washington Senators, who were a perennial last-place club. The lanky right-hander was considered to be one of the better pitchers in the major leagues, his 78–100 record notwithstanding. In addition to starting 184 games, he pitched in 215 games out of the bullpen, with a 17–14 record and 20 saves.

Claude Osteen was a smooth southpaw pitcher who combined with Sandy Koufax and Don Drysdale to give the Los Angeles Dodgers an unbeatable pitching trio in 1965 and '66. Osteen, who began his major league career with the Cincinnati Reds in 1957, won ten or more games for ten consecutive years between 1964 and 1973. The most important victory of his long career came on October 9, 1965. The Minnesota Twins had just beaten both Drysdale and Koufax in games one and two of the World Series, and Walter Alston's boys had their backs to the wall when the 5' 10", 170-pound lefty came to their rescue. He shut out the Twins 5–0 on a five-hitter, and the Dodgers roared back to take the series in seven games. The man called Gomer combined outstanding control with a mean slider, a sinking fastball, and a curveball, to stifle the opposition. His 18-year career resulted in 196 wins against 195 losses, with 40 shutouts. With Los Angeles from 1965 to 1973 he compiled a record of 147–125, with two 20-victory seasons, 34 shutouts, and a fine 3.09 earned run average.

Jack Banta, a tall, skinny, 6' 3" right-hander, arrived in Brooklyn in 1949 at the age of 24. He led the National League in strikeouts in '49 with 193, and was second in fewest hits allowed per game with 7.4. The sidearm pitcher had a blazing fastball, a curve, and reasonable control. In fact, he had everything but luck. In 1950, he developed a sore shoulder and never recovered.

Hal Brown was a knuckleball pitcher with pinpoint control. He pitched in the major leagues for 14 years, starting 211 games, with 47 complete games and 13 shutouts. He also relieved in 147 games with 11 saves. He won ten or more games four times, including a 12–5 record with the Baltimore Orioles in 1960. His career record of 85 and 92 was better than it looks. He was a better than .500 pitcher most of his career, but he had the misfortune of pitching for an expansion team in 1963 and '64, going just 8–28 with the ninth-place Houston Colt 45s. He did have one claim to fame with Houston, however, walking just eight men in 141 innings in 1963.

Burt Hooton, the master of the knuckle-curve, was a major league pitcher from 1971 to 1985, compiling a record of 151 victories against 136 defeats. In 1981, he went 11–6 during the regular season and 4–1 with a sparkling 0.82 ERA in the post season. He was the MVP of the League Championship Series against the Montreal Expos, and he won the deciding game of the World Series against the New York Yankees, 9–2. He was the pitching coach for the Houston Astros from 2000 to 2004.

The Lively Baseball

Bob Feller, in *Bob Feller's Little Black Book* said,

Of course, the way the ball is made now — with the thin cover, the tight winding, and the lightweight bats — the hitters are still going to send the balls out of the ballpark like rockets. I'm not merely surmising that the balls are more tightly wound than they were when I played. I know it because I've gripped them. When you've pitched in the big leagues as long as I did, you know the way the ball should feel and you can tell if the cover is thinner and if the seams are stitched in a tighter fashion.

The Decline of Complete Games

Carl Erskine:

Complete games are not desired today. The starter is to give 6 or 7 quality innings. Then the bullpen specialists come in to close out the game. The pride of finishing a game is not important. Specialists are now the manager's options. The pitch count is a determining factor in how far a pitcher goes.

Bob Feller:

I pitched 36 complete games in 1946. That's the most complete games from today back to 1916. [Grover Cleveland Alexander threw 38 complete games for the Philadelphia Athletics that year.]

Dave Ferris:

Today pitchers are told, "Give me 5 or 6 innings and I'll come and get you with a set-up man and a closer." When I pitched, if I didn't go 9, I was disappointed with myself.

Sid Hudson:

We considered it an honor to pitch a complete game regardless of how many innings. In 1940, I beat Lefty Grove 1–0 in 13 innings. We didn't count pitches then. I also pitched a couple of 11-inning games—winning both of them. I believe I had 126 complete games in my career.

Elden Auker:

As a starting pitcher for 10 years, we were expected to pitch the entire game. I won 131 games and pitched 126 complete games. I would like to see more complete games today.

Pete Burnside:

We were made to believe that if you had the honor to start a game, your goal was to finish it. Don't look for help.

Hal Brown:

Games won and complete games were the basis for salary. A pitcher wasn't taken out unless he was getting hit or showing signs of being tired. A completed game meant a lot and it was hard to get a pitcher out of a game if he was pitching a shutout.

The Location of the Strike Zone

Bob Feller said,

Years ago, the strike zone was defined. The pitcher knew the strike zone, and so did the hitter. The base umpiring is good today, but the balls and strikes calls are lacking. Umpires today have few guidelines. Their strike zone is what they decide it is.

Dave Campbell, a television commentator and former eight-year major leaguer, was quoted in Seth Swirsky's *Every Pitcher Tells a Story*, as saying,

> It's also tougher to pitch today because of a much smaller strike zone, particularly in the American League.

Did Pitchers Pace Themselves During a Game When You Pitched?

Many present-day baseball historians and managers claim it was easier to pitch years ago, because the pitchers could pace themselves during a game without fear of having a batter hit a home run. Today, with the ball as lively as it is, a pitcher has to bear down on every batter, because they can all hit it out of the park. Former players commented on that theory.

Carl Erskine:

> I don't entirely agree with that theory. Very few pitchers can so-call 'pace' themselves. Every pitch I threw was the best I had. [Robin] Roberts could in fact reach back on occasion.

Bob Feller, when asked if he paced himself, said,

> Sure. You didn't try to strike every batter out. You wanted to try to make them hit your first or second pitch. You'd ease up on some of the hitters and, if they got a hit, then bear down on the next guy. But wait till you have one man out and wait till you have a lead in the middle of the game. Say you do that a half dozen times during a game, why that's quite a help, especially on a hot day.

Virgil Trucks:

> Historians are wrong about their claims that pitchers could go nine innings years ago because they could let up. Pitchers went nine innings because they had to, or someone would take your job. After I left baseball as a player, I became a roving pitching coach in the 1970s, and I was told never to let a pitcher throw more than 100 pitches, because they have pitchers in the bullpen that are good for three innings, and some they call closers are meant to be good for one and two innings.

Clem Labine:

> I do not know of any pitcher during my era who let up on his pitches because of a weaker hitter. Common sense should be enough to understand you have to work hard on weak hitters so the better hitters don't have extra at-bats. The problem with today's pitchers is that they have been led to believe that over 100 pitches is a big strain on their arms.

Dave Ferris:

> I can think of hitters in the lower part of the batting order that were plenty tough — know some of 'em gave me more trouble than the other batters — sure don't agree with the claim that pitchers 40 or 50 years ago had it easier than today's pitchers because they could pace themselves.

Sid Hudson:

> I never let up on anybody — even on a pitcher. I think that today's pitchers throw more pitches, trying to hit both corners, and about half of these pitches are balls.

Walter Masterson:

The claim that it was easier to pitch in my era is false. I didn't pace myself. Pitching is 90 per-cent mental — 10 percent physical. It is a mind game between the hitter and the pitcher, not a thrower and a dummy.

Burt Hooton:

As a pitcher 30 years ago, I never paced myself. It was all-out on every pitch. Anyone with a bat in major league batter's box could beat you. Letting up or "pacing" could cost you the game. I got myself in shape and kept myself in shape to do that.

Pete Burnside:

My record shows that I was a very average pitcher. I went hard from the start for I was not sure when I would get another chance. If you were lucky and had a big lead, one could pitch differently and be careful not to walk anybody. We were expected to do our best to complete the game and not be looking for help. If the helper got hot, he might soon take starts from you.

Claude Osteen:

I agree that hitting has progressed where the lower part of the order is more capable of produc-ing. But good pitchers get 'locked in' and I didn't care who was in the lineup. I didn't pace myself and I don't think good pitchers do. We were programmed to finish the game. Every pitch, inning, at-bat, is a work of art. Today's pitchers are programmed to give 6 innings. ... Doctors and agents have created that, not stronger lineups or better hitting.

Jack Banta:

I don't remember easing up on any hitter except maybe the opposing pitcher. If I remember right, I threw as hard as I could for as long as I could.

Satchel Paige, in his book *Pitchin' Man*, might have had the best explanation about how he paced himself, when he said,

Y'understand when I go nine or more innin's, I don't try to strike out nobody. Just give 'em all a piece of the ball so they pop up on the first or second pitch. No use wastin' time. But when I go in for relief, that's different. Then I go in for strikeouts.

The Pitch Count and Pitch Count Limit

Tom Seaver said that every pitcher has a different pitch count limit. He said his limit was about 135 pitches, but that Jerry Koosman could throw 145 pitches, and Nolan Ryan was good for more than 150.

Carl Erskine:

I can't be too critical of pitch counts because those who endorse it (agents) and some coaches, seem to know that exceeding a certain number of pitches has some negative effect on the next start. I think it has a weakness in assuming that 'one size fits all.' Each pitcher is different. There are about 15 pitches per inning — or about 130–135 for 9 innings. Strikeout pitchers throw more — lots of fouls balls. I pitched some extra inning games — 12 innings the longest. In the 1952 World Series, fifth game, I pitched all eleven innings and on the last pitch, a curve to strike out Berra, I broke a blister on the second finger. That knocked me out of another start. I probably threw close to 200 pitches. The pitch count may have some value but it's over-emphasized. I often finished stronger than I started — getting a second burst in the eighth or ninth.

Bob Feller:

What do I think of pitch counts? Not much. Pitch counts have nothing to do with anything except to give somebody something to do. They should be doing something more important than sitting around counting pitches. It's like counting sheep at night. If you can't sleep, you'd be better off taking a good shower, then jump into bed. If I had a pitch count when I was in my prime, I'd have probably not gotten by the third or fourth inning. I've seen some guys who could throw over 150 pitches. That guy that used to pitch for the Red Sox, Mickey McDermott, he'd throw 150 to 175 pitches. He had good stuff but he didn't have good control. But against fastball pitchers, batters foul off a lot of pitches, skipping them off. Pitch counts depend on how much you've got on the ball. Sometimes you've got great stuff on the mound and when they swing their bat the ball's gonna fall between the fielders. There's a lot of luck in this game. A lot of things don't make any sense.

Virgil Trucks:

The pitchers of today are only doing what managers want them to do, throw a hundred pitches, and try to do it in six or seven innings. They have the bullpen set up for the next one or two innings. They have been doing this since 1970. I was the roving pitching coach for the Atlanta Braves in 1970 and '72. Paul Richards, the general manager of the Braves, required all pitchers to do that. As for going the distance of nine innings, they are not shaped for that. And the pitchers of today are talented because of good coaching from minor leagues to the majors. The reason for more rotator cuff injuries, etc., are due to not throwing enough, especially if they try to extend over the 100 pitches. I don't think six or seven innings makes you a quality pitcher. When we played, a pitcher would sometimes throw 200 pitches. If I pitched nine innings, and most times I did, I was always 150 or more. Pitches were never counted when we played, only we could guess after the game, and if you struck out nine or more, you were always over 140 or 150.

Clem Labine:

They were not counting pitches during my time in the majors.

Sid Hudson:

Nowadays, they usually ask pitchers to throw about 100 pitches in five, six, or seven innings. In my day, we were geared to go nine innings. I don't know the maximum number of pitches I threw. No one ever counted my pitches, but a normal nine-inning game required about 115 to 120 pitches. Some pitchers today are pampered, in that they know they are expected to pitch only five, six, or seven innings, according to the pitch count. In my era, our goal was to pitch a complete game. Today's pitch count that limits a pitcher to approximately 100 pitches a game should help him because he doesn't have to throw so many pitches. But I don't think six innings constitutes a quality start. The game just changed.

Burt Hooton:

Pitch counts are limits. Once you put limits on an athlete, you limit what he can do, physically and, more important, mentally. There are pitch counts these days — and seemingly more pitchers going into surgery. Weights may play a part in that. Throwing limits play a bigger part. In many instances, the pitch count becomes more important to the pitcher than winning the game.

Pete Burnside:

I feel pitch counts are important for each individual, but each individual's capacity differs. Pitches were not always counted when I pitched. Since I was wild, had my share of walks and strikeouts, a figure may be 110–120 pitches per nine innings. I don't know the maximum number of pitches I threw in a game, maybe 150.

Claude Osteen:

Pitch counts are O.K. today because of the specialized categories— middle man, long man, setup man, closer. I would say the average for starters was more than 100 pitches in my time. My average [pitch count] was low because pitch efficiency was a big thing with me and I threw strikes. I don't think I ever threw more than 135 [pitches in a game].

Pitching Inside

One day after a major league game in 2004, four Hall-of-Fame catchers appeared on the postgame show. They were Gary Carter, Yogi Berra, Johnny Bench, and Carlton Fisk. When they were asked why there were so many home runs today, they all said it was because pitchers don't pitch inside anymore. Unlike Bob Gibson, they don't feel the inside of the plate belongs to them. Sluggers such as Sosa and Bonds and Palmeiro therefore have no fear and dig in.

Eldon Auker:

The situation today is very different than the years I pitched. I think it is impossible to compare hitters of different eras. What has changed is the pitching. When I played, home plate "belonged to me," the pitcher. Today home plate "belongs to the hitter," with a plastic helmet, elbow pad, gloves, shin or leg guards. The pitcher is on the defense instead of the offense. If a hitter gave me too much trouble, I would see if he could hit me "layin' down."

Ned Garver, a teammate of Virgil Trucks in St. Louis, commented on Trucks' pitching philosophy, in Virgil's autobiography:

He loved being out there, but he was dead serious when he was pitching. The good lord blessed him with a lot of ability, and he could throw much harder than most of us. He had good control though — he could throw it right over the plate unless he wanted to throw it at your head! Back when we were pitching we threw at people pretty regularly. They expected it, and they knew how to get out of the way. Virgil was a good pitcher, and in order to be a good pitcher, he knew that he had to brush the hitters back. And he wasn't afraid to do it.

Trucks' nephew, Steve, volunteered this information:

I remember his attitude and demeanor was offensive toward batters. The closer a batter got to the plate, the harder he seemed to throw inside. I recall one game when he hit a batter and they had words as the batter trotted to first base. Virgil was on the grass as he walked toward first base with the batter. It was as if Virgil was telling him to stay off the plate and he wouldn't get hit.

Four-Man Rotation vs. Five-Man Pitching Rotation

Feller said,

What do I think of a 5-man rotation? I think I'd give the same answer as on the other question. Not much! There is no reason why a pitcher without an injury cannot pitch with three days' rest. If you're on a four-game schedule, you can do wind sprints and work out in between starts, with your big workout in the middle day of the schedule. Do some exercises and you might want to pitch a little batting practice like I did, or run along the sidelines and pick up balls, or maybe do your sprints. By the time you've worked out and changed your shirt, you waited in the bullpen, and if they needed you, fine. Otherwise, you'd do your throwing down there for about 15 or 20 minutes. The next day, do soft toss, pick up balls behind batting practice and maybe hit a few fungoes to the outfielders, do a couple of wind sprints that'll break a good sweat, and be ready to pitch your ballgame the next day.

Virgil Trucks:

I pitched every four days. And on my second day off, I was in the bullpen [Trucks started 328 games in the major leagues and relieved in 189.] If I didn't get into the game, I pitched for ten minutes in the bullpen.

Dave Ferris:

We pitched often, sometimes on three days' rest. They paid us to pitch and we pitched. You didn't look to the bullpen.

Sid Hudson:

I think a five-man rotation protects a pitcher's arm. It should. He has more rest than we had. In my time, we worked out, running the days after we pitched. The second day, we worked out; threw some to work on different pitches and get the stiffness out of our arm. The third day, we ran, worked out, and didn't throw any at all. The fourth day, we pitched.

Pete Burnside:

I was a slim kid. An extra day of rest would have been good for me.

Hal Newhouser was also a slim man, who packed just 180 pounds on a 6' 2" frame. His manager didn't want him to pitch in the four-man rotation because he thought it would be too hard on Newhouser's arm, but Hal persisted, with great success. He commented on the four-man rotation to Jim Sargent in *Oldtyme Baseball News*:

So I got into a nice pattern. I could rest one day. I would warm my arm up on the second day. I would rest on the third day. And I'd pitch on the fourth day. For the next 11 years, except for hurting my arm, I pitched every fourth day. I think I proved my point.

Prince Hal, as he was called, pitched in the major leagues for 17 years, compiling a record of 207–150. He pitched in 35 or more games for ten consecutive years, twice pitching more than 300 innings. From 1944 to 1946, he led the American League in pitching with records of 29–9, 25–9, and 26–9, with a combined earned run average of 1.99. His durability is reflected in the fact that he completed 57 percent of his 374 starts during his career.

The Emergence of the Setup Man and the Closer

Bob Feller, asked what he thought of the concept of a setup man and a closer, said, "Not much."

Virgil Trucks:

I think Casey Stengel started it, but not like they do today. He had a long man he'd relieve with, and then he brought in another one, and he went the rest of the way.

When we were in the fifth or sixth inning, and maybe one run ahead or maybe tied, they'd put in a pinch hitter for the pitcher, and maybe you wouldn't get the run or maybe you'd get the loss. And I didn't like that situation. They wanted to win the ballgame and they didn't care how it was done.

The Quality of Major League Pitching Today

Bob Feller:

The quality of baseball is not as good as it was 40 or 50 years ago. The hitting is not as good. Defense is better because of bigger gloves and better field conditions. There are a lot of throwers around and not too many pitchers. There are some good pitchers around like you saw in the World Series and some other postseason play but not nearly as many as there were when I played. They don't have the stamina. They don't have the desire to pitch complete games. ... The first time they expanded was all right, in my opinion, but that's when it brought the minor leaguers into the major leagues. And the second time they expanded was even worse. It's been a disaster and still is today. I don't think it has to do with the population growth. Baseball is not played as much as it used to be in high schools and colleges. They don't take it as seriously because baseball is not a revenue sport. They want money. They want the bottom line. That's why in colleges the best athletes go to football and basketball, and that's where the fans are, and the big crowds, the noise, and all the excitement. Baseball is on the back burner.

There are more injuries now caused by trainers. There are more pitchers on the disabled list now because their arms are not as strong. Players don't know the fundamentals. Agents and players may think they can extend their careers if they take more time off. I used to pitch a complete game every four days and throw between starts.

Virgil Trucks:

I think there is some good pitching today but, as I see it, they don't work enough. They don't pitch nine innings, or very seldom, and if they're in a close ballgame where they can go nine and probably win, they'll do that, but they've got that other thing set up now with the long man, short man, and closer, and pitchers should win a lot more games and not be stretched out as much. When I pitched, I wanted to pitch the whole ballgame. And right on top of that, we relieved. After starting, we would be in the bullpen the second day, and we would relieve, ... but I didn't know I had 30 saves in my career [saves were not tabulated until about 1969].

I don't like the D.H. because I liked to hit. I think one year I hit around .270. And I don't like the way they bunt today. They're the worst bunters I've ever seen. And especially in the National League where the pitcher hits. And that's all we did in spring training. We'd go out and bunt — do our running and get in shape — and bunt, and cover first. When I was playing, any hitter in the lineup, other than the cleanup hitter maybe, was a good bunter. And if they needed a sacrifice to move a man over, they did that. And like today, when a hitter gets two strikes on them, they still try to hit the ball out of the ballpark. You don't hit like that. You hit where the ball is pitched. Nine times out of ten, when they hit into a double play, they hit into it because they're hitting an outside pitch, and they're trying to pull it, and all your gonna do is hit a big hopper to the infield. There's a few of them who will go to the opposite field when they've got two strikes on them. They don't try to pull that ball and I bet 50 percent of the time they get a base hit to right field if he's a right-handed hitter, or left field if he's a left-handed hitter. I've seen home runs hit to the opposite field 370 to 400 feet when they hit the ball where it's pitched. It'll jump off that light bat too, you know. The bats only weigh about 31 or 32 ounces. In my day some of the guys had 35, 36 ounce bats.

Carl Erskine:

I think it's more difficult for pitchers today for these reasons: (1) No high strike. The strike zone as set forth in the rule book is armpits (actually slightly lower now) to knees. Umpires are out of control. (2) Batting gloves—a tremendous aid to hitters. (3) Baseballs are machine stitched — makes them tighter and harder and more lively. (4) Bats are dried to take out weight — more bat speed, more power — also that's why bats explode when a pitch is mis-hit.

Free agency and multiyear contracts and big money have changed the way baseball is played. Agents now pressure managers to not overuse their client — or on the other hand pressure the manager for not using his closer more often. Bonuses dictate how players perform — Lasorda told me he can't get a player to bunt if he needs a couple more extra base hits to get his bonus. The old days were great, but these are new times and they are not necessarily better or worse — just different.

Dave Ferris:

Today, with 30 teams, pitching seems a little thin. There aren't enough bonafide major leaguers. I don't like the designated hitter. I liked to hit. [Dave was a lifetime .250 hitter.]

Sid Hudson:

I think there were just as many talented pitchers in my day.

Hal Brown:

Baseball is different today. First, there are so many more major league teams—with only 16 teams, I think the teams played a better quality of ball, not throwing to the wrong base, throwing behind runners, etc.

Burt Hooton:

There are plenty of good pitchers, but there are more teams than there were 30 years ago. If you expand two teams, that's 20 to 24 more pitchers in the major leagues that would otherwise be in the minors. Pitching has become more specialized and the concept of what constitutes a good outing has changed. In other words, giving up three earned runs in five or six innings every outing was a quick ticket to the bullpen or the minors 30 years ago. An ERA above 4.00 was horrendous. If you averaged five innings per start, like many starters do today, you didn't remain in the rotation long, much less on the team. Now, pitchers who give up three runs in a five-inning outing [a 5.40 ERA] consider it a great job. Relievers who come in and give up a run per outing are thought to have done an acceptable job. Starters are mentally programmed at early ages to go five innings— or a certain number of pitches per outing. There are long men, middle men, setup men, left-handed specialists, closers, etc. Thirty years ago, you had ten-man pitching staffs. Now there are 11, 12, even 13 pitchers to a staff. Are the hitters better, or the pitchers worse? One thing however, is still true — 30 years ago or today. A good pitcher (which there are several today) will always stop good hitting.

Larry Jansen said, in *Oldtyme Baseball News*,

Let's say I think the scouts today are making a big mistake. They are signing players who can throw hard, and they don't seem to care if they can't hit the wall. I probably wouldn't have got a chance to play professional ball under those conditions. All they want now is a bunch of kids who can throw hard, and they try to teach them something. If they can't, they get someone else. They should sign more kids who can throw strikes. They are not signing the kids who are "junkers" like I was.

Dave Campbell told Seth Swirsky,

I'd say the biggest difference watching baseball in the 1990s compared to the '60s and '70s was the depth of quality starting pitching. In the National League, almost every team had at least two quality starters, and many had three or four. There weren't too many soft touches. They also went deeper into the game so one didn't get to face a lot of [the] watered down mid-relief pitching so prevalent today.

12

Pitcher Injuries and Conditioning — Then and Now

Injuries

In the early days of baseball, there were no team doctors, no specialized pitching coaches, no disabled list. That was true in the 1890s and it was still true in the 1950s. In fact, until the 1970s, treating an injury was a hit or miss proposition. There were no surgical procedures that could be used to repair a torn ligament, a rotator cuff injury, or cartilage damage. There were not even satisfactory methods for diagnosing an injury. One of the early baseball victims of the primitive medicine practiced in the nineteenth century was the great Addie Joss, a sidearming right-hander who threw smoke. The 6' 3", 185-pound Joss overpowered major league batters for nine years before hitting the wall. In 1910, coming off a sub-par 14–13 season, the 29-year-old native of Woodland, Wisconsin, struggled through a 4–5 record in April and May, before complaining of a sore elbow on June 5. He still took his regular turn on the ninth, but shut himself down after that outing, a 4–4 tie in which he was hit hard. His injury was finally diagnosed by the team trainer as a torn ligament, and he was told to rest his arm for one month. Once his prescribed rest period had expired, he attempted to come back, as reported by Scott Longert:

> On July 11, he tested the elbow, beating Boston 5–4. But he couldn't throw the sharp breaking stuff without a shooting pain up and down his arm. He could not survive on his fastball alone and he knew it. When the team left Boston, Addie remained in town to be treated by a specialist. The same doctor had helped Eddie Cicotte recover from arm problems. He left for Philadelphia after a week of treatment, unsure if his arm felt any different. On July 25, he gutted out five innings against the Athletics, but he had to leave the mound when the elbow swelled up again.

The medical treatment in the early part of the twentieth century didn't involve long rest periods. And Joss was anxious to test his arm every month or so. He even pitched an exhibition game against the Cincinnati Reds in October, with his manager's blessing. He pitched six innings and left the game feeling pretty good, with just a minimum of pain, and was optimistic about 1911. Over the winter, the team trainer visited Joss, and massaged his arm twice a day for a month. But it was all for naught. As soon as spring training got underway, the Cleveland hurler put his arm to the test, and it failed. After a vigorous pitching workout, Joss's arm was as sore as it had ever been. Tragically, the story ends there. Not long after his workout, he collapsed on the field with what was eventually diagnosed as tubercular meningitis. On April 14, 1911, 31-year-old Addie Joss died.

Two years later, when Smokey Joe Wood injured his arm in a freak spring-training accident, his experience was the same as Joss.' After struggling through three years of pain and frustration, with short rest periods followed by successful but painful starting assignments, Wood eventually became an outfielder and played five years for the Cleveland Indians before retiring in 1922. Even in his most painful days, Smokey Joe Wood was a sensational pitcher. Between 1913 and 1915, he pitched in 64 games, starting 48 and relieving in 16. He pitched 33 complete games, representing 64 percent of his starts, and he had an earned run average of 2.10. His career ERA of 2.03 is the third best all-time.

Twenty-five years later, there still hadn't been any improvements made in treating arm injuries. Satchel Paige, the great Negro league legend, came down with a sore arm in

Mexico in 1938 after trying to break off a curveball in the rarefied air of Mexico City. He was out of action almost a year, while he tried to get his arm working again. He took hot water baths several times a day, following these with attempts to stretch his arm out by throwing the ball gently underhand, sidearm, or overhand if he could raise his arm above his shoulder. One day, in the summer of '39, he threw a ball and the pain was gone. He went on to pitch professionally for another 28 years, including five years in the major leagues, and he never had another sore arm.

By the 1950s, major league baseball teams were still in the primitive stages of diagnosing and treating injuries. They now had team doctors, but they had no acceptable medical

Satchel Paige was a legendary pitcher in the Negro League for more than 30 years. Late in his career, at the age of 42, he joined the Cleveland Indians, going 6–1 down the stretch, to help them capture the 1948 American League pennant (AUTHOR'S COLLECTION).

Karl Spooner, who set a two-game National League strikeout record in his first two major league games, had to retire after just two seasons because of arm problems (AUTHOR'S COLLECTION).

procedures for treating sore arms. The usual treatment was the application of heat to the affected area, combined with rest. One of the biggest advancements in the field of player health at that time was the introduction of the disabled list. The DL, as it was called, permitted teams to remove players from their 25-man playing roster while they were recovering from an illness or injury. There were actually two DLs, a 15-day DL and a 60-day DL. If a player was placed on the 60-day DL, his team could replace him with a healthy player until he was ready to return. In order to be placed on the disabled list a player had to be certified unable to play by a doctor.

Jack Banta arrived in Brooklyn in 1949 as the pitcher with the most potential in the Brooklyn Dodgers minor league system. Fresh out of Montreal where he had led the International League with 19 victories, Banta excelled for the Dodgers, going 10–6 with a fine 3.38 earned run average, pitching in 48 games, 36 of them out of the bullpen. In the most memorable game of his career, he pitched 4⅓ innings of scoreless relief against the Philadelphia Phillies on the last day of the season, and he became the winning pitcher when the Dodgers clinched the National League pennant with a dramatic 9–7 victory in ten innings. He went on to pitch 5⅔ innings in three games in the World Series that fall, with a 3.18 ERA. But that was his swan song. The talented right-hander injured his shoulder the following year, and disappeared from the major league scene after going 4–4 in 16 games. As he noted in Peter Golenbock's *Bums*, "Course in those days, they didn't have athletic doctors. They assumed it was some kind of a tendonitis type thing. And I never came back. To this day, I can't throw a rock. Still hurts in the same place."

Karl Spooner burst upon the major league scene at the end of the 1954 season after dazzling the fans in the Texas League, leading the league in strikeouts with 262 in 238 innings pitched, and victories with 21. He pitched two games for the Dodgers during the last week of the season, blanking the National League champion New York Giants 3–0 on three hits, with 15 strikeouts, and, four days later, shutting out the Pittsburgh Pirates 1–0 on four hits with 12 strikeouts. His two-game total of 27 strikeouts set a new National League record. Clem Labine commented on Spooner's talent in Golenbock's *Bums*: "That man had a fastball that was unbelievable, not for sheer speed, but for how much the ball moved. He was one of the toughest left-handers that I've ever seen." In *Bums*, Ed Roebuck also remembered Spooner. "He was very cocky. We used to call him 'King Karl.' He thought he was the best pitcher ever to put on a uniform. And he proved his cockiness. What was remarkable about him was his deception. He was very long-armed, and the hitters would think they had him timed good, but they didn't." Eight days into spring training the next year, Spooner pitched in an exhibition game against the Chicago White Sox and, trying to throw too hard, too soon, he pulled a muscle in his shoulder pitching to "Jungle Jim" Rivera. The Dodgers pitcher told Peter Golenbock, "[The trainer] rubbed me down real good, put some diathermy on me. Of course back then they didn't know near what they know today about arms." King Karl struggled through the regular season, more with guile than speed, winning eight games and losing six, as the Dodgers swept to the title. He pitched the pennant-clinching game against the Milwaukee Braves on September 8, winning 10–2. It was the earliest pennant-clinching date in major league history. But Spooner's arm never healed. He finally had an operation in 1957, which he told Golenbock about. "I went to Long Island Hospital in Brooklyn, and before I went in, the doctor said the chances were less than fifty-fifty that I'd be able to pitch good again. He operated and I didn't pitch again until 1958. Over the winter, the Cardinals bought my contract off the Montreal roster, and they let me bring it along as I saw fit, real slow, which I did, and I was in real good physical shape. But any time I tried to extend myself, it just wasn't there. It was the same feeling I had before they operated. Tendonitis is what they called it. What this is, I don't know, even to this day. Even today, when I work, if I have to get into a certain position, I can feel it."

Sandy Koufax was another pitcher whose career was cut short because of an injury, but at least he had 12 years to stake his claim as a baseball legend before he called it quits. The 28-year-old Koufax, at the peak of his career, injured his pitching arm sliding into second base in 1964. It was initially diagnosed as an elbow inflammation and a slight muscle tear in the left forearm. With today's technology, his elbow might have been saved before it developed arthritis, but at that time, all he got was a few cortisone shots, ice packs, hot whirlpool baths, and ultrasound. And early in the 1965 season, after being sidelined with a sore arm once again, his arthritic condition was diagnosed. He pitched in constant pain over the next two years, going 26–8 in 1965 and 27–9 the following year. But that was it. Koufax retired at the end of the 1966 season, fearing permanent injury if he pitched any longer. As short as it was, his career was sensational. Over his last four years, he went a fantastic 97–27, for a .782 winning percentage, and a 1.85 ERA. He set a major league single season strikeout record with 382 strikeouts, pitched four no-hitters including a perfect game, and compiled a 4–3 World Series record, with a miniscule 0.95 ERA.

Today, with the tremendous advances in medical procedures, a pitcher with a serious arm problem can be treated surgically, and can return to his team as good a new — and sometimes better. The first breakthrough in the medical treatment of a pitcher's arm injuries was probably the revolutionary elbow surgery that salvaged the career of Tommy John. The elbow reconstruction operation relocated a tendon from his right forearm to replace an elbow ligament that had been destroyed. The procedure, which has become commonplace over the last 30 years, is now known as Tommy John surgery. Before he tore the ligament in his elbow, John had pitched in the major leagues for 12 years, compiling a win-loss record of 124–106. After surgery, he came back better than ever. He missed the entire 1975 season, but pitched another 14 years, from 1976 to 1989, winning 164 games against 125 losses. Included in his post-injury record were three 20-victory seasons, and three World Series appearances, in which he went 2–1 with a 2.67 earned run average.

John Smoltz, another potential Hall-of-Fame pitcher, suffered painful elbow injuries for several years before undergoing Tommy John surgery. Smoltz, one of the pitching triumvirate of the powerful Atlanta Braves over a 14-year period, helped pitch the Braves to 13 division titles, five National League championships and one world championship.

Sandy Koufax, perhaps the game's greatest southpaw pitcher, retired at the age of 30 because of arthritis in his elbow (AUTHOR'S COLLECTION).

After struggling with recurring elbow problems in the late '90s, Smoltz underwent Tommy John surgery in 2000, following which he gave up his starting pitching job for one in the bullpen. For three years, from 2002 through 2004, Smoltz was one of the top closers in the major leagues, saving 144 games against just 13 blown saves, for a 92 percent success rate, the second highest percentage of all time. In 2005, he returned to the starting rotation.

One of the most common pitching injuries over the years has been the rotator cuff injury. The treatment of this type of injury, including surgery, has become routine in recent years. Some of the pitchers whose careers have been saved by having this or other types of reconstructive surgery include Jim Palmer, Bert Blyleven, and Bruce Sutter.

The number of years of active service for selected pitchers is shown below.

Years of Service

Pitcher	Years Played	Years of Service
A. Spalding	1871–1877	7
Charles Radbourne	1881–1891	11
Cy Young	1890–1911	21
Christy Mathewson	1900–1916	17
Walter Johnson	1907–1927	21
Grover Cleveland Alexander	1911–1930	20
Lefty Grove	1925–1941	17
Bob Feller	1936–1956	18 (plus 4 years in the U.S. Navy)
Warren Spahn	1942–1965	21 (plus 3 years in the U.S. Army)
Sandy Koufax	1955–1966	12 (retired because of an arm injury)
Bob Gibson	1959–1975	17
Phil Niekro	1964–1987	24
Don Sutton	1966–1988	23
Tom Seaver	1967–1986	20
Nolan Ryan	1966–1993	27
Greg Maddux	1986–2005	20+
Roger Clemens	1984–2005	22+
Randy Johnson	1988–2005	18+

It is uncertain whether or not today's pitchers can expect to have a longer playing career than pitchers from other eras. The average length of service for major league pitchers in general, from 1933 to the present, is summarized below.

Year	Avg. Major League Years per Pitcher
1933	8.0
1944	6.1
1953	5.0
1959	4.6
1964	5.5
1972	5.3
1981	5.7
2004	6.5

The advances in medical and surgical procedures today do not mean there are fewer injuries today than there were 40 or 50 years ago. In fact, statistics going back to 1953 suggest otherwise. The following table, listing the percentage of major league pitchers that have been on the disabled list at some time during their careers, indicates there are more pitching injuries now than there were decades ago, and the number of injuries continues to increase.

Year	No. of Pitchers	Pitchers on the DL	% Pitchers on the DL
1952	Ellis Kinder was on the Inactive List. There was no DL.		
1953	154	5	3
1959	195	14	7
1964	221	38	17
1972	263	62	24
1981	330	165	50
1992	462	313	68
2004	342	248	73

The above list confirms that the number of players appearing on the disabled list more than doubled after free agency was granted to major league players. It may be that agents and owners are being more cautious in their approach to a pitcher's health and, in an effort to extend his career, put him on the disabled list at the slightest hint of a problem. Or it may be an indication that modern conditioning regimens have been harmful to a pitcher's health rather than improving it.

Injuries: Former Players Speak

Bob Feller:

Well, they don't do manual labor before their teenage years. They don't milk cows. They don't work in the fields. They don't work shoveling the grain or cleaning the barn, and doing all the heavy manual labor around the farm. I had a team of horses to plow the field and I was doing the work I needed to do, throwing bales of hay or straw around before I was even a teenager. Today, the first thing they see in high school or in college is a Nautilus machine. They don't do that manual labor when they're seven, eight, nine, or ten years old, before they're teenagers. If you don't do it then, why you've lost a lot. I don't know if there are more injuries today, but I know that the disabled list is pretty long most of the time. I notice that they all have more injuries when they're getting their brains beaten out than they do if their team is winning. If they're having a bad year, they're always on the DL. It may be psychological. If you're having a bad year, get hurt so you don't have to play much, and wait for the next year. If you're having a bad year and your pitching average is bad, pitch batting practice and don't get in the game. Wrap a towel around your arm and go get an x-ray taken. If you're having a bad year, you want to stay out of the lineup.

Carl Erskine had a potential Hall-of-Fame career cut short because of an arm injury that might have been repaired if today's technology had been available in 1948. Erskine, who in 1950 joined the Brooklyn Dodgers to stay, after four outstanding seasons in the minor leagues and two brief stays in Brooklyn, had this to say:

I pulled a [shoulder] muscle in my first start, pitching in the rain against the Cubs. Burt Shotton [the manager] wouldn't listen when I complained. As a rookie, I didn't say much—after all, I won my first five games—at 5–0 no one could believe I had arm trouble. I did a lot of damage continuing to pitch after the injury.

Erskine's roommate, Duke Snider, told the author that Carl had a knot the size of a golf ball behind his right shoulder. He said Carl couldn't throw between starts because of the discomfort. But Erskine continued to take his normal start until he couldn't stand the pain any longer. Then he retired. He was just 32 years old.

Carl Erskine also had this to say:

I don't think there are more injuries today. It seems that way because the disabled list is used extensively. And why not? Teams have lots of money invested in these pitchers and rehab is a necessity. In my day, the Dodgers and others had extensive farm systems. The Dodgers had about 800 players under contract with 26 farm teams. Players were signed cheap and were expendable. If you couldn't perform, you were sent back to the minors or traded. It was almost impossible to get on the DL. You had to have a broken bone or a major injury. Pitcher's arms are injured and they look normal.

Virgil Trucks:

There are more arm problems today. I think they have these problems with rotator cuffs now because they don't throw enough. Players today are not in good condition, so when they get to the fifth inning, they are tired, and if they try to put too much on the ball, they hurt their arm. And if it's the sixth or seventh inning, and they try to reach back for a little extra, they're in more danger of hurting their arm. I never heard of a rotator cuff until I finished playing ball. I can't remember anybody having a rotator cuff problem. Of course, they may have had a rotator cuff injury and treated it for some other reason. And this year I've noticed more hamstring injuries. There again, all baseball players do not run enough in spring training, or during the season. I ran every day that I didn't pitch. The first thing that goes with a ballplayer is his legs. And I never had a pulled groin, hamstring, or leg.

Dave Ferris:

I had arm trouble. Hughson had arm trouble about the same time. And Mickey Harris had arm trouble. Did we have arm problems from pitching too many innings? There's no answer to that. I tore something in my shoulder in a night game in Cleveland in 1947. I tried to snap a 3–2 curveball and I heard something pop. I finished the game and Bobby Doerr hit a home run in the ninth and we won, 1–0. The next day, I couldn't get my arm up to my three-quarter delivery. I could only pitch sidearm. Next start against Chicago, I lost the zip on my fastball. I never had the power again. I lost velocity and I pitched with a little pain. I never was a power pitcher. My fastball was in the high 80s, but I had a curve and a change. I threw a sinking fastball that was effective. We had a team doctor, but the treatment for a sore arm was two weeks of rest and put heat on it. An orthopedic surgeon has told me that today they could probably have done orthopedic surgery on my arm and I could have returned as good as new. There was no DL in my time. You either pitched or you were out—released or sent to the minors. We didn't do too much work on arms. Everything was heat. If there was something wrong with your arm, you put heat on it.

Joe Garagiola was quoted as saying,

We always played hurt. You didn't want to take a day off because you knew there was someone down in Columbus [the St. Louis Cardinal farm team] just waiting to take your job.

Clem Labine:

Most pitchers would not hurt their arms due to a lot of pitches if they had a sound arm. There seem to be more arm injuries today. I cannot understand why.

Walter Masterson:

Injuries are part of the game. Your arms swing many times in a day, in a relaxed manner, as you walk. To throw a ball, your throwing elbow and shoulders must be in the same plane or you develop a sore arm. Centrifugal force creates the velocity — Newton's third law. The balance point is behind the umbilical cord — exceed 84 percent of physical force and you are out of control. Balance is the key. The ability to relax under pressure makes you a better pitcher. Who is teaching it?

Elden Auker:

The pitchers today are conditioned to pitch only five to six innings. Many have pulled groins, hamstring injuries, sore arms and legs. In my opinion, many of them are not in condition. They work out on treadmills and other machines. Sprinting 50–100 yards and run and run would solve many of their problems.

Pete Burnside:

I don't know why there are more injuries now. Are pitchers trying to throw too many freak pitches — overthrowing — not in as good shape as they think they are? Trainers used to tell me the fewest guys on the training table were farmers and those who worked physically hard as kids outside baseball.

Claude Osteen:

We are more aware of injuries today because we know more today. However, with agents, big money, and liability, doctors, trainers, and medical specialists are going to protect themselves when it comes to letting pitchers throw more. Weaknesses in the arm are there because most pitchers do not throw enough to develop the natural pitching strength. The strength developed in the weight room is not like the strength developed by throwing. Of course, the throwing needs to be supervised for proper throwing mechanics. It is hard today to get a starting pitcher to work more than ten minutes in doing a side between starts and they work every five days instead of four.

Hal Brown:

I think there are more injuries today because of the number of teams and the amount of money the players get. When there were 16 teams in both leagues, there was always someone waiting to get a chance to play — therefore a lot of players played hurt. It's still a great game and I'm so grateful for the years I was able to play in the majors.

Larry Jansen said in *Oldtyme Baseball News,*

I hurt my back slightly in 1951. Then I made the mistake of trying to pitch with it. The following year I pitched awhile and it bothered me again. I kept trying to pitch instead of resting it. If I was playing today, I think they would have gotten me over that sore back before they'd let me pitch again. I ended up trying to pitch with a belt around me. And by doing that, I hurt my arm.

Leo Mazzone had this to say about a pitcher's injuries:

The main cause of an arm injury is not a fastball, a slider, a curve, a change, or a split-finger fastball. In fact, I will allow any pitcher to throw any pitch as long as he can throw it properly.

Most arm injuries result, not from a particular pitch, but from overexertion, "muscling up" [trying to throw too hard in a given situation], or overextension.

Conditioning

When major league baseball was being played in the eastern half of the United States over 100 years ago, a pitcher's training regimen consisted primarily of running and of throwing a baseball. Christy Mathewson, in his book *Pitching in a Pinch*, talked about the New York Giants' spring training regimen. He said on the first day of camp, he did loosening-up exercises and wind sprints. On the second day he began to throw, but only straight balls: "I never try to throw a curve for ten days at least after I get South, for a misplaced curve early in the season may give a man a sore arm for the greater part of the summer, and Big League clubs are not paying pitchers for wearing crippled wings." Beginning about the third week, Mathewson would pitch some batting practice to get used to pitching to a batter and, when the team began playing intrasquad games in the afternoon, he started to get some actual game experience. Most of spring training consisted of games of "pepper," wind sprints, and pitching batting practice or in exhibition games. It was a time to get into playing condition, strengthen the legs, work on new pitches, and smooth out the delivery.

There wasn't much change in the spring training regimen in the major leagues over the next 40 years. For members of the mound corps, it was pretty much run, shag fly balls, play some pepper, and pitch. Apparently that program worked reasonably well as many starting pitchers were able to throw 30 or more complete games a year as well as relieve on their second day off. Things began to change in the early 1950s when the disabled list was created. Suddenly more and more players were coming down with nagging injuries that required rest or treatment, and prevented them from playing. It is interesting to note that, in the early days of integration, no former Negro league pitchers spent time on the disabled list. The reason may be simply that the Negro league pitchers, before integration, were used to pitching 365 days a year.

The Negro leaguer's lot was not an easy one. The players made very little money, and many of them played baseball all over the Western Hemisphere — in the United States, Mexico, Puerto Rico, the Dominican Republic, Venezuela, or anywhere else baseball was being played — 12 months a year, just to make ends meet. In the U.S., they played in the Negro leagues from March through September. Then they barnstormed across the country with major league all-star teams in the fall and, often played winter ball in California or Florida between October and February. They didn't have Nautilus equipment. They didn't have heavy weights. They kept in good physical condition by playing baseball. They ran every day, and they threw a baseball every day. And they almost never suffered from a sore arm.

Once black pitchers began to follow the same conditioning regimen as their white teammates, they began to have the same arm problems as the other players, as shown in the table below. Apparently race has no effect on the number of severe injuries experienced by major league pitchers. It is strictly a matter of conditioning.

THE EFFECT OF RACE ON A PITCHER'S TIME ON THE DISABLED LIST

Date	Teams	ML Pitchers		Pitchers on DL		Percent on DL	
		White	Black	White	Black	White	Black
1953	16	146	8	5	0	3	0
1959	16	180	15	14	0	8	0
1964	20	202	19	38	0	19	0
1972	24	237	26	53	9	22	35
1981	26	293	37	143	22	49	59
1992	26	420	42	287	26	68	62
2004	30	255	87	182	66	71	76

Nolan Ryan, one of the pitching fraternity's most famous members, in his book *Nolan Ryan's Pitcher's Bible*, said,

> When I signed back in 1965, the standard approach was quite simple: just throw off a mound, do some sprints, and you're all set. Based on the information available in the 1960's, this training program wasn't too far off course. A pitcher has to have really strong legs naturally. And you do need to get used to throwing off a mound to get your arm in shape and build up your stamina.

Ryan followed this regimen for several years, but as more information began to surface about how to prepare the body to withstand the rigors of a long season, he gradually turned more and more to weight training in the gym, and to the use of the Nautilus and Universal gym equipment to develop and strengthen specific muscles in his arms, legs, chest, and back. His individual conditioning program was developed over the next 20 years with Houston's strength and conditioning coach, Gene Coleman, and the Texas Rangers' strength and conditioning coach, Tom House. His off-season program, between October and January, concentrated on building strength, while avoiding actual throwing. After New Year's Day, Ryan would start to pitch on flat ground, as a prerequisite to the more rigorous spring training program. By the time training camp opened, Ryan was ready to begin pitching off a mound. The big right-hander continued his strength and conditioning program during the season. His conditioning program, as outlined in his autobiography, included icing his arm for 20 minutes immediately after pitching, then spending 30 minutes on the stationary bike. The next day, he would do heavy weight work, abdominal work, 20 minutes of wind sprints, ball throwing, and bike riding. On day two he would concentrate on throwing long toss, pitching on flat ground, and riding the bike. The next day, he would repeat his day-one regimen as well as pitching off the mound at full speed for 15 minutes. Finally, on day four, he would do a light program of weights, abdominals, and running. And even on his scheduled pitching day, he would do some light weight work, some sprints, and some long toss, before warming up in the bullpen. He also had a few helpful tips on how to prevent a sore arm:

1. Don't try to learn a new pitch too quickly.
2. Don't try to overthrow the ball by trying to make a curveball break more than it normally does, or trying to get a few more miles-per-hour on your fastball. Anytime you overthrow, you risk injury.

3. Many injuries occur because players aren't in shape, so take care of yourself physically.
4. In the spring, don't start throwing hard, or curveballs, until your arm is in good shape.

Ryan's conditioning coach at Houston, Gene Coleman, was quoted in Ryan's book:

> Young pitchers should aspire to throw harder, but never without a good base of conditioning. Lifting weights and running are tools to increase velocity, but only throwing can build the endurance required to hurl 100–150 pitches on a regular basis. The Red Sox, White Sox, and Blue Jays have experimented with using a four-man rotation throughout their minor league systems. The theory is that arm strength and velocity can be improved by throwing more times per week. Al Rosen (San Francisco Giants) and Harry Dalton (Milwaukee Brewers) believe that young pitchers are underworked. Rosen said that coaches and managers are too protective of young arms, while Dalton pointed to the increasing number of pitchers disabled each year as a signal that something is wrong with conventional training procedures. ... Experience indicates that most pitchers with below-average velocity do not train properly.

Larry Jansen, an outstanding major league pitcher, and one of the former major leaguers who participated in this study, was also a successful pitching coach for the San Francisco Giants from 1961 to 1971, and he helped develop such world-class pitchers as Gaylord Perry and Juan Marichal, as noted in the previous chapter. Jansen's approach to pitcher conditioning centered on throwing a baseball. In spring training, he had his pitchers begin throwing on the first day, including breaking pitches. They would warm up for 10–15 minutes, and then throw about 50 pitches to batters. Half of the pitches were thrown from the stretch since about half of all pitches thrown in a game have to be thrown from the stretch, requiring different muscles than are used when throwing from a windup. He believed in conditioning all the muscles a pitcher would need, from the very first day. In his book *The Craft of Pitching*, Jansen said,

> The pitcher who withholds his "breaking stuff" until later in the spring frequently experiences an unpleasant rebound in muscle physiology. The pitcher who starts spring training by throwing both straight and breaking pitches will naturally suffer muscle soreness and stiffness which eventually (in about seven days) resolves.

Jansen also favored pepper games to aid a pitcher's muscle flexibility. An indication of the success of Larry Jansen's programs can be found in the careers of his two most famous students, Juan Marichal and Gaylord Perry, both Hall-of-Fame pitchers. Marichal pitched in the major leagues for 16 years, winning 243 games against 142 losses, for a winning percentage of .631. He completed 53 percent of the 457 games he started and spent just 57 days on the disabled list, and that in his last season. Gaylord Perry had an even more remarkable career, pitching for 22 years, with 314 victories against 265 losses. He pitched 303 complete games in his career in 690 starts, and he spent just 15 days on the disabled list in 23 years. Burt Hooton, who broke in under Jansen in Chicago, enjoyed a 15-year career, going 151–136, and never spent time on the DL because of an arm injury. Perhaps more teams should adopt Larry Jansen's conditioning regimen.

There were many conditioning programs being developed and fine-tuned around the country during the 1970s and '80s. The program outlined by Pat Murphy and Jeff Forney of Arizona State University is typical. Their program for pitchers in the off-season included three days in the gym working with the medicine ball, doing calisthenics to improve agility, strengthening the abdominals, and doing 220-yard sprints. The other two days were spent with small weights, doing bench presses, biceps curls, leg curls, and leg extensions, as well as doing another round of sprints. The in-season program was similar. It was a vigorous workout program, but it had one puzzling aspect. Although the program emphasized building leg strength, which is critical if a pitcher is to be successful, the pitcher never actually threw a baseball, which is his stock in trade.

The man responsible for customizing conditioning programs for Big League pitchers and for monitoring their progress is the pitching coach. And the most successful major league pitching coach during the 1990s and into the new century has been Leo Mazzone, the pitching coach of the Atlanta Braves. Mazzone believes that pitchers don't throw the ball enough. His program revolves around throwing a baseball regularly. He actually favors a four-man pitching rotation, but he has had to work within the directives of his organization, which favors a five-man pitching rotation. Mazzone, a former minor league pitcher, worked under Johnny Sain, the former Boston Braves pitching ace, when Sain was a major league pitching coach during the 1960s. Sain, and later Mazzone, believed that pitchers have to throw frequently to keep their arms in good condition. Mazzone's conditioning program with the Braves, as described in his book *Pitch Like a Pro*, begins with a throwing regimen. He gives the Braves pitchers a day off following a start, then has them throw off the mound for 10–15 minutes at 65–75 percent of full velocity on days two and three, then gives them another day off before their next start. If the pitchers want to play catch on their days off, that's fine with Mazzone. He said he never discourages pitchers from throwing a baseball.

Other than the throwing program, Mazzone has his pitchers run frequent wind sprints during spring training. They begin with ten wind sprints from the foul line to center field, and add two sprints a day until they reach 20. The goal is to get the pitcher's legs in condition over a period of time, not all at once. It is important for the pitchers to run all out during the sprints, and not to jog or dog-it during the exercise. During the season, more emphasis is put on actual pitching than on wind sprints. Also, in addition to throwing, Atlanta's pitchers utilize the weight room several days a week. The regimen there includes lower body exercises and upper body exercises designed to increase the strength, flexibility, and cardiovascular fitness of the legs, back, and shoulders. Braves pitchers also work with weighted balls or lightweight dumbbells, in the three to five pound range, to strengthen their shoulders.

Johnny Pesky, a coach with the Boston Red Sox, who has been a witness to all the training programs from the 1940s to the present, thinks today's weight training is beneficial to a pitcher.

Ray Berres, a former catcher and pitching coach for the Chicago White Sox, talking to David Condon in *Baseball Digest*, contributed these observations:

> It's the guys with the herky-jerky motions who have shoulder and arm problems and short careers. Another great help to a long career is running. Show me a pitcher with weak legs and I'll show you a pitcher who'll come up with a sore arm. I got to believe what everyone tells me: Bob Feller kept his legs in great shape. His record testifies to it. Advice for today's young pitchers? Work on a smooth delivery, and realize that a negative mental attitude is your worst enemy.

Conditioning: Former Players Speak

Warren Spahn was quoted in Kahn's *Head Game* as saying,

I don't think pitchers throw enough today. They go once a week. They pitch five innings. They don't throw batting practice between starts. We're in an era pre-occupied with jogging, getting your heart rate up, weightlifting. I think a lot of players lift and run instead of doing what's necessary to stay in pitching shape. Throw and throw. I'd pitch a game and the following day pitch batting practice, fifteen minutes for stamina. The next day I'd run some in the outfield. Day after that, I was ready for another start.

Randy Johnson, in *Randy Johnson's Power Pitching*, says that after recuperating from a serious back injury, he realized that he had to follow a conditioning regimen that was specific for the way he pitched. He noted that he was not a drive-off pitcher like Tom Seaver or Roger Clemens, who need exceptionally strong legs to push off the mound, maximizing their power. Johnson, who stands 6' 10" tall, is an upper body pitcher who slings the ball plateward with a three-quarter to almost sidearm motion. He said he

puts more emphasis on shoulders, rotator cuff and posterior delts, in particular, as well as abdominals, lower back, and hamstrings (the three areas that I refer to as my core). I need to keep those areas strong to maintain my velocity over the 100-plus pitches I throw in a typical start.

Johnson's conditioning program includes leg curls for hamstrings, leg extensions for thigh muscles, and lower back exercises. On the second day after he pitches, he does ten minutes of long toss beginning at 100 feet, and then stretches it out. The next day, he pitches on flat ground and does some dumbbell exercises. And the day before he is scheduled to pitch, he does more dumbbell exercises and rides the stationary bike. In the off-season, he begins throwing the ball easily after Christmas, progresses to long toss in mid–January, and starts pitching off a mound about two weeks prior to spring training.

Bob Feller noted,

I did a lot of calisthenics, and a lot of wind sprints, not jogging. Jogging's for old men. But wind sprints all out for 90 or 100 yards, then around the ballpark once or twice. I worked with weights, but not more than 10 to 25 pounds for dumbbells and not more than 125 pounds for other weights. I believe in the philosophy that you shouldn't build up big biceps or big muscles in your legs. You need long, lean muscles. I don't think most pitchers throw enough. It's up to the individual how much to throw. I believe pitchers should be doing long distance throwing in spring training and during the season to strengthen their arms. Pitching during batting practice will help strengthen your arm and improve your control. I used to pitch batting practice on my middle day during the rotation, and would still pitch on three days' rest. I didn't throw much before the game, but I did wind sprints between starts.

In the winter I walked a lot, did a lot of hunting, ice skated, played basketball. I threw in the gymnasium some, maybe two or three times a week. I didn't try to get anybody out in spring training. I just tried to work on my pitches. I did a lot of running and calisthenics and practiced the fundamentals such as backing up bases, fielding bunts, fielding come-backers, and throwing to bases. A pitcher can get in condition, if he takes care of himself, in a month. Of course, pitchers rarely pitch nine innings any more, so it takes longer to get your arm in shape. If you work out all winter, then you can get in condition in the month of spring training to be at the top of your game. I would bear down the last two times on the mound in spring training if there was a good mound on a warm day in a good ballpark in an exhibition game.

Regarding today's conditioning programs, Feller said,

I see it all. I think it's fair. I don't think it's anything sensational. I think they have great equipment. I think that some individuals are in as great shape as anybody else. They have a little bit different concept. They work on the extender muscles in the arm, then the leg you shove off with. You've got to build up the strength. You've got to have rhythm from the tip of your finger all the way down your left or right side, depending on which side you're throwing from. You have to practice rhythm and you have to practice coordination, which is very important to smoothness. Baseball is not a game for weightlifters.

Virgil Trucks, in his biography, said,

I believe that pitchers today don't throw enough. They only throw so much, and then that's it — they shut it down. The coaches count pitches and when a guy gets to 100, they take him out — no matter what the game situation is. I pitched many games where I threw over 200 pitches and I never had any chronic arm trouble. Now, I wouldn't pick up a ball on the day after I pitched, but I ran every day that I wasn't pitching. Some pitchers would take the day off from running after they pitched, but not me. That's why I feel that Atlanta's pitching staff of the 1990's was so good. Leo Mazzone, their pitching coach, had the old school philosophy that you throw more to keep your arm in condition. I agree with him — a pitcher's arm has to be in top condition in order to avoid injury, and I believe that throwing more is what keeps your arm in top condition. Many guys believe that it's just as important that a pitcher's legs be in top condition, too, and I agree with that. Marty Marion, my manager when I was with the Browns in 1953, was like that and he ran us a lot. I threw as much as anyone and I ran as much as anyone and I feel that that really contributed to my success on the mound.

Trucks also wrote:

We kept in condition by pitching 9 innings, and if we didn't have to relieve, we would have to throw about ten minutes down in the bullpen for the next game. That's the way it worked and we pitched every 4th day. As far as weights were concerned, we were told not to do so. And we never had a weight room or facilities to do so. We only had one trainer, and none in the minor leagues. They wouldn't let us lift anything heavy in the winter. They were afraid it would tighten up our muscles. I had a ball made up just like a baseball but it was made up of metal. It weighed about 10 pounds, anywhere from 5 to 10 pounds, more like 5 — and I used to flip that around, and that's the only thing I ever did for my pitching arm. They wouldn't even let us drink a lot of water. Now they fill themselves up with Gatorade.

Carl Erskine:

Weight training is a science, and done properly should give good results. Pitchers' legs need good conditioning. We got ours running sprints, but I'll bet weight training, in addition, would be better. We were always told weight training on arms and shoulders was not good for pitching arms— no muscle bulk. One aspect of the game has been overlooked. Before the early 1950s, managers and coaches were exclusively non-pitchers. There were no former pitchers as coaches— pitching coaches were usually catchers (former). I had four, Paul Cherrinko, Clyde Sukeforth, Bobby Bragan, and Joe Becker. These catcher "pitching coaches" could not help a pitcher with mechanics— didn't know the emotion or physical feelings a pitcher lived with — they could only evaluate his "stuff." Telling the manager his curve is lazy or his fastball isn't moving. Seems strange that baseball for a hundred years never used ex-pitchers on their coaching staff. Now the pitching coach is the manager's right arm.

Dave Ferris:

I did a lot of sprints and throwing. Some players did pushups. Ted Williams did 100 pushups every morning to strengthen his wrists and forearms. We exercised our arms by pitching. Your arms get stronger by pitching. You had to keep your legs in shape. The legs were the main thing pitchers did off-season—a lot of running. We ran sprints all the time in spring training. There wasn't too much joy sometimes, but a pitcher is just as good as his legs.

Clem Labine:

I believe the training of today's pitchers is 100 percent better than during my time.

Sid Hudson:

I think heavy weights are not good—maybe some light weights are ok. Pitching coaches today are teaching pitchers to throw from high overhand—throwing downhill to the batter (they claim it makes the pitcher harder to hit). He should be throwing around three-quarter—driving off the mound with his legs and body—throwing straight at home plate. Standing straight up and not using their legs and body to drive off the mound will be a grind on their shoulder. I was taught three-quarters—or sidearm now and then—which is the natural movement of the arm—good mechanics. Pitchers today fall off the mound—right-handers fall to the left and left-handers fall to the right. Neither are in a position to field the ball. Their mechanics are terrible. A pitcher should not be all "muscled up"—he needs a loose arm.

Elden Auker:

I do not know anything about today's training routine. We did not have any type of machines for conditioning. I conditioned my arms and legs by running, not jogging, but sprinting 50–100–200 yards every day when I was not pitching. Chasing fungoes hit to me by a coach. I also threw every day (batting practice). I never had a sore arm or shoulder during my entire career because my legs were in perfect condition. Pitchers will never hurt their arms if their legs are in condition. If their legs are not in condition, the result will eventually be a sore arm or a pulled muscle. In 1999, Dr. McFarland, Johns Hopkins University, conducted a research study on the mechanics of pitching a ball. His conclusion was "strengthening the lower extremities was vital in generating the velocity of the pitch." This is also true for the other players to eliminate hamstring injuries, pulled groins, etc. Did you ever hear of a hockey player unable to play because of a hamstring injury?

Pete Burnside:

I never lifted weights (I believe Bob Feller did and he was great). Many other hard throwers and successful pitchers didn't lift weights as far as I am aware. I'm certain present day training programs are superior to those of 50 years ago.

Claude Osteen:

The weight training is more rigorous and body building. Supervised training for isolated muscles in the arm and shoulder is okay but upper body bulk gets in the way of elasticity and would be better spent working on the legs, which are the foundation for good control in pitching. We did not mess with the upper body too much in weight training in my day.

Jack Banta:

Players today go to gyms and physical trainers during the off-season, and are consequently bigger, stronger, and in better shape than the players of 50 years ago.

Hal Brown:

I don't know the training program today. When I played, it was always thought that your arm was no stronger than your legs. Therefore, a pitcher did lots of running between starts.

Harry Danning told Al Smitley in a 1995 *Oldtyme Baseball News* story:

I think the training is overdone. All the years I played, I never had a charley horse. I think they are overtrained. I've never seen so many hurt legs and arms. I've never seen so many chips and so many guys on the disabled list. I caught in the World Series with a broken hand. They didn't know it, but I did. I got three hits in one game hitting one-handed. We didn't come out. I think we trained right. We did a lot of running. John McGraw's system was run and walk, run and walk, run and walk. Then they'd hit fungoes. These guys were so good, they'd hit them where you couldn't catch it and make you go all out. I think the biggest improvement is that now all people can play baseball. That's the biggest improvement, and secondly getting rid of the Reserve Clause. These fellows should get paid for their talents.

13

The State of
Major League Pitching

What Happened to Major League Pitching: A Final Review

Major League Baseball will begin its 131st season of operation in 2006. Over that period of time, there have been many changes and modifications to all aspects of the game, including fielding, batting, pitching, umpiring, and even to the ballparks themselves. But the area most affected by the changes has probably been the pitching, and what has affected the pitching the most have been modifications, legal and otherwise, to the baseball itself. These changes have had a significant effect on the relationship of the pitcher to the batter, and on the evolution of the pitching position.

THE BASEBALL

The actions of the major leagues to deaden the baseball in the 1930s contradict the argument of some baseball historians that the ball has never been juiced up, even back in 1920 when the so-called lively ball era began. Several ballplayers whose careers covered the early part of the twentieth century commented about the condition of the baseball at that time, including Frank "Home Run" Baker, as reported in chapter 5. The great Cy Young also believed the 1920 baseball was juiced. And Charles Ebbets, owner of the Brooklyn Dodgers, was quoted in the *Los Angeles Times* in1921 as saying, "From my observation and my judgment, the ball in use this season is livelier than any ball that has been used during all the years I have been in baseball." New York Giants manager John McGraw was one of the first people to complain about the liveliness of the ball in the mid–1920s, but his complaints were ignored by major league baseball for several years, after the manufacturer of the balls stated that no changes had been made to the ball. But after the 1930 offensive explosion, all parties had to admit that something had changed. Both leagues made several changes to the ball during the following decade in an effort to deaden the ball to its pre–1930 level.

Greg Maddux is the modern game's greatest control pitcher. He has won 305 games in 19 years, and he is still active (JAY SANFORD).

It is a fact that since the baseball manufacturing operation was moved to Costa Rica in 1994, home run production has increased by 35 percent. The liveliness of the Costa Rican baseball has been confirmed in several professional scientific studies, by such agencies as the University of Rhode Island and Larchmont Corporation. A representative of the Rawlings Sporting Goods Company has stated that the baseball has undergone very little change since the early days of the game. Unfortunately, that statement is incorrect. The baseball owners established the weight and dimensions of the ball in 1878, but there have been many changes to the structure and construction of the ball over the past 128 years. The first baseballs had a rubber center. Then a cork-center baseball was introduced in 1911, and a cushioned cork-center baseball in 1925; the liveliness of the ball increased with each change. Rawlings, the present supplier of major league baseballs, presently stores the wool that is used in the windings for the baseball under controlled temperature and humidity conditions. That procedure represents an improvement in the manufacturing process, as far as producing a more consistent ball is concerned, but when did that procedure begin, and what effect did it have on the liveliness of the ball? The wool for the first three windings of the baseball was obtained in the United States until after World War I, when it was reportedly replaced by Australian wool. The woolen yarn is manufactured in the United States at several different locations. The present wool windings are 75 percent virgin wool and 25 percent reprocessed wool that can include oil and 1 percent synthetic material. The fourth winding, which was originally cotton, is now a cotton/polyester yarn that produces a livelier ball than a 100 percent cotton yarn would produce. The thickness of the outside covering of the ball was changed several times during the 1930s, and the covering itself, which was originally horsehide, was changed to cowhide in 1975. There have been changes to the type and formula of the latex adhesive applied to the wound balls over the years, and to the numbers of strands in the yarn used for the seams. The equipment used to manufacture the balls has also been improved as technological advances have been made. Today's new state-of-the-art winding machines produce tighter windings, and recently installed baseball-rolling machines compress the seams, producing a ball that is glossier and more slippery. Finally, the finished baseballs are now tested for their Coefficient of Restitution (COR), which has become Major League Baseball's most critical specification, even though it has only been in use for the past decade or so. Prior to that time, the weight and circumference of the ball were the most critical specifications. And to further complicate matters, MLB changed suppliers in 1976, replacing long-time supplier Spalding with Rawlings Sporting Goods Company. Since that time, Rawlings has changed baseball manufacturing locations twice, moving the operation from the United States to Haiti in 1980 and then to Costa Rica in 1994, with predictable changes in the finished product.

Jim Sherwood, director of the Baseball Research Center at the University of Massachusetts at Lowell, during a study contracted by Major League Baseball to compare the differences between the 2000 baseball and the 1999 baseball, noted that two balls, both within specifications, could vary in the distance traveled when hit by as much as 49 feet — the difference between a routine fly ball and a home run. He further discovered that most baseballs tested were on the higher side of specifications, producing a livelier ball, as reported in *ASEE Prism* magazine.

A physicist from New York University, Richard Brandt, found that the present-day baseball has even more variability than Sherwood discovered. Brandt, hired by MacGregor Sporting Goods to test major league baseballs, "found 20 percent of the balls to have coefficients of restitution higher than the major league maximum specification of .578 — in one case as high as .607," according to Stephan S. Hall in his article "Baseball's Dirty Tricks," written for Thorn's *Armchair Book of Baseball II*. Brandt went on to say, "If you compare today's baseballs with ones from the past, the old ones were twenty-five to thirty percent less lively. What that means is that if you went back to 1927, when Babe Ruth hit sixty home runs, and you used the modern ball, Ruth would have hit eighty home runs."

The following summary lists all the changes that have been made to the baseball over the past 115 years that may have contributed to the increase in the liveliness of the major league baseball:

• The cork-center baseball was introduced in 1911.
• Tension settings on the baseball winding machine, which were increased in 1917 in order to obtain a tight wind on the cheap wool that had to be used during World War I, were kept at the higher settings after the war, even though high quality wool was available again. This condition resulted in a harder, livelier ball, a fact that was confirmed by John Curtis of Spalding.

- The spitball and other freak deliveries were banned in 1920. No foreign substances could be applied to the ball, including the rosin that pitchers had used to take the sheen off the ball.
- Balls that were scuffed or became dirty were replaced immediately, beginning in 1921.

The combination of the changes that were made to the ball between 1911 and 1921 may have been contributing factors in producing the lively ball that has been discussed over the past 85 years. The so-called lively ball may not have been the result of any one change. It may have been the result of a combination of changes.

- The cushioned cork-center baseball was introduced in 1925, adding a little more juice to the ball.
- Changes to the thickness of the leather covering, and the thickness of the seams, were made throughout the decade of the 1930s in an effort to deaden the baseball. In 1939, both leagues adopted the number-four ball, which had a thicker cover than the 1920s baseball, and five strands in the seam instead of four.
- In 1938, umpires began to use a special mud to rub-up the baseballs prior to each game, to take the sheen off the ball.
- Cowhide replaced horsehide as the leather covering for major league baseballs in 1975.
- The Rawlings Sporting Goods Company replaced Spalding as the official supplier of major league baseballs in 1975.
- Rawlings moved the baseball manufacturing operation to Haiti in 1980.
- Rawlings moved the baseball manufacturing operation to Costa Rica in 1994.
- Sometime during the last decade or two of the twentieth century, the Coefficient of Restitution (COR) began to be used as the most critical manufacturing specification for major league baseballs. During this same period, a ball-rolling machine was added to the manufacturing process to compress the seams on the finished balls, creating balls that, according to many major league pitchers, were much more slippery and difficult to grip than balls manufactured previously.
- After the last modifications were made to the cover and seams of the baseball in 1939, home runs remained relatively stable for the next 47 years, but as soon as the baseball manufacturing operation was moved to Costa Rica, the home run rate exploded, averaging 166 home runs per team per 154 games from 1994 through 2004 compared to 123 home runs per team per year between 1947 and 1993. Research studies conducted by the University of Rhode Island, the Larchmont Corporation, Penn State University, the University of Massachusetts at Lowell, New York University, and SGS U.S. Testing Company all confirm the above findings. The Costa Rican ball is much livelier than major league baseballs manufactured prior to 1993, in some cases as much as 35 percent livelier.

This is not to say that the baseball was the only cause of the home run explosion over the ensuing eight decades. There were other contributing factors such as the size of the ballparks and the size of the players. A complete chart of all the factors that have led to the present home run outbreak can be found in the appendix.

The Bat

The contribution of the baseball bat to the home run epidemic is yet to be determined, but it is doubtful that the bat has played a major part in the lively ball debate. As noted in chapter 9, the bat produces a striking force against the ball that sends the ball hurtling through space according to Newton's Second Law of Motion. The Bambino, who was exceptionally strong and had strong wrists, wielded a bat that weighed 42–44 ounces to hit his 714 home runs. Most modern sluggers, like Hank Aaron, swing bats that weigh between 31 and 34 ounces and, since the force applied to the ball from the bat is a function of both weight and swing speed, they would have to have an exceptionally high swing speed to match Babe Ruth's force at contact. Mark McGwire used one of the heavier bats of recent times, a 35-ounce bludgeon. Barry Bonds wielded a 32-ounce bat when he set the home run record. It was also pointed out previously that corked bats probably do not add to a player's home run totals for the same reason: the lighter weight of the bat resulting from the hollowed-out area might essentially neutralize the advantage of the increased swing speed.

Jim Sherwood, however, suspects that bats may be a factor in the increased home run distance. And Daniel A. Russell's research conducted at Kettering University seems to support that theory according to Alan M. Nathan's June 10, 2003, report, "Some Remarks on Corked Bats." Russell's study indicated that the velocity of the batted ball increases as the weight of the bat increases, with a corresponding decrease in the bat swing-speed, until it eventually levels off to an optimum velocity. According to Russell, the bat weight that would produce the optimum batted-ball velocity is 32 ounces, which, interestingly, is the bat weight that most major league players are using. However, in a practical test, Roger Maris once hit baseballs using five different bat weights between 33 and 47 ounces, and he hit the longest balls with the heaviest bat, indicating that his bat weight more than compensated for any loss in bat swing-speed he might have experienced swinging the heavier bats. One other point of interest is the fact that the wood used in today's bats is dried before the manufacturing process begins; this removes the moisture from the wood, effectively increasing its density. And some bats are roasted after manufacture to bring out the grain. Obviously, the bat is one of the variables in the lively ball debate that has been almost totally ignored.

The Strike Zone

From 1887 to 1950, the strike zone was defined as that area over the plate from the shoulders to the knees, but over the past 55 years it has been modified four times. Today the upper limit is vague. It is defined as halfway between the top of the shoulders and the top of the uniform pants, allowing umpires too much latitude in determining whether the pitch is a strike or a ball. The lower limit is defined as the top of the knee, giving the batter a decided edge in the war between him and the pitcher. The modern strike zone is at least 20 percent smaller than the pre–1950 strike zone, making this era the most batter-favorable era in the history of the game. The current strike zone strongly resembles the strike zone of the 1850s and '60s, when the pitcher was directed to toss the ball over the center of the plate so the batter could get a good cut at it. For a pitcher to throw a strike today, he has to put it in the batter's wheelhouse, where the batter can hit it with all the energy he can muster. And the batter can crowd the plate because he knows that most pitchers will not pitch inside for fear of being ejected from the game by the umpire. For 63 years, the strike zone was from the shoulders to the knees. Since 1988 it has been the size of a postage stamp.

PLAYER SIZE

As noted in chapter 10, players have been getting bigger every year since the early days of the game. But today's players are viewed with suspicion because of the actions of some of them who cheated by taking steroids in order to bulk up. Ken Caminiti, who was the National League MVP in 1996, said he took steroids during his MVP season. Jason Giambi and Barry Bonds admitted to a government investigating committee that they also took steroids, although Bonds qualified his confession by saying he didn't realize he was taking steroids, and that he only took them in 2003. He is still denying he took steroids during his record-breaking season of 2001, although a former mistress, testifying before the grand jury, said he told her he started taking steroids in 1999. Bonds' career statistics are shown below.

BARRY BONDS' STATISTICS BASED ON 550 AT-BATS

Years	Age	H	D	T	HR	RBI	BA
1986–1992	22–28	151	34	6	27	85	.275
1993–2000	29–36	167	33	5	45	118	.303
2001–2004	37–40	192	38	3	70	147	.349

One look at the above statistics is enough to boggle the mind. At his present pace, Barry Bonds will be hitting over 100 home runs a year by the time he's 50 years old. The numbers are absolutely staggering. It is well known that wine gets better with age. But ballplayers, obviously with the exception of Barry Bonds, do not. Coincidentally, Bonds' rise to a power icon began after his move to San Francisco. The big slugger has claimed that the above batting and slugging statistics are the result of his weight-lifting program. But people don't bulk up by 40 pounds and get puffy faces from lifting weights.

Jose Canseco, baseball's first and only 40–40 man before Bonds, admitted in his book *Juiced*, published in February 2005, to taking steroids throughout his career. He also named several players that he knew took steroids, although, to a man, the players named denied they ever took steroids. The United States Congress, probably as a result of the Canseco book, conducted a hearing in Washington, D.C., on St. Patrick's Day, 2005, to investigate the severity of the problem around the country. It has come to light that children down to high school age, and even younger, have begun to emulate their major league heroes by taking steroids, with serious side effects. At least two youngsters, one a high school student from Texas, have committed suicide because of depression resulting from their steroid use. The congressional hearing invited Baseball Commissioner Bud Selig; several of his executives; Donald Fehr, head of the Major League Players' Union; and baseball superstars Jose Canseco, Mark McGwire, Sammy Sosa, Rafael Palmeiro, and Curt Schilling to appear before the committee. Canseco confirmed his use of steroids, while Sosa, Palmeiro, and Schilling all denied, under oath, that they ever took steroids. Sadly, Mark McGwire refused to answer questions about whether or not he ever took steroids, causing one AP news story to report, "A hero shamed, diminished not just in size, but in stature, reduced to answering questions from Congress like some fidgety Mafia don — and the game he once dominated unable

Lefty Grove, another contender for the title of the game's greatest southpaw, compiled a 300–141 record during his 17-year career (AUTHOR'S COLLECTION).

to crawl out from even that shrunken shadow." As a result of his testimony, Mark McGwire, guilty or not, has been labeled a former steroid user by the majority of baseball fans across the country. This tragedy is just beginning to play out, and it will probably be several years before the entire truth is known. Until then, all slugging records from 1988 through at least 2004 will be viewed under a cloud of suspicion, particularly Mark McGwire's and Barry Bonds' home run records. And there is a clamor from the fans, reporters, and historians, to strike all records from all known steroid users from the record books and to ban all former steroid users from the Baseball Hall of Fame. As of April 2005, 47 minor league players have been suspended for taking steroids, but only three major league players have been suspended. The reason for the huge discrepancy between the number of major league offenders and minor league offenders is puzzling, but it needs to be determined and understood.

UMPIRES

Umpires today do not do a good job at calling balls and strikes. Each umpire has his own strike zone, both for height and for width. Very few umpires call only pitches over the plate strikes. Most of them call pitches several inches off the plate strikes, as noted above. A batter couldn't reach some of the pitches with a telephone pole, and Leo Mazzone, the pitching coach of the Atlanta Braves, has been taking advantage of the umpire's loose strike zone for more than a decade. When Greg Maddux and Tom Glavine pitched for the Braves, they hardly ever threw a ball over the plate. They usually pitched outside, often several inches off the plate, but they always seemed to get a favorable call. And that played a significant part in their success.

BALLPARKS

Major league baseball stadiums are getting smaller every year. Today, they are approximately 20 percent smaller than they were in 1927, when Babe Ruth set the modern single season home run record of 60. Calculations made by several baseball researchers determined that if Barry Bonds played in the same stadiums that Babe Ruth played in, he would have averaged 59 home runs for every 550 at-bats in 2001, even hitting the twenty-first century version of the lively ball. Conversely, if Ruth had hit against the rabbit-ball that Bonds hit against, he would have hit 81 home runs in 1927, not 60.

EXPANSION

The population has not grown at the same rate as the number of major league teams has grown, and this uncontrolled expansion has outstripped the ability of the minor leagues to channel talented ballplayers up to the major leagues. Because of the lack of promising baseball prospects, there are less than 20 minor leagues in operation today compared to almost 60 minor leagues 50 years ago.

The Overall Quality of Major League Pitchers Today

STARTING PITCHERS

The overall quality of major league pitching is not nearly as good as it was 40 and 50 years ago. In fact, it is in a state of chaos at the present time, with a lack of qualified pitchers, small baseball stadiums, juiced baseballs, a tiny strike zone, out-of-control umpires, and the ever-widening steroid scandal. The state of the game is best exemplified by the experience of Kyle Lohse, the number-four starter on the American League Central Division champion Minnesota Twins. The 6' 2", 190-pound, right-handed pitcher received a raise from $395,000 to $2,400,000 through arbitration in 2005, after compiling a 9–13 record with a 5.34 ERA in '04. Fifty years ago, a pitcher on a league championship team who posted a losing record and had an ERA that was 71 points higher than the league average would have been released outright or, at the very least, sent down to the minor leagues to hone his skills. In today's game, he becomes a millionaire.

There are, however, many outstanding starting pitchers today such as Roger Clemens, Greg Maddux, Pedro Martinez, Randy Johnson, and Curt Schilling, who would have excelled in any era. The following list shows the career ERA differential between individual pitchers and the league average.

Pitcher	DERA
Lefty Grove	1.48
Randy Johnson	1.36
Roger Clemens	1.29
Greg Maddux	1.19
Walter Johnson	1.00
Cy Young	0.99
G.C. Alexander	0.89
Sandy Koufax	0.87 (1.42 1961–66)
Bob Gibson	0.79
Christy Mathewson	0.75
Bob Feller	0.72
Warren Spahn	0.56
Babe Ruth	0.49
Nolan Ryan	0.38

Lefty Grove, not surprisingly, exceeded the American League ERA by 1.48 runs during his career. In 1931, he exceeded the league average by a whopping 2.32 runs, posting a brilliant 2.06 ERA compared to a league ERA of 4.38. The next three places behind Grove are all active pitchers, which confirms the feeling that the top pitchers today could compete in any era. However, due to the fact that there are approximately 150 starting pitchers in the major leagues today compared to 64 starting pitchers 50 years ago (the result of expansion and a five-man starting pitching rotation), there is probably an average of one starting pitcher per team who should be either in the bullpen or the minor leagues.

STARTING PITCHER HISTORY, 1876 TO 2003

Year	Roster Size	Percent CG	Avg. Rotation	Pitchers per Team	Games per Season
1876	11	91	2	2	65
1885	14	87	2	4	111
1895	14	81	4	5	133
1905	14	80	4	5	154
1915	25	54	4	4–8	154
1925	25	49	4	5–8	154
1935	23	45	4	5–8	154
1945	25	46	4	6–8	154
1955	25	30	4	6–10	154
1965	25	23	4	7–10	162
1975	25	27	4	8–12	162
1985	24	15	4–5	9–12	162
1995	25	7	4–5	8–12	144
2003	25	4	5	10–12	162

THE PITCH COUNT AND PITCH COUNT LIMITS

The modern philosophy regarding starting pitchers dictates that a pitcher be removed from the game when his pitch count exceeds 100 pitches. This practice may be partially responsible for the increase in arm injuries that have plagued the major leagues in recent years. The feeling of many former pitchers, pitching coaches, and baseball historians, is that pitch count limits cannot be dictated for an entire pitching staff. Each pitcher is different, according to those who have played the game, with a different body structure, different stamina, and different musculature, and each has a different pitch count. Some pitchers are finished after 100 pitches, while other pitchers can throw more than 150 pitches and still be strong. Tom Seaver said his pitch count limit was about 130 pitches a game, but Jerry Koosman's limit was 145 pitches, and Nolan Ryan's limit was more than 150 pitches. Jack McKeon is one manager who thinks pitchers don't throw enough, and he extends his pitchers throughout the season, letting them throw complete games whenever possible. Manager Frank Robinson of Washington is another old-school advocate of individualized pitch counts. In one early 2005 game, he let Livan Hernandez throw 131 pitches in a complete-game victory over the Los Angeles Dodgers. And the Giants' Jason Schmidt has exceeded 140 pitches several times.

COMPLETE GAMES

The decrease in the number of complete games thrown by a pitcher is not a modern phenomenon. It has been decreasing since the first game was played on the Elysian Fields in 1845. The decrease has nothing to do with the quality of pitching in the modern era. It is strictly a matter of a team attempting to win a baseball game, using the freshest arms available. In today's game, the emergence of the world-class closer has reduced the number of complete games to almost nothing. There may, however, be a correlation between the mental preparedness of pitchers and the disappearance of complete games. Today, pitchers are taught that a quality start on their part consists of six or seven innings. If a pitcher goes six innings and yields three runs or less, that is considered a quality start; at this old-timers only shake their heads and laugh. Three runs in six innings represents a 4.50 ERA, which is hardly high-quality pitching in any era. The following chart shows the complete-game comparisons between the regular season and the postseason, for select pitchers.

STARTING PITCHERS' POSTSEASON RECORD

Pitcher	GS	CG	W	L	WS % CG	Career % CG
Lefty Grove	5	4	4	2	80	65
Whitey Ford	22	7	10	8	32	36
Bob Gibson	9	8	7	2	89	53
Sandy Koufax	7	4	4	3	57	44 (58 percent 1963–66)
Don Drysdale	6	3	3	3	50	36
Tom Seaver	8	2	3	3	25	36
Greg Maddux	29	2	11	14	7	18
Roger Clemens	30	1	10	7	3	19
Randy Johnson	14	3	7	8	21	20

Pitcher	GS	CG	W	L	WS % CG	Career % CG
Pedro Martinez	11	0	6	2	0	13
Curt Schilling	15	4	8	2	27	22

KEY:

GS: Games Started

CG: Complete Games

W: Win

L: Loss

WS Percent CG: World Series, Percent Complete Games

Career Percent CG: Career, Percent Complete Games

The chart reveals a major change in thinking in recent years regarding the value of a complete game, from both a manager's and a pitcher's point of view. Prior to 1970, most starting pitchers were programmed to pitch complete games during the season, and even more so in the World Series. Bob Gibson, the ultimate warrior, is of course the prime example of finishing what you start. But other pitchers, such as Grove, Drysdale, and Koufax, were always prepared to go nine innings. It is obvious that today's pitchers are not prepared to go the distance, and only pitch longer than six or seven innings if they have a shutout going, or are involved in a historic event like a no-hitter or the possibility of a new strike-out record. Randy Johnson and Curt Schilling are exceptions. They are throwbacks to the hardy pitchers of the pre–1970 era. Pitchers such as Maddux, Martinez, and Clemens however, expect to pitch six or seven innings and then retire to the comfort of the clubhouse, their day's work successfully completed, although the game may still be in doubt. This modern attitude, which has been adopted by major league management, is hurting the game and is preventing many of the outstanding pitchers of the era, such as Maddux and Clemens, from achieving their full potential. If Clemens, for instance, had pitched in the pre–1970 era, in a four-man starting rotation and with a nine-inning mind-set, he might well have won in excess of 400 games during his career, as well as set many other records. And the Boston Red Sox might have won the world championship 19 years earlier. Greg Maddux probably would also have been in the upper echelon of pitchers for games won.

DO PITCHERS PACE THEMSELVES?

It has been said that it was easier for a pitcher to pace himself in the old days because he could let up on a batter in the lower part of the batting order without fear of the batter hitting a home run, whereas in the modern game, every batter has the ability to hit a home run at any time, so a pitcher has to pitch all-out on every pitch. That is a fallacy. It was difficult to pitch in the old days too, when the games were played during the day under oppressive summer heat and in heavy flannel uniforms. Many pitchers did pace themselves in those days, to conserve their energy for the eighth and ninth innings. Other pitchers, who didn't think they paced themselves, were doing it unconsciously. And those pitchers who didn't pace themselves didn't pitch many complete games. It is still possible for pitchers to pace themselves today, and the smart ones do that. A home run today is not as critical as it was years ago, because teams score many more runs today. Eric Gagne, one of the major leagues' premier closers, said his new role saved his career. Originally he was a starting pitcher for Los Angeles but, as he admitted, he couldn't cut it as a starter because he never learned to pace himself. As a result, he always ran out of gas by the fifth inning. In *Randy Johnson's Power Pitching,* he said he tries to retire the batter on his first or second pitch in order to conserve his energy for the late innings. And so do the Florida Marlins triumvirate of Burnett, Willis, and Beckett.

FOUR-DAY VERSUS FIVE-DAY ROTATION

Based on the statistics developed by baseball researchers such as Richard D. Cramer, David W. Smith, and

Dennis Eckersley is one of the game's most unusual pitchers, a 20-game winner with a no-hitter to his credit, who evolved into baseball's foremost closer between 1988 and 1997 (BRACE PHOTO).

Pete Palmer, and the testimony of former pitchers such as Bob Feller, Leo Mazzone, and Hal Newhouser, the baseball establishment seems to have overreacted to pitching related injuries in the 1960s and '70s and, in a rush to judgment, blamed the four-man pitching rotation. The change to a five-man rotation did not solve the problem. In fact, it may have made the problem worse. Today's pitching arms seem to be less well conditioned than they were 40 or 50 years ago, and the 100^+ pitch-count limit has exacerbated the problem.

There does not seem to be any advantage for a team to have a five-man pitching rotation rather than a four-man pitching rotation. Leo Mazzone, a former minor league pitcher, pitched in a four-man rotation and he favors the four-man rotation, feeling it keeps a pitcher fresh and strong. The number of pitching injuries has not been reduced over the past 50 years, and the service time of pitchers has not significantly increased. Any increase that has been realized in service time is due to the high salaries that players command today, which entices them to play longer than their counterparts did years ago. On the other hand, the increase in the total number of starting pitchers, 150 today versus 64 pitchers 50 years ago, has diluted the overall pitching talent in the major leagues today.

Pete Palmer concurred that teams today face dangerously diluted pitching staffs. "I can't see how pitching is so much more difficult today than when they had the four-man rotations and 250 innings. So now they relegate 30 games to the fifth and worst starter instead of splitting [them] up among the top four."

PITCHING INSIDE

The key to successful pitching has always been the ability to pitch high and inside, and low and outside. Today most pitchers are afraid to pitch inside, for fear of being ejected from the game by the umpire if their pitch hits the batter. That situation has emboldened batters to crowd the plate, knowing the umpire will protect them. The strike zone includes both sides of the plate. The inside of the plate belongs to the pitcher, as well as the outside of the plate, and both the batter and the umpire need to recognize that fact. But the pitcher, being human, occasionally misses his spot, so it is the batter's responsibility, as it has always been, to protect himself at all times and to be ready to get out of the way in the event of an errant pitch.

RELIEF PITCHERS

Richard D. Cramer conducted a study of relief pitching for SABR's *Baseball Research Journal*, with the following results.

AVERAGE NUMBER OF RUNS SCORED PER INNING

1895	1901	1911	1929	1958	1972	1973
0.78	0.59	0.60	.058	0.48	0.40	0.48

RUNS SCORED PER INNING, 1895 TO 1973
RUNS SCORING RELATIVE TO AVERAGE

	1895	1901	1911	1929	1958	1972	1973
1st Inn.	1.08	1.17	0.97	1.08	1.12	1.19	1.22
2nd Inn.	0.99	0.88	0.70	0.77	0.80	0.84	0.87
3rd Inn.	0.93	1.14	1.01	1.15	1.12	0.96	1.01
4th Inn.	0.83	0.83	0.98	0.96	0.93	0.99	0.96
5th Inn.	0.93	0.87	1.03	1.04	0.95	0.94	1.12
6th Inn.	1.00	1.01	1.18	1.00	1.09	0.97	1.12
7th Inn.	1.22	0.92	0.98	0.95	0.97	1.03	0.73
8th Inn.	1.06	0.76	1.11	1.00	1.05	1.24	1.11
9th Inn.	0.95	1.42	1.04	1.06	0.95	0.83	0.87

RUNS SCORING IN INNINGS 7–9 RELATIVE TO AVERAGE

1895	1901	1911	1929	1958	1972	1973
1.08	1.03	1.04	1.00	0.99	1.03	0.90

Cramer concluded that there was no significant difference between runs scored in the seventh through ninth innings in 1973 than the runs scored in earlier years. He said, "In other words, by the usual statistical criteria, the differences among these three values are not statistically significant. Neither are they practically significant."

David W. Smith came to the same conclusion when he analyzed data from 1901 through 2003. He was looking for obvious patterns showing the effectiveness of relief pitchers. His data showed the team winning percentage when leading after one, four, and eight innings. As he said, "there are no discernible differences from 1901 through 2003." In general, a team leading by one run after eight innings will win approximately 86 percent of the time. If the lead is two or more runs, the team will win 94 percent to 99.5 percent of the time, closer or no closer. And a team leading by one or more runs after seven innings will win approximately 90 percent of the time.

Smith uncovered some additional information:

1. The number of relief pitchers used per game increased from 0.1 in 1900 to 0.9 in 1930, 1.5 in 1960, 2.0 in 1990, and 2.5 in 2000.
2. The batters faced per appearance has decreased from 11.13 batters in 1921 to 5.08 batters in 1998.
3. The number of innings pitched per appearance has decreased from 2.54 innings in 1921 to 1.17 innings pitched in 1998.

Pete Palmer, referring to these and other studies, said it more succinctly:

Studies have shown that teams don't win any higher percentage of games with a lead going into the ninth than they did 30 years ago when there was no closer, so the whole idea has been stupid from the beginning. Basically what you do is pay a pitcher millions of dollars to pitch 60 innings and help win 40 or 50 games that you had a 95 percent chance of winning anyway (and of course they still don't win them all), when you could use him for 100 innings when it really mattered and probably win a few more games.

Modern closers such as Dennis Eckersley, Mariano Rivera, and Eric Gagne have created a niche for themselves and their successors. Every team that dreams of making it to the World Series today must have a reliable closer. That said, it is obvious that major league pitching has been spread too thin for the past three decades. Middle relievers and short relievers are, in many cases, minor leaguers who have won a spot on the roster by default.

As noted previously, there were approximately four relief pitchers per team in the major leagues 50 years ago, for a total of 64 pitchers. Today there are approximately six relief pitchers per team, for a total of 180 pitchers. Again, taking into account the increase in the U.S. population in the past 50 years, there are approximately two relief pitchers per team that should be earning their stripes in the minor leagues.

In spite of all the questions about the need for such a large relief corps, relief specialists, setup men, closers, and their like will be with us for the foreseeable future, so a short review of their history is in order. The following chart lists some of the world-class relief specialists that have represented major league teams over the past 90 years.

RELIEF PITCHERS: GAMES PITCHED, SAVES, AND INNINGS PITCHED PER GAME

Pitcher	Years Pitched	Games	Saves	IPG
Firpo Marberry	1924–1928	243	101	1.73
Johnny Murphy	1932–1947	375	107	1.73
Hugh Casey	1942–1949	207	55	1.79
Joe Page	1947–1954	215	76	2.09
Hoyt Wilhelm	1952–1957	361	53	1.84
	1961–1972	958	227	1.83
Elroy Face	1953–1969	765	193	1.48
Ron Perranoski	1961–1973	736	179	1.59
Mike Marshall	1967–1981	699	188	1.88
Sparky Lyle	1967–1982	899	238	1.55
Rollie Fingers	1972–1985	790	341	1.65
Goose Gossage	1972–1994	971	310	1.63
Kent Tekulve	1974–1989	1050	184	1.37
Bruce Sutter	1976–1988	661	300	1.58
Dan Quisenberry	1979–1990	674	244	1.55
Jeff Reardon	1979–1994	880	367	1.29
		361	174	1.07 (88–94) C
Lee Smith	1980–1997	1022	478	1.25 C
		500	121	1.05 (89–97) C
John Franco	1984–2004	1088	424	1.14 C
		893	379	1.01 (87–04) C
Dennis Eckersley	1988–1998	641	374	1.05 (88–98) C
Trevor Hoffman	1993–2004	696	393	1.10 C
Mariano Rivera	1995–2004	567	336	1.16 C
John Smoltz	2002–2004	210	154	1.08 C
Eric Gagne	2002–2004	234	152	1.06 C

Relief specialists were still being referred to as firemen and stoppers in the late 1980s. The term closer didn't begin to gain in popularity until 1989 and later. A closer (C) has been defined as a relief specialist who can protect a lead over the last inning or two of a game. It has been said that closers, while typically possessing as much talent as any other pitcher on the team, may not have a wide enough variety of pitches or enough stamina over several innings to become a starting pitcher. There is some truth to that theory. Firpo Marberry noted that he didn't have enough variety to last late into a game. He said the batters caught up to him after one or two at-bats. And Eric Gagne admitted he wasn't a good starter because he ran out of gas after three or four innings. One source also noted that closers are successful because they remain calm under pressure and are effective against both right- and left-handed batters for an inning or two.

John Franco may have been the first true closer; he recorded 32 saves in 1987, pitching 82 innings in 67 games for a 1.22 IPG pace. If rating systems are developed to rate relief specialists, there should probably be at least two categories, one for firemen and another for closers. Firemen, such as Firpo Marberry, Joe Page, Ron Perranoski, and Bruce Sutter,

Roger Clemens, a 328-game winner through 2004, shows no sign of slowing down at the age of 43 (BOSTON RED SOX).

often pitched several innings in a game, some times as many as six. Closers almost always are limited to one inning or less. Occasionally they might pitch two innings, but rarely more than that. Eric Gagne pitched three innings in a game in 2004. After suffering through two successive mediocre performances following his three-inning stint, his manager was severely chastised by the press for overextending his valuable closer. Starting pitchers are in the game to win, and they are considered to be eminently successful if they win 55–60 percent of their games. Firemen usually entered the game in the fifth inning or later, with the game still in question. They had an opportunity to win the game, or occasionally save it. The top firemen in baseball history, such as Gossage, Perranoski, and Sutter, were generally successful 70–75 percent of the time. A closer, on the other hand, normally enters a game in the ninth inning with one goal in mind, to save the game. Rarely does he have an opportunity to gain a victory. The world-class closers have proven to be successful 80–90 percent of the time.

In an era when very few pitchers complete games, it is vital for a team to have a reliable closer who can come out of the bullpen to shut down the opposition in the eighth and ninth innings. This situation, however, could change in a few years if teams return to a four-man pitching rotation with more complete games, and starting pitchers are once again made available for relief duties in between starts.

Pitching Coaches

Professional baseball teams today, minor league as well as major league, employ former pitchers as pitching coaches, which is a tremendous advantage over what teams offered 40 or 50 years ago. Pitching coaches prior to the 1960s were, in many cases, catchers. And as Carl Erskine noted, they "could not help a pitcher with mechanics— they could only evaluate his stuff. Now the pitching coach is a manager's right arm."

Injuries, Medical Technology and Player Conditioning

Pitcher conditioning programs are increasingly coming under fire as a result of the numerous arm injuries that pitchers are suffering. There appear to be more injuries today than at any time in the past, as evidenced by the chart in chapter 10 that summarized the increase in the number of pitchers on the disabled list from 1953 through 2004.

Another injury summary, this one from Dan Gutman's *Way Baseball Works*, reported the following statistics:

Significant Injuries and Illnesses to Pitchers

Decade	Injuries and Illnesses	Decade	Injuries and Illnesses
1900s	6	1950s	3
1910s	3	1960s	6
1920s	3	1970s	15
1930s	10	1980s	17
1940s	5	1990s	28 (4 months annualized)

As noted earlier, the injury or illness rate increased by 250 percent after the introduction of free agency. It was also noted that new pitches, such as the split finger fastball, which puts additional strain on a pitcher's arm, may be a contributing factor to the increasing injury rate. This, in spite of the fact that there are more trainers working for major league teams today, and more conditioning programs are being utilized by the players. Many former major league pitchers think today's pitchers may have weak arms because they don't throw enough to develop the natural pitching strength they need to pitch nine innings. They believe that pitchers, both in the minor leagues and the major leagues, are conditioned to pitch only five or six innings a game, with a pitch count around 100 pitches. Fifty years ago, pitchers were continually stretched out through the season to strengthen their arms so they could routinely throw 135 pitches or more, and they were programmed to expect to pitch a complete game every time out. Some people feel that pitchers are building the wrong muscles for the work they do. In the past, the primary conditioning program for pitchers consisted of running wind sprints and throwing a baseball. Today it emphasizes using mechanical exercise equipment that develops specific muscles, but not necessarily the muscles required to throw a baseball 90 miles per hour.

Dr. Gene Coleman, director of conditioning for the Houston Astros, believes today's pitchers do not throw enough. He advocates a vigorous conditioning program followed by frequent throwing to strengthen a pitcher's arm, improve his stamina, and increase his velocity.

Leo Mazzone, the major league's most successful pitching coach, maximizes his pitcher's throwing exercises throughout the baseball season. And he stresses wind sprints for his players, particularly during spring training.

New surgical procedures, such as arthroscopic surgery, Tommy John surgery, and rotator cuff surgery, have allowed pitchers to recover completely from serious shoulder and arm injuries and to resurrect their careers. It has extended the careers of numerous players, starting with Tommy John, who had a tendon transplanted from his right forearm to his left elbow after he tore the tendon in the elbow while pitching. Fifty years ago, John's career would have been over after that injury. But in 1975, Dr. Frank Jobe conducted the experimental surgery with sensational success. In fact, the 33-year-old John was a better pitcher after the surgery than he had been before. He recorded 164 of his 288 career victories after 1975.

What Baseball Needs to Do to Give Pitchers a Level Playing Field

1. The baseball itself is a major culprit in the chaotic state of major league pitching today. The present manufacturing specifications for major league baseballs are too loose. And there are too many loopholes in the specifications, as they now exist. They need to be rewritten, and tightened considerably.

2. Major League Baseball should engage an independent laboratory to test baseballs on a regular schedule, in order to prevent the drastic changes in the composition or liveliness of the ball that have occurred periodically over the past 85 years. And they should maintain a scientific testing program to periodically compare baseballs from different eras.

3. The entire Costa Rican major league baseball manufacturing operation needs to be studied in great detail. It appears to be out of control.

4. Major league teams should consider returning to a four-man pitching rotation, with the starting pitcher available for relief duty on the second day after he pitches.

5. Teams should also consider eliminating the closer and reactivating the fireman, a pitcher who could pitch from one inning to seven or more innings, instead of relying on a closer who can only pitch one or two innings with questionable results. On average, there are approximately three pitchers on each team, one starting pitcher and two relief pitchers, who should be in the minor leagues learning their craft. The money saved by eliminating three pitchers could be better used to add more position players to the roster.

6. Conditioning programs for pitchers need to be reevaluated. The programs should concentrate on the practical components of physical fitness for pitchers, such as a vigorous throwing program and a vigorous wind sprint program as outlined by Leo Mazzone and others. The top priority should be to strengthen a pitcher's legs and stretch out his arm throughout the season, until he can comfortably pitch nine innings, or more, if necessary.

7. Conditioning programs in the gym, as described by Nolan Ryan, Tom House, and others, are excellent for conditioning specific muscles, but weight-lifting should be limited to light weights so as not to build unnecessary and dangerously heavy muscle mass.

8. Conditioning programs for pitchers need to begin at the minor league level. At the present time, young pitchers are coddled in the minor leagues, and their arms are not conditioned to withstand the rigors of pitching a nine-inning game over a 162-game major league season. This lack of conditioning may contribute to their later arm problems.

9. The 100$^+$ pitch-count limit should be scrapped. Every pitcher should be monitored to determine his personal pitch-count limit, which will allow him to pitch deeper into games and to pitch more complete games.

10. Pitchers need to be allowed to pitch inside without fear of being ejected from the game.

11. The strike zone needs to be redefined. It should at least be returned to the 1950 specification that identified the strike zone as the area over the plate between the batter's armpits and the top of his knees. And umpires should be ordered to follow the strike zone rule to the letter. A ball thrown over the plate between the height limits specified is a strike. A ball thrown six inches off the plate is not a strike. It is a ball.

12. Calling balls and strikes is the most difficult part of an umpire's responsibility, and it may be beyond the capabilities of some umpires. It may be necessary to have two separate and distinct umpiring categories, one for umpiring on the bases and foul lines and one for umpiring behind the plate. And a "plate umpire" might command a higher salary than a "position" umpire.

13. One variable in the lively ball debate that has been basically ignored to date is the bat the players are using to propel the baseball tremendous distances. An authorized scientific laboratory program should be initiated to compare the different bats being used today, as well as bats from different eras, to see if there is a difference between bats that could contribute to a batter's home run distance.

14. Major League Baseball and the players' union need to continue to strengthen the new steroid policy. It is time that the two organizations cease stonewalling problems such as this, stop fighting each other for territorial advantage at every juncture, and concentrate on what is good for the game and what is bad for the game. Eliminate the bad stuff as soon as it becomes obvious— not 30 years later.

Appendix A.
Major League Starting Pitchers

Pitcher	Years	G	GS	CG	IP	W	L	SO	W	HB	ERA
Al Spalding	1871–77	347	325	279	2,886	252	65	248	164	—	2.12
Pud Galvin	1875–92	697	681	639	5,941	361	308	1,799	744	—	2.87
C. Radbourne	1881–91	527	502	48	4,527	309	194	1,830	875	—	2.68
Amos Rusie	1889–01	463	427	393	3,779	246	174	1,950	1,707	112	3.07
Kid Nichols	1890–06	621	562	532	5,067	361	208	1,881	1,272	129	2.96
John Clarkson	1882–94	531	518	485	4,536	328	178	1,978	1,191	80	2.81
Jack Stivetts	1889–99	388	333	278	2,888	203	132	1,223	1,155	99	3.74
Cy Young	1890–11	906	815	749	7,356	511	316	2,803	1,217	163	2.63
Mickey Welch	1880–92	565	549	525	4,802	307	210	1,850	1,297	—	2.71
Tim Keefe	1880–93	600	594	554	5,050	342	225	2,564	1,233	—	2.63
Rube Waddell	1897–10	407	340	261	2,961	193	143	2,316	803	115	2.16
Ed Walsh	1904–17	430	315	250	2,964	195	126	1,736	617	52	1.82
Walter Johnson	1907–27	802	666	531	5,914	417	279	3,509	1,363	205	2.17
Smokey Joe Wood	1908–20	225	158	121	1,434	117	57	989	421	49	2.03
Rube Marquard	1908–25	536	407	197	3,307	201	177	1,593	858	39	3.08
Clark Griffith	1891–14	453	372	337	3,386	237	146	955	774	171	3.31
Christy Mathewson	1900–16	636	552	435	4,789	373	188	2,507	845	59	2.13
G.C. Alexander	1911–30	696	600	437	5,190	373	208	2,198	951	70	2.56
Babe Ruth	1914–33	163	148	107	1,221	94	46	488	441	29	2.28
Lefty Grove	1925–41	616	457	298	3,941	300	141	2,266	1,187	42	3.06
Guy Bush	1923–45	542	308	151	2,722	176	136	850	859	41	3.86
Vic Aldridge	1917–28	248	204	102	1,601	97	80	526	512	39	3.76
Bob Shawkey	1913–27	488	333	197	2,937	195	150	1,360	1,018	48	3.09
Herb Pennock	1912–34	617	419	247	3,572	241	162	1,227	916	36	3.60
Lefty Stewart	1921–35	279	216	107	1,722	101	98	503	498	18	4.19
Johnny Morrison	1920–30	297	164	90	1,535	103	80	546	506	28	3.65

Pitcher	Years	G	GS	CG	IP	W	L	SO	W	HB	ERA
Guy Morton	1914–24	317	185	82	1,630	98	86	830	583	22	3.13
Rosy Ryan	1919–33	248	75	29	881	52	47	315	278	11	4.14
Earl Whitehill	1923–39	541	473	226	3,565	218	185	1,350	1,431	101	4.36
George Uhl	1919–36	513	368	232	3,120	200	166	135	966	113	3.99
Wes Ferrell	1927–41	374	323	227	2,623	193	128	985	1,040	23	4.04
Bob Feller	1936–56	570	484	279	3,827	266	162	2,581	1,764	60	3.25
Warren Spahn	1942–65	750	665	382	5,294	363	245	2,583	1,434	42	3.09
Don Drysdale	1956–69	518	465	167	3,084	209	166	2,486	855	154	2.95
Sandy Koufax	1955–66	397	314	137	2,324	165	87	2,396	817	18	2.76
Bob Gibson	1959–75	528	482	255	3,884	251	174	3,117	1,336	102	2.91
Phil Niekro	1964–87	864	716	245	5,404	318	274	3,342	1,809	123	3.35
Steve Carlton	1965–88	741	709	254	5,217	329	244	4,136	1,833	53	3.22
Don Sutton	1966–88	774	756	178	5,282	324	256	3,574	1,343	82	3.26
Tom Seaver	1967–86	656	647	231	4,783	311	205	3,640	1,390	76	2.86
Nolan Ryan	1966–93	807	773	222	5,386	324	292	5,714	2,795	158	3.19
Randy Johnson	1988–04	489	479	92	3,368	246	128	4,161	1,302	156	3.07
Greg Maddux	1986–04	608	604	105	4,182	305	174	2,916	871	118	2.95
Roger Clemens	1984–04	640	639	117	4,493	328	164	4,317	1,458	147	3.18
Jason Schmidt	1995–04	252	243	17	1,568	104	74	1,383	601	37	3.90

KEY—

G: Games Pitched   **W:** Wins   **HB:** Hit Batters
GS: Games Started   **L:** Losses   **ERA:** Earned Run Average
CG: Complete Games   **SO:** Strikeouts
IP: Innings Pitched   **W:** Walks

Appendix B.
Major League Pitchers:
Comparisons by Era
Average Statistics per Year

Era	G	GS	CG	W	L	IP	SO	BB	HB	ERA
1890–1910										
Cy Young	41	37	34	23	14	334	127	55	7	2.63
Kid Nichols	15	41	37	24	14	338	125	85	9	2.96
1900–1920										
C. Mathewson	37	32	26	22	11	282	147	50	3	2.13
Ed Walsh	36	26	21	16	11	247	145	51	4	1.82
1910–1930										
Walter Johnson	38	32	25	20	13	282	167	65	10	2.17
G.C. Alexander	39	33	24	21	12	288	122	53	4	2.56
1930–1950										
Tommy Bridges	33	28	15	15	11	217	129	92	3	3.57
Carl Hubbell	36	29	17	17	10	239	112	48	4	2.98
Lefty Grove	36	27	18	18	8	232	133	70	2	3.06
Bob Feller	38	32	19	18	11	255	172	118	4	3.25
1950–1970										
Warren Spahn	38	33	19	18	12	262	129	70	2	3.09
Robin Roberts	36	32	13	15	13	247	124	47	3	3.41
Bob Gibson	33	30	16	16	11	243	195	84	6	2.91
Don Drysdale	40	36	13	16	13	264	191	66	12	2.95

Era	G	GS	CG	W	L	IP	SO	BB	HB	ERA
1970–1990										
Tom Seaver	33	32	12	16	10	239	182	70	4	2.86
Nolan Ryan	34	32	9	14	12	224	238	116	7	3.19
1990–2004										
Pedro Martinez	39	32	5	18	7	218	255	61	11	2.58
Randy Johnson	32	32	6	16	8	223	277	90	10	3.10
Roger Clemens	32	32	6	16	8	225	216	73	7	3.19
Greg Maddux	34	34	6	17	10	233	163	49	6	2.89

Appendix C.
Major League Pitchers with 5,000+ Career Innings Pitched

Pitcher	Years Pitched	Career Innings Pitched
Pud Galvin	1875–1892	5,941
Tim Keefe	1880–1893	5,050
Kid Nichols	1890–1906	5,067
Cy Young	1890–1911	7,356
Walter Johnson	1907–1927	5,914
Grover C. Alexander	1911–1930	5,190
Warren Spahn	1942–1965	5,294
Gaylord Perry	1962–1983	5,350
Phil Niekro	1965–1987	5,404
Steve Carlton	1965–1988	5,217
Don Sutton	1966–1988	5,282
Nolan Ryan	1966–1993	5,386

Appendix D.
Major League Relief Pitchers

Pitcher	Years	G	GR	CG	SHO	W	L	SV	BS	% SV
J. McGinnity	1898–08	465	84	314	32	246	142	24	—	—
Three-Finger Brown	1903–16	481	149	271	55	239	130	49	—	—
Jack Quinn	1909–33	756	313	243	28	247	218	57	—	—
Firpo Marberry	1923–36	551	365	86	7	148	88	101	—	—
Lefty Grove	1925–41	616	159	298	35	300	141	55	—	—
Jack Russell	1926–40	557	375	71	3	85	141	38	—	—
Wilcy Moore	1927–33	261	229	14	2	51	44	49	—	—
Clint Brown	1928–42	434	304	62	8	89	93	64	—	—
Johnny Murphy	1932–47	415	375	17	0	93	53	107	—	—
Mace Brown	1935–46	387	332	18	2	76	57	48	—	—
Hugh Casey	1935–49	343	287	24	3	75	42	55	—	—
Ace Adams	1941–46	302	295	2	0	41	33	49	—	—
Alpha Brazle	1943–54	441	324	47	7	97	64	60	—	—
Ted Wilks	1944–53	385	341	22	5	59	30	46	—	—
Joe Page	1944–54	285	240	14	1	57	49	76	—	—
Jim Konstanty	1944–56	433	297	14	2	66	48	74	—	—
Ellis Kinder	1946–57	484	362	56	10	102	71	102	—	—
Clem Labine	1950–62	513	475	7	2	77	56	96	—	—
Stu Miller	1952–68	704	611	24	5	105	103	154	—	—
Hoyt Wilhelm	1952–72	1,070	1,018	20	5	143	122	227	inc	78
Elroy Face	1953–69	848	821	6	0	104	95	193	—	—
Lindy McDaniel	1953–75	987	913	18	2	141	119	172	inc	67
Ryne Duren	1954–65	311	279	2	1	27	44	57	—	—
Luis Arroyo	1955–63	244	208	10	1	40	32	44	—	—
Don McMahon	1957–74	874	872	0	0	90	68	153	inc	73
Jim Brewer	1960–76	584	549	1	1	69	85	132	inc	72
Ron Perranoski	1961–73	737	736	0	0	79	74	186	inc	73

Pitcher	Years	G	GR	CG	SHO	W	L	SV	BS	% SV
Dick Radatz	1962–69	381	381	0	0	52	43	122	—	—
Dave Giusti	1962–77	668	535	35	9	100	93	145	39	79
Tug McGraw	1965–84	824	785	5	1	96	82	180	50	78
Mike Marshall	1967–81	723	699	3	1	97	112	188	74	72
Sparky Lyle	1967–82	899	899	0	0	79	74	186	86	73
Rollie Fingers	1968–85	944	904	4	2	114	118	341	109	76
Gene Garber	1969–88	931	922	4	0	96	113	218	82	73
Al Hrabosky	1970–82	545	544	0	0	64	35	97	32	75
Charlie Hough	1970–94	858	418	107	13	216	216	61	21	74
Goose Gossage	1972–94	1,002	965	16	0	124	107	310	112	73
Kent Tekulve	1974–89	1,050	1,050	0	0	94	90	184	81	69
Dennis Eckersley	1975–98	1,071	710	100	20	191	171	390	71	85
Bruce Sutter	1976–88	661	661	0	0	68	71	300	101	75
Dan Quisenberry	1977–90	674	674	0	0	56	46	244	60	80
Jeff Reardon	1979–94	880	880	0	0	73	77	367	106	78
Dave Righetti	1979–95	718	629	13	2	82	79	252	74	77
Jesse Orosco	1979–03	1,252	1,248	0	0	87	80	144	76	65
Lee Smith	1980–97	1,022	1,016	0	0	71	92	478	103	82
Tom Henke	1982–95	642	642	0	0	41	42	311	55	85
Doug Jones	1982–00	846	842	0	0	69	79	303	77	80
Jeff Russell	1983–96	589	510	11	2	56	73	186	45	81
John Franco	1984–04	1,088	1,088	0	0	90	86	424	101	80
Todd Worrell	1985–97	617	617	0	0	50	52	256	71	78
Randy Myers	1985–98	728	716	1	0	44	63	347	60	85
Rick Aguilera	1985–00	732	643	10	0	86	61	318	77	81
Bobby Thigpen	1986–94	448	448	0	0	31	36	201	52	79
Jeff Montgomery	1987–99	700	699	0	0	46	52	304	74	80
Jose Mesa	1987–03	762	667	6	2	70	91	249	43	85
John Smoltz	1988–04	602	201	47	14	163	121	154	14	92
John Wetteland	1989–00	618	601	0	0	48	45	330	63	84
Roberto Hernandez	1991–03	762	759	0	0	53	54	320	80	80
Rod Beck	1991–03	678	678	0	0	38	43	286	55	84
Rob Nenn	1993–02	643	639	0	0	45	42	314	54	85
Trevor Hoffman	1993–03	641	641	0	0	45	44	352	44	89
Troy Percival	1995–03	527	527	0	0	27	35	283	45	86
Billy Wagner	1995–03	464	464	0	0	26	29	22	38	86
Mariano Rivera	1995–04	586	576	0	0	47	31	336	49	87
Eric Gagne	1999–04	282	234	0	0	24	21	152	6	96

KEY—

G: Total Games Pitched
GR: Games in Relief
CG: Complete Games

SHO: Shutouts
W: Wins
L: Losses

SV: Saves
BS: Blown Saves
% SV: Save Percentage

Appendix E. Relief Pitchers' Single-Season Save Records

NATIONAL LEAGUE

Year	Pitcher	Saves
1876	Jack Manning	5
1905	Claude Elliott	6
1909	Mordecai Brown	7
1911	Mordecai Brown	11
1931	Jack Quinn	15
1947	Hugh Casey	18
1950	Jim Konstanty	22
1954	Jim Hughes	24
1960	Lindy McDaniel	26
1962	Elroy Face	28
1965	Ted Abernathy	31
1970	Wayne Granger	35
1972	Clay Carroll	37
1984	Bruce Sutter	45
1991	Lee Smith	47
1993	Randy Myers	53
2002	John Smoltz	55

AMERICAN LEAGUE

Year	Pitcher	Saves
1901	Bill Hoffer	3
1905	Rube Waddell	4
1908	Ed Walsh	7
1912	Ed Walsh	10
1913	Chief Bender	12
1924	Firpo Marberry	15
1926	Firpo Marberry	22
1949	Joe Page	27
1961	Luis Arroyo	29
1966	Jack Aker	32
1970	Ron Peranoski	34
1972	Sparky Lyle	35
1973	John Hiller	38
1983	Dan Quisenberry	45
1986	Dave Righetti	46
1990	Bobby Thigpen	57

Appendix F. Factors Contributing to the Increase in Major League Home Runs from 1919 to 2004

AVERAGE MAJOR LEAGUE HOME RUNS PER TEAM PER 154-GAME SEASON

Year	No. of Home Runs
1915–1919	24
1920–30	68
1940	93
1955–59	138
2004	173

Factor	Percent home run change team/year	Number of home runs change team/year
Player size, weight training, supplements	15	22
Lively ball — 1920	23	35
Babe Ruth syndrome	23	34
Ralph Kiner syndrome	22	33
Integration	9	13
Designated hitter	4	6
Night baseball	-7	-10
Expansion	0	0
Miscellaneous — travel, free agency, etc.	-11	-17
Homer friendly parks, dimensions	4	6
Atmospheric conditions, Colorado, Atlanta, etc.	4	6
New livelier baseball — 1994	14	21
Total	100	149

Home runs have increased by 149 homers per team over a 154-game schedule from 1919 to 2004. Of that total, approximately 56 home runs can be attributed to livelier base-balls from the 1920 and 1994 periods. Two other significant factors are the Ruth and Kiner syndromes, which are the effects these two sluggers had on later generations of hitters who held the bat at the end and swung for the fences, emulating their heroes. Integration accounted for 9 percent of the increase due to the big Negro League sluggers such as Easter, Aaron, Campanella, Banks, Doby, Irvin, and Mays, who brought their slugging style to the major leagues. Players are getting bigger every year and, on the average, for every 2.4 pounds of weight they add to their frame, they will hit one more home run.

Bibliography

Adelman, Melvin L. *A Sporting Time*. Chicago: University of Illinois Press, 1990.

Allen, Maury. *Baseball's 100*. New York: Gallahad Books, 1981.

_____. *You Could Look It Up*. New York: Times Books, 1979.

Altherr, Thomas L. "A Place Leavel Enough to Play Ball." *Nine* 8, no. 2 (spring 2000).

Alvarez, Mark. "An Interview with Smokey Joe Wood." *Baseball Research Journal* 16 (1987).

"Atlantic Club vs. Mutual Club." *New York Times*, July 31, 1860.

Auker, Eldon. Correspondence with author. June 22, 2004, November 3, 2004.

Babicz, Martin C. "Pitching Triple Crown Sign of Real Good'un." *Baseball Research Journal* 14 (1985).

Banta, Jack. Correspondence with author. June 22, 2004, November 1, 2004.

"Base Ball." *New York Times*, July 6, 1860.

"Base Ball, Excelsior Club vs. Putnam Club." *New York Times*, August 7, 1860.

"Base Ball, Great Match Between the Atlantic and Excelsior Clubs of Brooklyn — Fifteen Thousand Persons Present — The Atlantics the Victors." *New York Times*, August 10, 1860.

Berra, Yogi, and Dave Kaplan. *When You Come to a Fork in the Road, Take It*. New York: Hyperion, 2001.

Bert, Ray. "Stepping up to the Plate." AAEE Prism Magazine, www.prism-magazine.org, October 2000.

Bowman, John, and Joel Zoss. *The Pictorial History of Baseball*. New York: Smithmark, 1993.

Briggs, Lyman J. "Methods for Measuring the Coefficient of Restitution and the Restitution and the Spin on the Ball." From "Eminent Scientist Reports How Far a Baseball Curves," March 29, 1959 (reprint), National Institute of Standards and Technology, www.100.nist.gov/curverelease.htm

Brown, Hal. Correspondence with author. June 22, 2004.

Burnside, Pete. Correspondence with author. July 1, 2004, November 5, 2004.

Carter, Craig, ed. *Daguerreotypes*. 8th ed. St. Louis, Mo.: Sporting News, 1990.

_____. *The Series*. St. Louis, Mo.: Sporting News, 1989.

Caruso, Gary. *The Braves Encyclopedia*. Philadelphia: Temple University Press, 1995.

Carver, Robin. *The Book of Sports*. London, 1827.

Clarke, William. *Boy's Own Book*. London, 1829. Reprint, New York: World Publishing House, 1877.

Coberly, Rich. *The No-Hit Hall of Fame*. Newport News, Cal.: Triple Play, 1985.

Cohen, Eliot, ed. *My Greatest Day in Baseball*. New York: Simon and Schuster, 1991.

Cohen, Richard M., and David S. Neft. *The World Series*. New York: Collier, 1986.

Condon, David. "Ray Berres: He Taught Pitchers How to Win." *Baseball Digest*, Evanston, Ill.: Century, 1988.

Couzens, Gerald Secor. *A Baseball Album*. New York: Lippincott and Crowell, 1980.

Cramer, Richard D. "Effect of Relief Pitching." *Baseball Research Journal*, 1975, pp. 82–86.

Curran, William. *Strikeout*. New York: Crown, 1995.

Danning, Harry. Correspondence with author. 2002–2004.

Davids, L. Robert. "The Best Games Pitched in Relief." *Baseball Research Journal*, 1978, pp. 111–116.

"Dead Ball for Coast Loop." *Los Angeles Times*. December 11, 1936.

"Death of a Baseball Player." *New York Times*, October 20, 1862.

DiMeglio, Steve. "A Whole New Ballgame." Sports Weekly.

Durant, John. *The Story of Baseball*. New York: Hastings House, 1973.

Erskine, Carl. Correspondence with author. June 16, 2004, July 22, 2004, November 3, 2004.

"Excelsior vs. Atlantic — The Excelsiors Victorious — The Champion Club Beaten." *New York Times*, July 20, 1860.

"Excursion of a Brooklyn Club." *New York Times*, July 13, 1860.

Fagan, Herb. "The Larry Jansen Interview." *Old-tyme Baseball News*, Vol. 7, Issue 3, pp. 28–29. McKinstry, 1995.

Feller, Bob, with Burton Rocks. *Bob Feller's Little Black Book*. Chicago, Ill.: Contemporary, 2001.

Feller, Bob, and Bill Gilbert. *Now Pitching*. New York: Kensington, 1990.

Feller, Bob. Correspondence with author. May 9, 1999, November 30, 2004.

Ferris, Dave. Correspondence with author. June 11, 2004, July 1, 2004, November 19, 2004.

Frommer, Harvey. *Baseball's Greatest Managers*. New York: Franklin Watts, 1985.

Gallagher, Mark, and Walter LeConte. *The Yankee Encyclopedia*. Champaign, Ill.: Sports Publishing, 2000.

Gettelson, Leonard. "Iron Man Pitching Performances." *Baseball Research Journal*, 1977, pp. 19–25.

Gibson, Bob, with Lonnie Wheeler. *Stranger to the Game*. New York: Viking, 1994.

Gilbert, Thomas. *Elysian Fields*. New York: Franklin Watts, 1995.

Gold, Eddie, and Art Ahrens. *The Golden Era Cubs 1876–1940*. Chicago, Ill.: Bonus, 1985.

Goldstein, Richard. *Superstars and Screwballs*. New York: Dutton, 1991.

Golenbock, Peter. *Bums*. New York: Putnam's, 1984.

Grayson, Harry. *They Played the Game*. New York: A.S. Barnes, 1945.

Gutman, Dan. *The Way Baseball Works*. New York: Simon and Schuster, 1996.

Henderson, Robert W. *Ball, Bat and Bishop*. Urbana, Ill.: University of Illinois Press, 2001.

Hershiser, Orel, with Jerry B. Jenkins. *Out of the Blue*. Brentwood, Tenn.: Wolgemuth and Hyatt, 1989.

Holway, John. *Josh and Satch*. New York: Carroll and Graf, 1992.

Honig, Donald. *A Donald Honig Reader*. New York: Fireside, 1988.

Hooton, Burt. Correspondence with author. November 10, 2004.

House, Tom. *The Pitching Edge*. Champaign, Ill.: Human Kinetics, 1994.

Hudson, Sid. Correspondence with author. June 15, 2004, November 12, 2004.

Ivor-Campbell, Frederick, ed. *Baseball's First Stars*. Cleveland, Ohio: Society for American Baseball Research, 1996.

James, Bill. *The New Bill James Historical Baseball Abstract*. New York: Free Press, 2001.

James, Bill, and Rob Neyer. *The Neyer/James Guide to Pitchers*. New York: Fireside, 2004.

Jansen, Larry. Correspondence with author. June 11, 2004, October 30, 2004, December 1, 2004.

Jansen, Larry, and George Jansen. *The Craft of Pitching*. Indianapolis, Ind.: Masters, 1997.

Johnson, Lloyd, and Miles Wolff, eds. *The Encyclopedia of Minor League Baseball*. Durham, N.C.: Baseball America, 1993.

Johnson, Randy, with Jim Rosenthal. *Randy Johnson's Power Pitching*. New York: Three Rivers, 2003.

Kaat, Jim. "Baseball's New Baseball." PopularMechanics.com, October 1, 2000.

Kahn, Roger. *The Era*. New York: Ticknor and Fields, 1993.

Kahn, Roger. *The Head Game: Baseball Seen from the Pitcher's Mound*. New York: Harcourt, 2000.

Kaplan, Jim. *Lefty Grove, American Original*. Cleveland, Ohio: Society for American Baseball Research, 2000.

_____. "The Best Pitcher Ever." *Baseball Research Journal*, no. 27 (1998), pp. 62–65.

Kermish, Al. "The Babe Ruth Beginning." *Baseball Research Journal*, 1975, pp. 45–51.

Labine, Clem. Correspondence with author. June 11, 2004, November 16, 2004.

Lane, F.C. *Batting*. Cleveland, Ohio: Society for American Baseball Research, 2001.

Lang, Jack. "These Were Baseball's Eleven 'Meanest' Pitchers." *Baseball Digest*, January 1989.

Leavy, Jane. *Sandy Koufax, A Lefty's Legacy*. New York: Perrenial, 2003.

Light, Jonathan Fraser. *The Cultural Encyclopedia of Baseball*. Jefferson, N.C.: McFarland, 1997.

Longert, Scott. *Addie Joss, King of the Pitchers*. Cleveland, Ohio: Society for American Baseball Research, 1998.

Lyle, Sparky, and Peter Golenbock. *The Bronx Zoo*. New York: Crown, 1979.

"Major Leagues Act to Curb Home Run Hitters." *Los Angeles Times*. February 4, 1931.

"Major Leagues Split on Issue of 'Rabbit' Ball." *Los Angeles Times*. December 7, 1937.

Marzano, Rudy. Correspondence with author. July 15, 2004.

Masterson, Walt. Correspondence with author. June 20, 2004, November 3, 2004.

Mathewson, Christy. *Pitching in a Pinch*. New York: Stein and Day, 1912.

Matus, Irv. "Fifteen Pitches per Inning — More or Less?" *Baseball Research Journal*, 1978, pp. 92–97.

"Mays/Chapman Incident: An Accident Waiting to Happen." http://thedeadballera.com/accident waiting.html.

Mazzone, Leo, and Jim Rosenthal. *Pitch Like a Pro.* New York: St. Martin's, 1999.

McConnell, Bob, and David Vincent, eds. *The Home Run Encyclopedia.* New York: Macmillan, 1996.

McNeil, William F. "Backstop: A History of the Catcher and a Sabermetric Ranking of 50 All-Time Greats." Jefferson, NC: McFarland, 2005.

McNeil, William F. "Baseball's Other All-Stars: The Greatest Players from the Negro Leagues, the Japanese Leagues, the Mexican League, and the Pre–1960 Winter Leagues in Cuba, Puerto Rico and the Dominican Republic." Jefferson, NC: McFarland, 2005.

McNeil, William F. *The California Winter League.* Jefferson, N. C.: McFarland, 2002.

McNeil, William F. *The Dodgers Encyclopedia.* Champaign, Ill.: Sports Publishing, 2003.

McNeil, William F. *The Single-Season Home Run Kings.* Jefferson, N.C.: McFarland, 2003.

Mitchel, Jerry. *Sandy Koufax.* New York: Grossett and Dunlap, 1966.

Moreland, George L. *Balldom.* New York: Balldom, 1914.

Murphy, Pat, and Jeff Forney. *Complete Conditioning for Baseball.* Champaign, Ill.: Human Kinetics, 1997.

Mussill, Berrnie. *Oldtyme Baseball News.* Petoskey, Mich.: McKinstry, 2000.

Nash, Bruce, and Allan Zullo. *Baseball Confidential.* New York: Pocket Books, 1988.

Nemec, David. *The Beer and Whiskey League.* New York: Lyons and Burford, 1994.

Newbury, John. *A Little Pretty Pocket-Book.* Worcester, Mass., 1787.

"News Item: October 18, 1862 — James Creighton dies at his father's house in Brooklyn, at the age of 21 years, seven months and two days." All-baseball.com, September 23, 2004.

Okkonen, Marc. "Pitchers Who Could Hit." *Baseball Research Journal,* no. 28 (1999), pp. 80–83.

Osteen, Claude. Correspondence with author. June 11, 2004, November 1, 2004.

Paige, LeRoy (Satchel), as told to David Lipman. *Maybe I'll Pitch Forever.* Lincoln, Nebr.: University of Nebraska Press, 1993.

Paige, LeRoy "Satchel," as told to Hal Lebovitz. *Pitchin' Man.* Cleveland: Cleveland News, 1948.

Palmer, Pete. Correspondence with author. 2003–2004.

Palmer, Pete, and Gary Gillette. *The Baseball Encyclopedia.* New York: Barnes and Noble, 2004.

Peary, Danny, ed. *Cult Baseball Players.* New York: Fireside, 1990.

Pesky, Johnny. Correspondence with author. June 11, 2004.

"Play Ball! Baseball in the Nineteenth Century." Conner Prairie, www.connerprairie.org/.

Powers, Jimmy. *Baseball Personalities.* New York: Rudolph Field, 1949.

Reichler, Joseph, ed. *The Baseball Encyclopedia.* 4th ed., New York: Macmillan, 1979.

Reichler, Joseph, and Jack Clary. *Baseball's Great Moments.* New York: Gallahad, 1990.

Reidenbaugh, Lowell. *Baseball's Hall of Fame, Cooperstown.* New York: Arlington House, 1988.

"Researchers Find Evidence of Livelier Balls in Major League Baseball." University of Rhode Island Pacer, http://advance.uri.edu/pacer/december2000/story1.htm.

Rickey, Branch, with Robert Riger. *The American Diamond.* New York: Simon and Schuster, 1965.

Ritter, Lawrence S. *Lost Ballparks.* New York: Viking Penguin, 1992.

Ritter, Lawrence S. *The Glory of Their Times.* New York: Quill, William Morrow, 1984.

Rossi, John P. *The National Game.* Ivan R. Dee, Publisher, n.d.

Rudolph, Jack. "The 17-Inning No-Hitter." *Baseball Research Journal,* 1978, pp. 82–86.

Ryan, Nolan, and Tom House, with Jim Rosenthal. *Nolan Ryan's Pitcher's Bible.* New York: Fireside, 1991.

Ryan, Nolan, with Jerry Jenkins. *Miracle Man Nolan Ryan.* Dallas, Tex.: Word Publishing, 1992.

Ryan, Nolan, and Joe Torre, with Joel Cohen. *Pitching and Hitting.* Englewood Cliffs, N.J.: Prentice-Hall, 1977.

Saccoman, John T. "The Most Dominating Pitcher of All Time?" *Baseball Research Journal,* no. 27 (1998), pp. 66–68.

Sanford, Jay. Correspondence with author. September 1, 2004.

Santa Maria, Michael, and James Costello. *In the Shadows of the Diamond: Hard Times in the National Pastime.* Dubuque, Iowa: Elysian Fields, 1992.

Sargent, Jim. "Hal Newhouser." Oldtyme Baseball News, 1995, pp. 13–15.

Schott, Tom, and Nick Peters. *The Giants Encyclopedia.* Champaign, Ill., 1999.

Seymour, Harold. *Baseball.* New York: Oxford University Press, 1960.

Shatzkin, Mike, ed. *The Ballplayers.* New York: Arbor House, William Morrow, 1990.

Shieber, Tom. "The Evolution of the Baseball Diamond." *Baseball Research Journal,* no. 23 (1994), pp. 3–13.

Sloat, Bill. "They're Lively to the Core, Tests Reveal." Cleveland Plain Dealer, September 29, 2000.

Smith, David W. "Coming from Behind: Patterns of Scoring and Relation to Winning." Paper presented at SABR 34, Cincinnati, July 16, 2004.

Smitley, Al. "A Chat with Harry Danning." *Oldtyme Baseball News,* 7, no. 4, Petoskey, Mich.: McKinstry, 1995.

Smitley, Al. "Straight from the Horse's Mouth." *Oldtyme Baseball News*, vol. 7, no. 4, 1995.

Society for American Baseball Research, www.sabr.org.

Spalding, Albert G. *Baseball, America's National Game, 1839–1915*. San Francisco: Halo Books, 1991.

Sporting News. December 23, 1920, February 12, 1931, December 16, 1937, January 5, 1939, St. Louis, Mo.

Staten, Vince. *Ol' Diz*. New York: HarperCollins, 1992.

Steinberg, Steve L. "The Spitball and the End of the Deadball Era." *The National Pastime*, no. 23 (2003), pp. 7–17.

Stockton, J. Roy. *The Gashouse Gang*. New York: A.S. Barnes, 1945.

Strutt, Joseph. *The Sports and Pastimes of the People of England*. London: Methuen, 1903.

Swirsky, Seth. *Every Pitcher Tells a Story*. New York: Times Books, 1999.

Thorn, John, ed. *The Armchair Book of Baseball II*. New York: Scribner's, 1987.

Thorn, John, ed. *The National Pastime*. New York: Bell, 1987.

Thorn, John. *The Relief Pitcher*. New York: E.P. Dutton, 1979.

Thorn, John, Pete Palmer, Michael Gershman, and David Pietrusza, eds. *Total Baseball*. 5th ed., New York: Viking, 1997.

Tiemann, Robert L., and Mark Rucker, eds. *Nineteenth Century Stars*. Cleveland, Ohio: Society for American Baseball Research, 1989.

Trucks, Virgil, as told to Ronnie Joyner and Bill Bozman. *Throwing Heat*. Dunkirk, Md.: Pepperpot Productions, 2004.

Trucks, Virgil. Correspondence with author. June 17, 2004, November 1, 2004, November 30, 2004.

Twombly, Wells. *200 Years of Sport in America*. Maplewood, N.J.: Hammond, 1976.

Votano, Paul. *Late and Close*. Jefferson, N.C.: McFarland, 2002.

"World Soccer History," www.soccernova.com.

Wray, J.E. *How to Pitch*. American Sports, 1931.

Wright, Russell O. *Crossing the Plate*. Jefferson, N.C.: McFarland, 1998.

Zimmerman, Tom. *A Day in the Season of the Los Angeles Dodgers*. New York: Shapolsky, 1990.

Index

DATE DUE
